June

Seattle 2022

THE WORLD IS GOING TO LOVE THIS

Up From The Basement
with THE STROKES

by

Gordon Raphael

Wordville

First published in the UK in 2022
by Wordville
London
NW1 6BP

ISBN: 978-1-8384036-7-6

Edited by Tedd George
Cover artwork by Karen Marcus Design
Front cover image by Kurt Graham from the video *Eternal Love*
starring Mary Jane Chocolat, Philip Forrest and Gordon Raphael.
Back cover images listed on www.gordotronic.com

Wordville
www.wordville.net
info@wordville.net

Directly From My Heart To You

This book is dedicated to the little girl, Frankie Weingart,
who grew up to be my mom, the frangipani-scented candle maker—
and the little boy, Larry Halpern, who grew up to be my dad: scientist
and jazz saxophone player. Oh, and the painter Hieronymus Bosch,
whose artwork I discovered to be magically enchanting.

TABLE OF CONTENTS

0: Why Now?

I have been meaning to write this stuff down for a long, long time. One of my lifelong friends, Mr. Forrest Kinney, came to visit me in Berlin a few years ago. After I'd told him ten stories in a row over breakfast on Weinbergsweg, he stopped me, shook his head and laughed. He proposed that we go somewhere together for a month, like Hawaii, and he'd shoot videos of me telling my stories. Forrest observed that it was more than just the words, it was how animated my face got and the many crazy voices I used to represent different characters involved in the comedies and dramas of my life. Forrest had already authored twelve books, having spent his life writing about piano teaching and creativity, but he'd also helped two other people write their own life story.

The mere thought of going away by ourselves to focus and actually DO THIS scared the daylights out of me. I mean, I've always loved talking about my adventures and realize that I do tend to put on a show, but that's always been spontaneous, when I've got a curious, responsive mind and friendly face right there in front of me. Just imagining being away from my beloved coffee shops and well populated sidewalks was petrifying to me. The vision in my head of talking to a camera or having to sit still long enough to write down my experiences (even just the parts of my life involved with *The Strokes*) felt so lonely and forced.

A short list of sweet friends and family members had already insisted that I write my story and, since Forrest left Berlin to visit the European home cities of his favorite composers, more and more people have told me, "You really should write a book, write this shit down!"

A loud, growing chorus of voices by now, echoes repeating until I just can't ignore them any longer.

In a line that I'm sure we'll all be seeing/hearing over the next years, describing countless films, books, songs, albums, paintings, sculptures and babies: The pandemic of 2020 made me realize that it was time to do it!

1: Back In New York City

I'm sitting at a table in Orlin, my favorite cozy café on St. Marks Place in the East Village, ordering their $5 breakfast special. Since moving here from Seattle, most of my life savings are disappearing quickly on my apartment rent and this new recording studio I just became a partner in. I never thought I'd be moving back to New York, no way, after the tragic misadventures (read: DRUGS) my girlfriend, Debe Lazo, and I embarked on exactly ten years ago. Yet here I am in 1998, completely excited to try again. After all, my intervention and drug treatment at The Lodge in Port Angeles, Washington worked out well and I have managed to stay clean and sober for almost eight years so far.

As soon as I made the commitment to NOT use drugs, I was asked to join a beautiful band in Seattle called *Sky Cries Mary*. While the grunge times were famous for long-haired boys in plaid flannel shirts, cutoff jeans and army boots, we rose to prominence as a seven-piece, tribal space-rock band. Our line-up consisted of a male and female singer, DJ Fallout spinning beats, live drums, bass, guitar and I was in charge of generating space sounds and subliminal messages from my electronic keyboards. We were fortunate to be one of the most loved bands in Seattle, with our 1960s style psychedelic light show and wild body-painted dancers; playing sold-out shows in the best venues, with lines around the block of ecstatic fans who sang along with every word. As a member of that band, I signed my first-ever record deal, a nice music publishing deal, experienced multiple tours across the USA and Canada, even once played in Tokyo, without relapsing or getting high at all. In 1995, *Sky Cries Mary* was enlisted by (Microsoft co-founder) Paul Allen's company, Starwave, to become the first band to have a live concert broadcast over the internet, one week before *The Rolling Stones*. We also worked with Microsoft, helping them develop one of the first CD-ROM products.

The grunge scene in Seattle had recently deflated following the horrible death of Kurt Cobain, the announcement that *Soundgarden* was disbanding, Jeff Buckley's freaky drowning in the Mississippi River and the sad deterioration of one of my favorites, Layne Staley, the singer of *Alice in Chains*.

Sure, I'd returned to my beloved New York City several times in the past years, performing with *Sky Cries Mary* at Limelight and Roseland, even appearing on the Jon Stewart and Conan O'Brien late night TV shows. One of the most magical peaks was when my good friend in Seattle, Serge Gubelman, sent me to stay for a week in Manhattan with magnificent theatre director Tom O'Horgan (*Jesus Christ Superstar, Hair, La Mama*). His home, an entire floor of a building on Broadway in downtown NYC, was filled with thousands of rare musical instruments from around the world. There was a glass harmonica, which is a wooden keyboard (invented by Benjamin Franklin, used by Mozart and Beethoven) which plays spinning glass bowls submerged in water! Then there was his hallway of tuned gongs, leather saxophones from the Renaissance, wooden Polynesian frog percussion and a PIPE ORGAN.

The very first night I stayed at Tom's, he took me to dinner with one of my biggest musical heroes—synthesizer pioneer Wendy Carlos. She then invited me back to her wonderful studio, where I was thrilled to see the original Modular Moog used on her revolutionary soundtrack to the film, *A Clockwork Orange*, now decorated with peacock feathers and a Siamese cat named Pandy sleeping on top of it. She also showed me a circular theremin she created and four giant handmade speakers hanging from the ceiling, in a surround-sound array. Wendy played me her new album, *Switched on Bach 2000*, featuring a 3D sound process she had invented and unusual tuning systems which were the exact ones used in the 18th Century, when that music was written.

New York runs in my blood. My mom was a Brooklyn girl, and my dad grew up in The Bronx, where I happened to be born as well. But really, "HOW DID I WIND UP HERE AGAIN"?! I thought my Manhattan days, my East Village wanderings were over and done with. I'd fucked up so badly last time, yet here I sit at Cafe Orlin, wondering how I'm possibly going to survive this time. What the hell will my next steps be?

2: Absinthee

Near the end of my time in *Sky Cries Mary*, I started a new musical project called *Absinthee*, which I loved with all my heart. My bandmate was a wonderful singer named Anne Hadlock, who also captivated my imagination with her poetry, painting and photographs. She grew up thirty minutes from Seattle, in a farmhouse on breathtakingly beautiful land, surrounded by giant pine, fir and cedar trees.

This place was called Bear Creek and their old barn had been converted into a world class, state-of-the-art, recording studio. *Soundgarden* had recently recorded *Badmotorfinger* there, and *Foo Fighters* were working on *The Colour and the Shape* when Anne and I began writing songs together. Our first *Absinthee* album was recorded on her farm, using a 24-track Studer tape machine. The sound quality was a gigantic leap up from what I'd been achieving in my own basement studio, and I was so blown away, that I actually howled in laughter when I heard how great Anne's voice sounded at Bear Creek. Her vocal tone reminded me of an old Ella Fitzgerald jazz record, thanks to the rare, vintage AKG C-24 microphone they had in their collection. Anne grew up singing into that mic, so it was no wonder that she'd developed such a smoky style at such a young age. We were also lucky to receive generous support and encouragement from her family.

My first meeting with Anne was at Cafe Paradiso, on Seattle's Capitol Hill. She was recommended to me by her brother Ryan when I told him I was looking for "a real screamer!" to sing on some dense, industrial electronic music I was recording. She was attending Cornish College of the Arts, studying painting, and the hardbound sketchbook she showed me during our first meeting was full of her own mesmerizing photos. They were eerie black-and-white self-portraits, quite macabre and seemed to have been made in the distant past. I have always been drawn to the visual arts and, for me, her work was striking—already shining with artistic mastery. I told Anne about my latest musical ideas and sent her home with ten instrumental songs on a cassette tape.

When we met again, just a week later to record her first ideas, she'd already written melodies and lyrics for four songs. Her crystal clear, WIDE singing voice and blood curdling screams fit perfectly with the dark, grinding sounds and haunted chord progressions in my songs.

Apart from her art and music, Anne had a job training horses for showjumping. I watched admiringly, in amazement, as she'd put those sleek, powerful beings through their daily routines. One day, while driving home from one of those training sessions, my new bandmate revealed an insanely good eye for real estate. This was a topic I knew nothing about as I had only recently, since getting signed with *Sky Cries Mary*, started paying my own rent for a spacious, inexpensive basement apartment. Before that, I was a penniless couch surfer, always relying on the kindness of others as I maniacally pursued my music and songwriting through a marijuana haze. But now I was drug-free, in Anne's silver Volvo, driving past a broken down old Victorian house on Capitol Hill.

She looked out her window and exclaimed, "Oh, look Gordon, that one's for sale!"

I had no idea what she was doing when she pulled over and slammed her car into park. We got out and she knocked on the door. An elderly man answered, and Anne asked if we could take a look around. I followed her inside. Every room was broken, dusty, filled with junk and newspapers. One of the back downstairs rooms had partially collapsed and a family of raccoons was now living there. The man who'd let us in was living upstairs, in a single bedroom partially filled with newspapers, while the rest of the house was inaccessible, scary and rundown. I felt uncomfortable in that house, anxious to leave, but Anne's face was lighting up, noticing small details in the house's 'bones', and beautifully-crafted old window frames. After all, she'd seen her family take a dilapidated old barn and turn it into a multi-million dollar recording studio. This stuff was in her DNA.

Anne bought the house with money she'd made from her horse training business (she was nineteen at the time). During the next months, the foundation was leveled, walls restored and painted, new wood floors put in and the kitchen was remodeled with colorful, floral Mexican tiles. Finally, the exterior of the house was painted pink, with green trim, and we both moved in to our new *Absinthee* headquarters. I instantly loved living there. My bedroom was painted a rich, dark magenta color, with a shiny wood floor and fitted with a custom-made, antique looking closet with rectangular glass windows to display my vinyl record collection. WOW! I'd never lived anywhere as elegant as this before and I was ready to settle in for a long, long time. All through the 1990s my life in Seattle had been incredibly fun. I'd felt creatively on fire, satisfied and successful during my five-year run in *Sky Cries Mary*, fully enjoying our shows, tours, videos and record releases. Sharing the pink *Absinthee* mansion with Anne, in the coolest area of Seattle, was the perfect next step on our musical adventure.

Anne's brother, Ryan Hadlock (who is now a mega-famous US record producer) and her father Joe, helped us finish and mix our album, but we were still struggling to book decent shows. The sad fact was that, by 1997, Seattle's rock scene had returned to being a shadow, just like it had been before that one bejeweled window opened (1989-1994). That was the time when fantastic international attention, opportunity and craziness flooded our city. During those glorious years, it was rumored that any person with long hair, carrying a guitar, would be approached by a record label, taken out to dinner, plied with unlimited drinks and then be offered a deal. Musicians and bands moved from all over the USA to try and get a piece of that action. I'd been living in Hollywood when the scene kicked off, but I boarded the next Greyhound bus out of Los Angeles after I saw *Pearl Jam* (then called *Mookie Blaylock*) and *Alice in Chains* play together at The Florentine Gardens. No one in the audience that night had expected the audacity and impact that both those bands delivered, and I reasoned, "If this is what's happening in Seattle right now, I MUST be part of it."

━━━━◆◆◆◆━━━━

And what exactly was that vision of early 90s Seattle, Washington that drew the masses and attracted fans from all over the world? The town is located on a powerfully spiritual inlet of salt water called Puget Sound, enclosed to the west by the magical Olympic Mountains and guarded to the east by the jagged, high, snow-peaked Cascades. To the North is the crystal magician, Mount Baker, always gleaming white with snow, while down south, Mount Rainier, so tall and wide, looming like an apparition or guardian angel.

Precisely what makes a body of water 'spiritual' or a mountain range 'magical'? Clouds and water vapor, trapped between those two mountain ranges, cover the entire Pacific Northwest region of the United States with mist, fog and rain showers, that appear then disappear within minutes; this area also specializes in being sunny AND raining at the same time. To stand at Pier 59 or Victor Steinbrueck Park at Pike Place Market, gazing out over Puget Sound through that rainy haze, you perceive that the nearest civilization out there is Japan, straight ahead 5,000 miles away. Orcas, seals, trout and salmon can be seen on the surface of water that goes down to 930 feet deep, while octopi, squid, geoducks, clams and oysters choose to stay hidden below.

There is also the palpable history of Native American culture, with physical reminders such as totem poles and longhouses; the air itself is layered with invisible trails of shamans from the past. As for magical mountains, the Wonderland Trail around Mt. Rainier takes ten days to hike, covering 93 miles of rivers, glaciers, lakes and panoramic vistas. For only two months in summer, when the snow melts, can the lupines, alpine asters and other wildflowers come up to bloom. Over on the other side, the Olympic Mountains hide a prehistoric rainforest, with fallen, ancient moss-covered trees giving birth to new ones, while giant fungi and colorful Amanita muscaria mushrooms flourish all around.

When we step back from the macro-cosmic zoom lens of these impressive natural surroundings, the social scene in Seattle during the time I was growing up was pretty unusual. Being alone in that Northwest corner of the USA felt very cut-off and isolating, unlike the cluster of big cities up and down the East Coast. People were generally friendly and laid back, but we encountered lots of attitude, verbal abuse, threats and outright violence from citizens with redneck, conservative, homophobic and uptight mentalities.[1] It wasn't too uncommon to hear, "What are you, some kind of fag?" being shouted from a passing muscle car, before dodging the eggs that were being thrown at us.

Heavily contrasted with that were pockets of bright young scientists, heavy intellectuals reading massive amounts of books and creative geniuses busy with their music, art and filmmaking. Many of our fathers worked building airplanes at Boeing, taught at the university or went fishing and crabbing from Seattle to Alaska. The rain, being so prevalent, directed the youth to either join sports teams at school or drink beer in their family basements, where they started their own rock bands. Los Angeles and New York, where the US record companies operated, were far away and far out of reach, so no one in our scene expected anything more than to play in front of a few hundred like-minded scenesters at The Vogue, Central Tavern, Rainbow Tavern or

---

[1] These were cowboy vibes; farmers' kids driving into the big city to harass any freaks or weirdos they hoped to come across. Often this redneck aura resulted from the many beers acting upon brains that were limited by strict punishing regimes in their 1950s-influenced evangelical / religious homes. There were also athletic high school guys dead set upon beating up anyone veering from their expectations of appropriate gender expressions.

small venues in restaurants that popped up and then closed down every six months.

During the punk years, young bands playing highly inventive, urgent yet poetic music started to emerge. That small group of bands and fans was fertile creative ground. *The Telepaths*, one of the most creative and volatile bands from our city, innovated by hosting their own concert which featured the screening of Jean Cocteau's art films, followed by pure live rock MAYHEM. The personalities were SO distinctive in that crowd; their fashions so unique and beautiful. This same group of fifty to sixty people partied together for almost five years.

One venue opened up, dedicated to cultivating this artistic, punk-rock approach—it was called The Bird, run by Roger Husbands, manager of local band, *The Enemy*. The city of Seattle via its police department was quick to shut down this 'cultural threat'. Things really kicked off on a higher level when Terry Morgan and his company, Modern Enterprises, opened The Showbox, which is still going strong to this day.[2]

---

[2] This was the first wave of original music in Seattle. These 'pre-grunge' bands paved the way to an independent music scene. They existed for the sheer love of creating something outrageous. The performers listed here had incredible force of personality and powerful self-belief in their different musical expressions: *The Macs, Three Swimmers, The Meyce, The Moberlys, The Knobs, Clone, The Fags, The Enemy, Mental Mannequin, Little Bears from Bangkok, The Telepaths, The Lewd, The Blackouts, Young Scientist, Student Nurse, Audio Letter, X-15, Ze Whiz Kidz, Chinas Comidas, The Refuzors, Malfunkshun, Red Dress, The Tupperwares, The Pudz, The Fastbacks, The Mentors, The Feelings, UVC* and *The Look*. There were two very important fanzines, *Chatterbox*, run by Lee Lumsden & Neil Hubbard, and the amazing *Stelazine* by Stella Kramer. Both of these provided deep insight as well as historical documentation of this scene. For the most complete book on this topic, I urge you to read Clark Humphrey's *Loser: The Real Seattle Music Story*.

From 1986 on, whether it was because of *The Cult*, *Guns 'n Roses* or *Jane's Addiction*, long hair for boys came flashing back into style, which had been strictly verboten since the arrival of the *Sex Pistols* (except for *The Ramones*).

The miserable weather and the lack of social encouragement for creative minds led to several branches of local music. *Soundgarden* offered a *Black Sabbath*-guitar texture served up with screaming, nightmarish, psychological frustration, through the Jim-Morrison-on-steroids, dark poetry of Chris Cornell. *Mudhoney* took the low road through punk rock, filtering it through *The Stooges*, serving up the kind of social angst that only rainy Seattle in the mid-80s could induce.

Many great bands were coming up around the same time (*Cat Butt*, *Green Pajamas*, *Tad*, *Bundle of Hiss*, *Feast*, *The Melvins*, *Skinyard*, *Mother Love Bone*, *Fastbacks* and *Nirvana*, for example). This new generation had the ability to break out beyond both mountain ranges for the first time since the mid-1950s (*The Wailers* and *The Frantics* were the pioneers of an earlier Seattle garage rock sound). One major rock guitarist, a certain James Marshall Hendrix (aka Jimi), was indeed from Seattle, but suffered through the US Army, toured the south as a backup musician and starved in New York before finally being 'discovered'. Chas Chandler brought Jimi to London where he began a brilliant, fiery, four-year career. The innovative music he created then endures for absolute eternity.

Sub Pop Records, the brainchild of Bruce Pavitt & Jonathan Poneman, built the foundation that launched the 'Seattle' brand of rock. One of their signings, *Nirvana*, went on to send the first rocket to the moon (so to speak, in rock 'n' roll terms). Their mates, geographically, though probably not as friends, *Pearl Jam* and *Soundgarden* then planted the flag (Seattle USA) and did the moonwalk, respectively. Importantly, the United Kingdom was the first territory to really support this musical movement. Later, after the glowing sales figures resounded through New York and Hollywood, all the major record labels, which previously only owned warehouse space on the outskirts of Seattle, now ran to rent plush offices in town. They were about to get serious and grab some MONEY from this upstart, atypical music scene.

What about the look, the fashion? Seattle's thrift stores were filled with vintage 1960s clothing. I was thrilled to find discarded wide-buckle belts, psychedelic paisley shirts, original flared Levi's jeans and platform saddle shoes. A combination of guitars, long hair and second hand 60s clothing added a revival hippie element, blended and strained through the recent aggressions of punk rock. *Sky Cries Mary* performed with a multi-projector light show run by Stray Voltage, the team of photographer Cam Garrett and Michael Laton. Laton was an original light wizard from the real 60s San Francisco psych-scene and he once gave this comparison of the Seattle grunge musicians with the San Fran hippies: "The California musicians had a very cowboy, gunslinger look, while the Seattle bands are more like Valhalla Viking warriors."

During the grunge heyday, record deals were abundant, and the number of live music venues more than doubled. All the nightspots and dive bars were packed every single night with musicians and fans who came from all around the world to dive into this raging Northwest party.

Seattle bands were mostly not at home for five years, as they were out on the road either in the USA or Europe. The dark side was—as often happens where music and success, or music and failure, combine—drugs and alcohol. Addictions and tragic overdoses became rampant in our scene, and people's lives changed forever, rarely for the better.

———◆◆◆———

When that window of iridescent, guitar-driven world domination slammed shut, Seattle drifted back to being a ghost town. Suddenly there wasn't much opportunity to build one's musical career. My days were spent in a luxurious, artistic reverie—

making samples, programming beats and writing songs for Anne to sing. At the same time, we became increasingly aware that there was no vital scene to be part of anymore. *Absinthee* played at The Showbox, Weathered Wall and even once out at The Gorge, but to me there was a sadly familiar 'nowhere to go' feeling that I painfully remembered from before the grunge hysteria. For Anne, however, it was unfathomable that the powerful and supportive music scene she'd grown up listening to and watching record at her family's studio had now dissipated. She did not take this loss well, gradually losing hope and becoming despondent about our band's future.

Two weeks before St. Patrick's Day / Anne's birthday, she asked me if we could have a talk. She proceeded to tell me that she'd made a deal with herself that if she wasn't famous by the time she was twenty, that she was going to QUIT music. I'd already experienced her bouts of depression. These manifested during our album recording sessions, and we had some flare-ups over the topic of 'success' during our long drives between Seattle and Bear Creek. I took her words very seriously, searching for something helpful to say. I thought about how important our music was to me, how much I enjoyed playing my guitar while she threw herself on the floor, wearing a lovely dress with army boots, screaming her lungs out—so what could I possibly do to stop this? How could I reassure her so that we could move forward as a musical team?

I had one idea, in a flash, blurting out, "Have you ever been to New York?" She hadn't, so I offered to take her there to celebrate her birthday, adding that I would try to find somewhere in Manhattan that we could play a show on short notice. I still had money left over from a publishing advance, *Sky Cries Mary* income and some that my mom left me before she passed away, so this idea seemed doable. She agreed to this trip, smiling slightly. Crisis resolved for the time being.

As luck would have it, Anne's family had a friend on New York City's Upper West Side who agreed to let us stay in one of his apartments, and another friend, Alan Bezozi, landed us a show at Luna Lounge, a place that would have great resonance later in my life's story.

Everything went fabulously well. Anne and I had happy times together exploring the East Village, Central Park and the Guggenheim Museum. Our performance as a duo, with my keyboard (Ensoniq ASR-10 Sampler) and her singing, went smashingly and even led to a conversation with an A&R agent from a major label after our set. It was all quite exhilarating and good medicine for our souls.

We returned to the pink house on Capitol Hill after a week away. I was glad to go on writing music and rehearsing to record two new songs, *Moonsong* and *Prelude*, at the dreamy Bear Creek Studios. A few days later, Anne asked me again to the front room for a chat.

I had no idea what was coming this time, but she used these words: "We have to move to New York, there's nothing for us here. You know we can play shows there and meet with record companies."

This was the furthest thing from my mind and, honestly, the last thing in the world that I wanted.

I'd moved to New York in 1987, after an old church that my friends and I were living in (all of us broke, unemployed musicians on drugs) burned down mysteriously one day. Debe Lazo and I were out having a fancy lunch (on her grandmother's credit card) at downtown department store Frederick & Nelson's. When we returned to the church for my band practice, there were fire trucks parked out front. Luckily none of our housemates were hurt, but everything inside was burned and turned to ashes.

We moved to New York two weeks later because friends of mine, producer John Holbrook and photographer Ray Charles White, offered me the use of their musical equipment when they heard that mine had all been destroyed. I had great confidence that I'd be successful in New York with my crazy 'West Coast' sounds and weird recording ideas. Instead, we wound up barely surviving, in total poverty, while strung out on hard drugs.

It was a miserable situation and, as a junkie in the East Village, I was repeatedly robbed; once with a gun to my stomach in an abandoned building on Avenue D; once by a guy holding a butcher's knife to my back, and once with a razor knife to my throat. The weirdest experience was when I was robbed by a guy with long black hair, who looked like me! We were even wearing the same black leather jacket, torn jeans and army boots as he chased me down East 7th Street. I was running as fast as I possibly could to get away from him, but my army boots felt like lead weights, thanks to being extremely dope-sick. Finally, when I reached a well-lit corner on Avenue B, I sat down in front of a bodega, with many people walking by on the sidewalk. My lookalike caught up with me and shouted to everyone that I had stolen his wallet! Then a crowd gathered around me, convinced that I WAS THE ROBBER, shouting "kick his ass" to my assailant. He rifled through my pockets taking my last dollar bills and my freshly scored drugs, before running away.

Other highlights of our horrific New York lifestyle included: cocaine overdoses, ambulances, jails, me giving a massage to Persian restaurant owners in exchange for lamb soup...and other HIGHLY unglamorous missteps. It ended with my girlfriend at St. Vincent's hospital for an entire summer. After that horror, in November of 1989, we were both tricked by our families into returning to Seattle for an intervention and sent to separate drug treatment centers. Yeah, I didn't have fun memories of trying to make it BIG in the Big Apple, and I wasn't interested in going back there for a potential round two!

Anne let me know that I had a clear choice. She would go to NYC with or without me, to attend the School of Visual Arts. I could stay in Seattle and lose our music together or go with her to New York, where I would need to find an apartment of my own, new musicians to work with and a place to rehearse.

I was totally passionate about the music we were making as *Absinthee*. I'd left *Sky Cries Mary* while we were signed with Warner Bros. Records, because all I wanted to think about was making my own music and hearing Anne's voice. It took one day of racking my brains and searching in my soul before I finally agreed, still with worries and doubts, to move with her in six weeks. Out of our sweet pink mansion and onto the streets of Manhattan.

3: Welcome to Chateau Relaxo

Anne and I arrived in New York with a couple of suitcases. I brought guitars: Gibson SG, Les Paul, Fender Stratocaster. I also brought some keyboards: ASR-10, Arp Odyssey and Mini Moog. She brought along her new Jack Russell puppy, named Petal.

The black car that picked us up from JFK Airport had to stop several times on the way back to the city, so that Petal could wee by the side of the road. We stayed with her friend Bill Mullen on the Upper West Side for a few days, until Anne got her own apartment in his building. I found a place to stay in the East Village, sleeping on someone's couch. For this privilege I had to pay $900 a month, which was "ouch!", as the total rent for my luxurious basement flat in Seattle had been an easy $150.

To make matters even more irritating, the couch was right under a window on a busy street, with a bus stop right outside that was jarringly noisy all night long. I was glad to be back living in my sacred, holy East Village, but the apartment owner used my room as her office, coming in to work every day at 9am. This meant that I was required to be awake, ready to hit the streets by then, which was not at all in keeping with the musician's hours I'd been cultivating. I checked my Seattle bank balance to calculate how long my leftover money was gonna last, as I pondered how to get my music and *Absinthee* rolling again.

Anne and I discovered a cool rock scene with attitude going on at Continental Club, featuring a phenomenal band called *Honky Toast*. We were both impressed the first time we saw them perform, and I recognized their incandescent guitarist, Richard Fortus. He had previously been playing in *Love Spit Love* starring Richard Butler, gravelly voiced singer of *The Psychedelic Furs*, which was the last show I'd seen in Seattle before leaving town.

I remember that no one could keep their eyes off Richard Fortus.[3] Not only did he look so damn cool, but he struck his guitar like he was psychopathically assaulting it. He had techniques that only a highly trained classical musician might possess, because he was a cellist as well. That concert was also memorable for the opening band, *Subcircus*. They blew me away with their 'androgynous grunge Bowie in full drag' style, and I instantly became a hardcore fan.

Other than *Honky Toast*, another fabulous New York band at the time was *Halcion*, featuring my friends Chad Swahnberg and Dorit Chrysler. They were a killer, intelligent, visceral band, who had toured with Marilyn Manson before headlining their own shows in Brooklyn and the East Village.

One of the most popular nightspots downtown was Luna Lounge, presenting three bands a night with free admission. The East Village was still teeming with creative artists, the shops, cafes and people providing a visual feast, around the clock. I always enjoyed the walk from my apartment to Luna Lounge—Arlene's Grocery, Mars Bar, Max Fish, Baby Jupiter and Mercury Lounge. This was the Ludlow Street circuit, majorly rocking and action-packed; to me it was the real heartbeat of the downtown nightlife, party and music scene. Chad Swahnberg was one of two friends from my earlier life in Manhattan (along with photographer Ray Charles White) that I was still in contact with when Anne and I moved back in May 1998.

Chad and Ray had both witnessed my heroin and cocaine-induced self-demise, yet still held out hopes that I would bounce back some day. During that very bleak period, Debe and I conducted a very bizarre photo-session on the rooftop of our 2nd Avenue apartment building. We both dressed up to the nines in freaky old clothes—me in a long, shiny, black leather trench coat, wearing a matching fuzzy black Russian hat, and Debe wearing

---

[3] Richard Fortus has been a member of *Guns N' Roses* since 2002, while former *Love Spit Love* and *Honky Toast* drummer Frank Ferrer has been in *Guns N' Roses* since 2006.

her dayglo green and orange polka dot 60s dress, with vampire eyebrows. We had found all these items of clothing either lying on the street, in the alleyway behind our apartment or in cheap neighborhood thrift shops. In these photos we truly look like half-alive rock 'n' roll skeletons, trying to be nonchalant and cool.

Chad Swahnberg came to greet Anne and I as soon as we landed in New York. Chad was always a beacon of intelligence, wit and musical expertise. We shared a studious fascination with a wide range of music: Avant-garde classical composers such as Arnold Schoenberg and Anton Webern, progressive rock, especially *Gentle Giant* guitar solos, and old 4AD (label) bands such as *Pixies* and *Cocteau Twins*. He was delighted to see me back in Manhattan, in much better shape than last time, and was also pleased to meet Anne. As we settled in, he began inviting us to parties, gatherings and social functions.

Soon we were going out with Chad and his crew two or three times per week. Interestingly, almost everyone we met through him was Austrian, German or Swiss. They were journalists, songwriters, musicians and writers, as it was still feasible at that time for bright, young, creative people from around the world to stay in Manhattan, enjoying the last real outpouring of counterculture on the streets there. Our new friends were mentally sharp, constantly discussing recent art and music. They certainly loved having parties, whether on their rooftops, under the star-covering haze of Manhattan's neon glow, or in a variety of small intimate bars. It was energizing to meet these Europeans, they were very welcoming towards me and took kindly to Anne, as well. I had no idea what impact on my future this festive community of Austrians, Germans and Swiss would have, never imagining that within seven years I would be living full time in Berlin!

My social circle in New York was expanding, but still I had no job, nor prospects. Even more pressing, I had nowhere to set up my music equipment to dive back into my passion—writing and recording music. I had my ASR-10 keyboard set up in my various short-term bedrooms but, after having a massive collection of instruments set up in *Sky Cries Mary*'s basement, I was craving more space. We had recorded *Absinthee* at Bear Creek, and I attended *Sky Cries Mary*'s *Moonbathing on Sleeping Leaves* mixing sessions at A&M Studios in Hollywood (on La Brea, in Charlie Chaplin's old movie studio), so I was seriously visualizing having my own studio, where I could really make loud NOISE.

Excitedly, Anne called me up to tell me that she'd found an intriguing ad in the *Village Voice*: "Partner wanted for day shifts in fully-equipped recording studio, downtown."

That was exactly what we needed and, after one phone call (no cellphones quite yet, they were called landlines!), the studio owner, Scott Clark, invited Anne and I down to look at the place, to see if we could make it work. Scott's studio was located at Ludlow and Grand in a basement. Since I was living in the East Village, Anne came down from the Upper West Side and we walked from 7A Cafe, where I had breakfast every morning, down Avenue A, over to our familiar Ludlow Street, then down through the Lower East Side to the beginning of Chinatown. We found 56 Ludlow, pressing the studio doorbell there.

According to history, this was the exact same building where, on the 5th floor in 1965, John Cale, Sterling Morrison and Lou Reed formed *The Velvet Underground* AND tape-recorded the original songs that became their first album. YES, this was a building with an inspiring musical past!

Scott buzzed us in and we climbed down some rickety stairs to a small door in the basement where he greeted us. He escorted us through a very small live room (just big enough for a drum set and a couple of guitar amps) and into the control room, where we met Joyce Lan (Scott's girlfriend at the time) and her twin sister Crystal. All three of them were very happy, smiling and full of bubbly energy.

Scott was a rock bass player and, from what I soon learned, a mega-brilliant, creative genius. He already possessed an advanced insider's knowledge of computers, in those early days. Having graduated from college at a young age, Scott first started teaching digital art and design at Parsons School of Design, but was now working full time at Scholastic, looking after two hundred publishing computers. We clicked instantly. Scott appreciated my Seattle rocker vibe and was interested in hearing my music. I was instantly impressed with his studio, which he called "Chateau Relaxo". It was like nothing I had ever seen before.

It wasn't exactly a flashy commercial studio. There was no grand mixing desk, no big speakers and the space was relatively small. Scott Clark, who was actually brand new to the art of recording, had spent months reading magazine interviews with all his favorite producers and audio engineers. Then he had both the vision and resources to search for all the best pieces of equipment, as recommended by his audio heroes. He had bought a few great microphones, a few great preamps, keyboards, compressors and the main innovation: a state-of-the-art Apple Power Mac computer running Pro Tools Hardware and Emagic Logic recording software. Emagic was a German company that had invented something incredible and world class—a software that could record audio from live instruments and microphones on one window and, simultaneously, record MIDI sequences controlling keyboards, samplers and synthesizers on a second window. This was a huge breakthrough and ingenious. Though these features are common now, it was cutting edge technology back in 1998.

Big recording studios around the world were going out of business because the cost of maintaining large vintage mixing consoles and old 24-track tape machines was astronomical. It was a rare breed of old-timer who knew how to repair that equipment (which always seemed to be breaking down), and those highly specialized technicians were becoming harder to find or going extinct from alcoholism. Most well-known studios were loaded with these costly, vintage machines, but Scott designed a studio utilizing only a few pieces of the best classic equipment, relying on new, ever-improving computer technology. This was clearly prophetic and very far ahead of its time. Go Scott Clark! Go Chateau Relaxo!

At the end of our cheerful, upbeat meeting, he offered Anne and I the dayshift, from 9am until 7pm, seven days a week, for $700. I did a small gulp, mentally adding the $700 to the $900 of rent I was already paying for my living space. But, of course, we quickly agreed. We envisioned all the songs we would write and record there and knew it would be a great place to audition musicians for *Absinthee*.

I had rarely used computers before. In fact, I had a very snotty and critical attitude towards their use in music. I'd been in recording studios since 1975, producing my own songs since '78, and my feeling was, "What, you're kidding me? You're gonna watch a TV while you record music? Fuck that." But now I was about to jump headfirst into Emagic Logic at Chateau Relaxo. His Kurzweil K2500 sampler, Manley Compressor, Neumann U87 condenser mic and PowerMac were all new concepts to me. I was facing a huge learning curve, but already knew I'd be crafting sounds on a much higher level, with a vastly expanded creative palette. Scott generously offered to help me with any questions I had or if I got stuck. And STUCK I did get, multiple times per day for the first few months.

I'd call Scott at his job at Scholastic,

"HELP. I just deleted the song I've been working on for two days. What do I do??"

"The Neumann microphone seems broken... Oh? Phantom power button, ahh! OK... Now it works, whew!"

He was there for every phone call, patiently and laughingly bailing me out of situation after situation, until I got the hang of high-end, analog recording equipment in conjunction with digital audio.

By September 1998, I was living in an Upper West Side sublet. Anne had sold the extraordinary pink house in Seattle to her brother Ryan, and used that money to buy her own studio apartment at 16th Street and 3rd Avenue, a beautiful area of

Manhattan. I would take the 1 or 3 train to Union Square, then walk down to Ludlow & Grand. Every day I would start my new recording experiments and songwriting as close to 9am as I possibly could, to maximize my time in the studio.

Sometimes I would run into Scott and his guitarist Eric Bruggemann (from their band, *The Inhabitants*) just finishing up a long night of rehearsing or recording. Once they left and I was alone, I'd play my Arp Odyssey synthesizer, generating infinite crazy sounds, and my Mini Moog for floor-vibrating low bass tones. Then I would hit Scott's Kurzweil for drums and pianos, before I dialed up mad, distorted, space guitar noises through his ART processor. I always wrote and recorded songs quickly, developing two or three songs a day, all week long.

Some songs were pure, synthetic instrumentals, taking advantage of the cool equipment I now had at my disposal. Some were long space jams with different musicians I would meet and bring over to play with. There were also plenty of powerful new *Absinthee* songs, ready for Anne's lyrics and singing. We received a huge boost when I boldly asked *Honky Toast*'s amazing guitarist, Richard Fortus, to help us with a guitar hook for our song, *Across the Water*. He kindly agreed and then played a divine and GODLY riff through his rare, filter-sequencer pedal, thus blowing our minds. Even though we were new in town, Richard was so kind in helping us. He even refused my small offer of $50 payment!

Absinthee became a fluctuating lineup of talented, stylish musicians playing live shows and recording at Chateau Relaxo. We were constantly trying to attract the attention of New York's music industry, with the end goal of signing to a record label that really believed in our music. Thanks to Anne's Bear Creek connections and my *Sky Cries Mary* affiliation, we were able to invite a small stream of managers, A&R scouts and producers to drop by and meet us.

I quickly learned to LOVE recording on computers as I was able to stack up many tracks, creating dense orchestrations just like in those big fancy studios I'd been in, but without having to pay the high daily rate. I was also getting really cool sounds from our drummer Dan Menke, using two or three good microphones and that Manley compressor-thing really gave an edge that I'd never achieved before.

By mid-December, when Anne and I were flying back to visit our families in Seattle for Christmas, I had written and recorded about forty new Gordon Raphael songs and ten others for *Absinthee*. Alas, the downside being that my money was almost completely gone. My girlfriend, Sheila, gave me $1,000 (out of sympathy) towards my studio rent, and another friend, Charmagne, paid me to pose as her husband in order to sign divorce papers at a Chinese lawyer's office downtown. Ah, the rock life, the glamour of being a musician, certainly!

On that flight back to Seattle, I was pleased with my newly improved recording skills and my year's worth of cool new songs but wondered how I was gonna survive going into 1999. My apprehension grew about living in NYC with no money coming in; $1,600 in rents due each month was daunting. I had lived most of my musical career with no money, but thanks to *Sky Cries Mary*, I had experienced seven years with cash in my pocket, my own place to live and music non-stop.

4: The Turning Point

That Christmas, Anne and I started a new tradition of flying back to Sea-Tac Airport, then driving out to stay with her family at Bear Creek.

I adored their beautiful old farmhouse with its comfortable bedrooms, huge well-stocked kitchen and living room with fireplace. My favorite space (other than the music studio across the pasture) was the dining room, with its long wooden table, old stone fireplace and worn antique floors, offering sweeping views of vibrant forest and the crystalline, winding Bear Creek itself. Peacefully nestled in trees, staring through large picture windows at the heavy Northwest cloud-show and misting rain showers flying by, this was the perfect antidote to daily life in New York.

After a few days on the farm, I would always make the trip into Seattle to visit my dad and sisters, Cherron and Lisa. I would walk up and down Broadway on Capitol Hill, grabbing a Nico Latte at Espresso Vivace, coffee so special that Anne had her family send bags of it to her New York apartment, monthly. Then I'd be walking the Ave in the U-District, noticing the new generation of punks panhandling around 45th Street, just like the hippies did when I first discovered that area. Continuing on, through the beautiful University of Washington campus, where my dad worked, I never missed a chance to see the cherry trees, the beautiful fountains or the stunning view of expansive Lake Washington with the Cascade Mountains in the background.

Before leaving the campus, I ritually stood between the Art and Music buildings, swooning over their impressive, cathedral-like, old European architecture.

I had been a student there for two years, as a way of appeasing my father and getting him to pay my half of the rent at Apt. F[4].

The art and music buildings were symbolic temples to my two favorite subjects and I spent countless hours in the library, poring through books filled with old European and Surrealist artworks. Without a doubt, the paintings I found in those books and the progressive rock music I was listening to from an early age, created an imaginary, mythological Europe that I began to inhabit, somewhere in my mind.

Late in the afternoon I'd board a Metro bus heading downtown, to hit Pike Place Market for the bright colors of the fruits and vegetables, the crazy mix of people in the crowd and, specifically, to replenish my supply of incense and perfume oils at Tenzing Momo, a witchy herbal supply shop with a heady ambience that I'd been in love with for decades.

Talking with my sister Lisa about my New York adventures brought a big smile to her face but, when I mentioned that I was nearly broke and kinda nervous about it, she looked worried. She tried to bolster my confidence by reminding me that I'd had a great run with my music and, ever since drug-treatment nine years earlier, I'd been successful at staying clean. She spoke highly of *Sky Cries Mary*, how their popularity helped me earn enough money to replace the keyboards and amplifiers I'd lost in the church fire and then continue on to acquire most of the musical instruments I'd ever dreamt of. Lisa reasoned that, with my skills and experience, including the straight jobs I'd had, she could help me write a solid resumé.

---

[4] Apartment F was located in the incredibly vibrant and wild neighborhood of Capitol Hill in Seattle. It was my first real apartment of my own and I shared it with my girlfriend Pony Maurice and the outrageous poet/punk rock guitarist Dahny Reed. This was a throbbing, vital center for our circle of musical friends; I wrote many of my best songs there and started my band *Colour Twigs*.

What were those "straight jobs"? Kids' birthday party clown, blueberry picker, medical research lab assistant, movie ticket taker/popcorn-maker, caterer, New York Public Library employee, serving sandwiches in a Hollywood restaurant, house painter; this is the complete list, with longest job lasting five months.

The thought of going back to working at a job outside of music was shocking and worrying to me. It had only been seven years since I was completely broke and without work, but my ultimate goal had always been to be free to think about music all the time and make my living exactly in that way. It was depressing to think that my rock 'n' roll glory days were behind me. I had followed my own path, being outrageous both visually and sonically onstage, playing synthesizers and teaching myself how to record music, writing hundreds of my own cryptic interplanetary songs. All experiences that I loved, wholeheartedly.

Back at the farmhouse, Anne's mom, Manny, was also giving me sage advice. Over the past three years she'd been instrumental in booking studio time for *Absinthee* at Bear Creek and hired me for several small jobs writing and recording music for Microsoft. She had also worked hard designing and decorating our pink house, adding marvelous details as it was being renovated. Now she was trying to guide me towards job contacts for when I got back to Manhattan. The gravity of my financial situation was that I had just enough money in my Wells Fargo checking account to pay my apartment and studio rent, food and train fare, for the first two months of 1999—the year Prince had been singing about since 1982. Scary Happy New Year. Goodbye Seattle!

I walked into Chateau Relaxo the morning after we landed in NYC to write new music, blasting off into the creative universe, that glowing, infinite space where I really felt I belonged. Scott had installed a new software plug-in called Amp Farm, which was designed to make your guitar sound like it was running though classic, vintage amplifiers. You could choose which amp head you wanted, Fender Twin, Marshall Plexi or Vox AC30, then add virtual speaker cabinets.

Amp Farm looked cool, so I took my 1980 Sunburst Les Paul (discovered at Trading Musician in Seattle), plugged in, turned a few knobs and, much to my immediate delight, I landed on a tone that sounded exactly like *Sunshine of Your Love* from my favorite *Cream* album, *Disraeli Gears*. After five minutes of improvisation (my specialty), I came up with four chords, a really heavy riff and snaking bass line. Tada! My song *View from Blue* was born. Three hours later, I had lyrics, singing and even a low goth vocal harmony, reminiscent of my beloved *Alice in Chains*.

I always feel elated when I finish making a song I particularly like and quite often the process of recording myself playing instruments and singing makes me feel as if I'm high on hallucinogens, subtle traces of tripping. My theory is that, because playing and singing are intuitive from the left-brain, while the technical part of recording is all right-brain; going rapidly back and forth between these activities makes a lightning storm connecting the two halves, thus creating that dream-like effect. I have played *View from Blue* at all my shows since the day I wrote it.

Working on several songs per day, my fluidity in guitar playing, singing, finding synthesizer sounds and songwriting was in top form. This workflow absolutely couldn't have been more enjoyable. Being in New York, working with Anne in *Absinthee* and having this particular studio to work in was doing wonders for my creative output, as fresh songs and exciting sounds were being born every day. This was truly the most continuous, uninterrupted time I ever had as an artist. Instruments and studio equipment had become an extension of my ideas and musical instincts. This had certainly NOT been the case earlier in my life, when wires, tape recorders and music itself seemed like a hopelessly insurmountable obstacle course.

I first attempted to record my own songs when I was twenty years old, but really made a mess of it for the first two years. I was always setting the recording level too HOT, making everything peak-out and distort in a horrible way, and then I would accidentally erase the parts I liked. My initial efforts with both synthesizers and tape recorders were frustrating, tense and sweaty!

I had celebrated my 19th birthday by joining a band called *Medusa*. The band leader was my friend Brian S. Phraner, who also played bass, sang and wrote all the songs. We lived in a converted convalescent hospital in the small town of Mount Vernon which was located in the Skagit Valley, north of Seattle. There were many interesting people living in that building, the main themes being tarot cards, magic, marijuana, mushrooms and meditation. Brian had completely taught himself to be a master musician by playing his Hagstrom bass along with all his favorite records (*Pink Floyd*, *YES*, *Deep Purple*). He also learned how to produce his own songs on a 4-track tape recorder that he borrowed from the music department at Skagit Valley College. My main motivation to learn how to use that 4-track machine was from hearing Brian's *Medusa* music. It was so layered, psychedelic and vast. His creations impressed me so much that I LUSTED to understand his techniques, to try and accomplish them myself.

I had another huge reason to learn engineering and production. All my life I'd been in bands with very domineering GENIUS figures. These were guys that, for whatever reason, had developed MAD skills on their instruments far beyond their young age. I was the polar opposite, struggling constantly for years to play the correct note, in the proper rhythm, with a good sound. For example, when I was seventeen my piano teacher, Donald Denegar (a brilliant, gifted music teacher), had eight-year-old students that could play more proficiently and musically than I! Along the way, I'd been kicked out of several bands simply because I didn't really understand 'rhythm counting', and made constant mistakes hitting the wrong notes, or the cracks between the keys. These errors were all made much worse from my early and constant pot smoking.

At age twelve I was assigned scales and easy pieces, using a loudly clicking wooden metronome. I was dumbfounded though—defeated in my efforts—because to me the damn metronome felt like it was speeding up and slowing down all the time (it wasn't). I felt deeply in my churning paisley and patchouli-scented soul that I was destined to learn guitar, play incredible keyboards, sing and write strange songs. The last thing I needed was some expert or know-it-all standing in the same room while I was trying to get all of this together, laughing at me, telling me I suck, played a wrong note or sang like shit.

If I could just make friends with the tape recorder, I could figure everything out on my OWN. With the TEAC 3340-S 4-track, you could 'bounce' tracks, combining parts you'd already recorded with new incoming performances, to free up space to layer more sounds and parts.

In the beginning, when I wrote my own songs, what held me back was that I'd run out of ideas! I would start with a raw burst of enthusiasm and marijuana-enhanced brilliance, spending hours performing the first parts correctly, yet with a certain magic. Then I'd add a few space sounds, then bass lines, before completely grinding to a halt, having no idea how to actually finish anything. But then came that glorious morning breakthrough, on January 1st, 1980: I actually COMPLETED my first-ever song, *Substitute Music*, in a blaze of LSD color swirls. Delirium amid clear impressions of reincarnation and past-life mental brainstorms. The lyrics, firmly and forever embedded on magnetic tape, included this choice couplet:

"We have seen the alien, and he is us.
Our worst enemy lies within the mirror..."

Classic acid rant. It went so well, that I recorded two more songs that same day.

The second piece, *Isolation Madness*, was three minutes of distorted, backwards guitar rock, sprinkled with ARP Odyssey synth explosions on top and me, singing in a fake, redneck, Texan accent, about sitting on my back porch ruminating about LIFE while watching all the people just walking around doing their thing. The third song was a sound collage built on layered interplanetary noises, jarring explosions, with synthetic sounds of melting metal flying through outer space. That really marked DAY ONE, when I first considered myself a songwriter, sound inventor and producer. I basically made songs and sound collages like these throughout the entire 1980s and 90s.

By the time our church/recording studio burned down and I relocated to New York for the first time (in 1987), I had boxes full of 'Gordon Raphael compositions' on cassette tapes. Though I lost my Hammond Organ, synthesizers, briefcases full of letters and love letters, my clothes, books and the psychedelic posters that had once adorned my childhood walls, those cassette tapes miraculously SURVIVED the fire.

The tragic irony came a year later, when I visited my friend Sigmund, with whom I had left several boxes of my tapes as we were on the way to start our new life in New York. Because I trusted him and he had a huge house of his own, I'd left with him a few boxes of cassettes that wouldn't fit in my suitcase. When I told him that Debe and I now had a steady place to live, so I could take those boxes of tapes back, he replied that GOD told him to throw them away, because I didn't need them anymore. And so, he did. My relationship with Sigmund, and his relationship with God, will be discussed in a later book. Suffice to say that I was fucking furious with him for getting rid of my songs, and never spoke with him again.

Cassettes of my first six years of original music that did survive the fire, smelled of acrid, residual smoke and the handmade artwork on their boxes were singed in sinister grey and yellowish shades. 90% of those tapes made it safely to New York and I still possess them. Over the years, friends who I'd given cassettes to as handmade presents, would send some back to me that contained lost songs. Two years ago, I was contacted online by someone I'd never met, who'd found one of these hand decorated tapes in a St. Vincent de Paul thrift shop in Renton, Washington. She googled the band name and traced it to me. She then sent me that cassette which had ten songs on it that were missing from my collection! It has been truly haunting to hear some of my own

31

missing songs vaguely playing in my head, but not be able to remember all the words, chords and sounds.

━━━━━◆◆◆━━━

Back at Chateau Relaxo, I continued my own experimental music, worked closely with Anne writing new songs for *Absinthee* and rehearsed with our band members for upcoming shows. The threat of my almost empty bank account and the advice I had been given to apply for jobs were weighing heavily over my days. In true Gordon fashion, I did my best to ignore the 'getting a job' bit and, a week after returning from our Seattle Christmas, I cut up magazine pictures of cool-looking keyboards and vintage microphones, assembling a collaged poster with felt pen writing that said something like "Record Producer with Cool Studio seeking Bands and Artists who want to record DEMOS." Then I ran to the copy shop on East Houston and printed twenty of these which I taped to phone poles and mailboxes down Ludlow Street, in the nightclub area. I also stuck some up on St. Marks Place and along Avenue A. No one called.

A week later it was clear that my poster idea wasn't working. As the last money was vanishing from my bank account, I tried to remember what Manny and Lisa had been telling me about finding a job. I resigned myself to the possibility that I could work at A&P supermarket or something similar, until *Absinthee* got our record deal. Then I would be back on my feet, back on the road in no time.

I sublet my friend's (Philippo Scrooge, part of our early artistic, punk rock social scene in Seattle) old-school New York studio apartment, facing Tompkins Square Park on East 7th Street between Avenues A and B. My rent there was only $500, a significant reduction from the previous year.

Around the same time, I got a call at home on my landline from a musician named Pamela Laws. She was living in New York but hailed from San Francisco, where she'd been a singer and electric guitarist during the grunge era in a rock band called *Seven*

32

Day Diary. The other guitarist in that band was one of my lifelong best friends, Kenneth V. Weller.

Ken and I were elementary school buddies; together in Cub Scouts, soccer team and later he was the bass player in all my high school rock bands (*Apple Corps, The Steve Kirk Band* and *The Musk Floral Ensemble*). We were proud to be in Boy Scout Troop 617 and, at the end of a long mountain hike, while the other kids were wrapping potatoes in foil and placing them under hot coals, Ken and I would pitch our tent and work to correctly position a loudspeaker plugged into his small transistor radio. While I hung that speaker with wire from the top of our tent, he was busy marinating steaks for our supper.

Ken told Pamela Laws to look me up because he was familiar with everything I'd ever recorded and thought I could help with her new solo project. She asked to come see the studio, to check out my sounds and see if we could potentially work together. I played her some pretty, moody songs that Anne had sung on, so she could hear what I could do with a female voice. Then I played her some of my own recent songs, finishing with two crazy experimental pieces, so she could hear a variety.

Happily, she was a bit impressed. Pamela told me she liked my style and thought that her songs would benefit from my production. She asked how much I charged and, well, I hadn't considered that part! I thought hard and fast and told her, "$25 per song?" She laughed and said she would pay me more than that and we could start recording drums a few days later.

The first band I had ever produced was *Mental Mannequin*, in 1980, and the second was *Colour Twigs*, in '83. Both of these were my own bands. Then in '86, I recorded a goth band called *Serious Dark Angels*, on a borrowed 4-track cassette deck, in our tiny one-bedroom Apartment F in Seattle. Drummer Ben Ireland had sat on the bathtub with one mic in the bathroom for his entire drumkit. I put one mic on a guitar amp and one on a bass amp which were both in my living room. The fourth microphone was for the singer, Fagin.

Also in '86, there was a small run of bands that I recorded in my friend Bruce Jones's basement on an Akai 12-Track; this odd beast of a machine used what looked like old video tapes. Those bands happened to be *Green River*, *Feast* and *Bundle of Hiss*; musicians that would grow to become vastly influential a few years later. The next year at our church/studio, before it burned down, I produced a few groups. Through the haze I can only remember one, inspired by *Beastie Boys*, called *Urban Rhythm Unit*. Years later, at Bear Creek Studio, I produced our first *Absinthee* album and one heavy metal TV commercial with Matt Cameron (*Soundgarden*, *Pearl Jam*) on drums. I also had a one-day session there with *Maktub* starring the astronomically zany, brilliantly talented singer, Reggie Watts.

Those bands, plus my own tripped-out songs, were the complete basis of my experience as a producer. Now, thanks to Pamela Laws, I was about to have my first professional recording session in New York City. I never considered being a producer for 'other people', as it was simply a process I learned to develop my own songs. Besides which, I did not think I would have patience for anyone else's musical ideas!

5: First Sessions For 'Other People'

Pamela Laws arrived at Chateau Relaxo with a very friendly, cool-looking Hispanic drummer from Brooklyn. Even though our studio was quite advanced, it was still the days of a single Digidesign 888 interface, which meant we could only record eight channels of audio at the same time.

Technically speaking, Scott Clark had installed a Pro Tools Mix Plus system (Mix Core and Mix Farm PCI cards were inside the computer), which brought the sounds from eight different microphones into the digital domain via the 888 interface. Emagic Logic version 3 was our preferred software because, unlike Pro Tools which needed to clumsily link to a second software (Cakewalk or Mark of the Unicorn, for example) for MIDI sequencing, Logic could already record both audio and MIDI perfectly well.

The way I was thinking about recording in January 1999 was very different to how I work now. At that time, I was sticking closely to time-honored studio techniques, procedures that most musicians and engineers followed. From the late 1980s all through the 90s, it was common to begin recording a song with the guitarist playing a 'scratch' version of the song all by themselves, in strict tempo with a click track. It would usually take a while to get that part done correctly, using an approximation of the actual sound that would be used 'later'. It would usually take up a significant amount of valuable studio time to get this first part sounding good enough for the other musicians to play along to. All the years that a band rehearses and performs a song, the whole band plays together. This is the feel-good, human way that bands naturally interact. Suddenly, in the studio, one musician was isolated, then needed to rock out to a mechanically perfect computer click. Afterwards, the singer would sing along to that, half-heartedly and rather quickly as a 'guide track'. Why singing half-heartedly? Because, again, the singer is used to howling over a room full of big amps and drums, not just accompanying a

35

single guitar and click, click, click! THEN the drummer would go into a room by themselves, wearing headphones. Under the scrutiny of the engineer, producer, fellow band members and their friends, the drummer would be required to play as perfectly as possible to these scratch tracks.

It was often a sweaty affair, even for a talented drummer who was rhythmically tight thanks to many hours practicing at home with a click. Engineers would spend an hour or two finely crafting the drum sounds before recording. What followed was a couple more hours of 'takes' (basically playing the song over and over). All this time, the rest of the band has been using up all their excited energy sitting on a couch with their friends, smoking cigarettes, often drinking beer for five hours. Finally, there would be one song's worth of well-played drums. Just when the other musicians wanted to rush and pick up their instruments, they'd be asked to sit for at least another hour or two while the drums were edited, to sound more 'perfect' and professional.

This nit-picky editing was done either because the drummer needed to feel better about his playing or the producer was super anal, insisting that everything be absolutely accurate to the 'grid'[5]. In the big days of yore, when studios charged $1,000 per day, producers and engineers received great salaries and so it was acceptable to luxuriously spend ALL those hours (on the clock) recording ONE song's worth of drums. From the band's point of view, I can tell you, it was excruciating and boring to sit there for five or six hours while the producer and drummer took turns hating each other. During a live concert, bands easily run through nine songs during a forty-five-minute set and, gosh, the drums sound just fine! Why, when they now had to pay so much for studio sessions, did drums suddenly take six hours for one song?

---

[5] A grid is a computer's visual and digital representation of perfect rhythmic timing. Software or producers can 'quantize', which involves moving just about all musical information onto the grid so it is theoretically correct. My issue is that humans have a nervous system (computers don't) and it's emotional to slow down and speed up.

In this old, tiring process, bass would be added to those highly labored drum tracks and the guitar and vocal scratch tracks would get ERASED, only to be performed AGAIN more seriously. I now see this method as time consuming, energy draining and it created music that is a bit lonely and sterile because no musicians were laughing and jumping in each other's faces while the song was being played. It often transmits the emotional power of solitary confinement!

Before moving to New York, I'd never set up proper microphones for drums by myself (putting ONE cheap mic in a bathroom for Ben's drums on *Serious Dark Angels* was... different!). Most of my songs used drum machines and, when I produced my own bands in big studios, a highly skilled engineer would do all the techie-stuff; mics, preamps and compressors. After seven months of deep experimentation with the Chateau Relaxo equipment, I felt totally confident and ready to make killer, unusual drum tracks.

Selecting six microphones, I placed two, spread apart, up over the drummer's head, one in front of the kick drum and individual mics over the snare, rack tom and floor tom. Then I added our fat Neumann U87 condenser mic to soak up the overall room sound, squishing that chaos through our Manley compressor. The U87 became a psychedelic ambience mic that made all the drums stick together and sound like they were breathing.

Pamela and her drummer looked surprised and happy when the soundcheck only took twenty minutes before the drums were ready to record. Yes, Pamela did perform a scratch guitar and vocal part using a click track, but it all went really smoothly. A couple hours later, the drums were finished for her first song and, as I played them back to her, I overheard the drummer on his cell phone (some musicians had them in 1999, but certainly not me):

"Whoa this guy Gordon can get good drum sounds FAST. We should cancel that other studio for Thursday and come here instead!"

Cool! That's exactly how it happened that I got my second job during the day of my first job.

Pamela booked in twelve more days, steadily building a collection of her own songs. Acoustic and electric guitars became layered with drums, bass and various guest instrumentalists, providing a serene natural backdrop for her clear voice and introspective lyrics. She was happy with the results, generously paying me $100 per session, not the $25 per song I had originally asked for. Her drummer did bring in his other band and soon people began coming down those basement stairs just about every day to work with me.

Many of these sessions were booked for only a few hours. On those shorter sessions, the artists might record an acoustic guitar part and some vocals, returning a few days later with a tambourine and a friend that would play a harmonica solo. Oh... why did I have to say harmonica solo? That instantly brings back the painful memory of the ONE time I accidentally deleted something that I had already been paid to record.

The studio had an elaborate information backup system which let us save copies of all the data from sessions onto tiny digital 'back-up tapes'. In those days not everyone had a computer and very few musicians owned a CD burner. So, this one painful day, an artist (forgot his name!) came to do further work on his song. I was able to reload his session from the tape backup, but for some goddamn reason, his harmonica solo's audio file had become corrupted! Lost for all time. He got really angry with me and I certainly was both sorry and embarrassed. I refunded his money for the previous session and gave him a couple hours for free the following week, to bring his harmonica player back to redo it. Unfortunately, with recordings it's very rare to redo something exactly the same way it was before. It's almost impossible to recreate 'happy accidents' and rare to tap into the same emotional feeling, one week later.

Chateau Relaxo was operating perfectly. Scott had built such a solid, good-sounding system that, even though that Power Mac was ON all day, every day, for two years in a row—it never crashed! I would stay until 7pm, then hand the studio over to Scott and Eric, who worked till dawn. Musicians were coming down, paying me to transfer their old cassettes onto the computer to burn CDs for them. Nine years earlier, I remember going to a studio in Pasadena, California where they charged me $50 dollars for a single CD copy of my songs. Now, I was charging $25 an hour to engineer and the CDs were free.

Artists would begin songs with a full ten-hour day in the studio and then return two weeks later, after they'd saved up enough money to spend another afternoon tracking or mixing their songs. By mid-March 1999, I somehow had a full-time job recording people. I was breathing great sighs of relief because I could actually pay my rent, bills, take buses and subway trains. There was even enough money left over to take occasional taxis, go to gigs, eat at Thai and Mexican restaurants (I was a long-term vegetarian) and soak up the exhilarating atmosphere at Cafe Orlin for breakfast. In between sessions and on my days off, I was still going hard, making my own music and arranging new songs for *Absinthee*.

Anne was attending the School of Visual Arts, doing a tremendous job of meeting people and going out to clubs and parties as often as possible. I almost always went with her, for there was tremendous fun to be had on those nights at The Vault (goth club), Luna Lounge, Fez, Club Motherfucker and various arty loft parties downtown. We attended the *Bauhaus* reunion concert at Hammerstein Ballroom and went frequently to see bands at Irving Plaza, conveniently located near Anne's apartment. Being so close to that venue meant that we could have crazy parties before and after, with our growing circle of New York friends. Baby Jupiter was one of the clubs on the way home from the studio and we were starting to know many local musicians who played there. Further up the road, Continental was still a pressure cooker of late-night rock action and public drunkenness (except for me, teetotaler). I was playing my music game full time, but I was seriously 100% off drugs and not interested in alcohol, which is a drug anyway. I was never really hyped on drinking alcohol. I mean—if it's completely legal and your parents did it— where's the danger? Where's the adventure? Where's the glory?

6: Bring on the Germans, Swiss and Austrians!

Now that I was up and running, with regular clients coming in to record with me, it wasn't long before my immediate group of party partners, as introduced to me by Chad Swahnberg, started booking time at the studio. Several of them had their own musical projects, choosing to work with me because they imagined it would be fun.

The first guy in was the very kind, funny and intelligent Swiss writer, Frank Heer. We recorded his epic, ten-minute odyssey called *Did You See Me Riding On That Horse?* He named his group, *Bingo Palace*. I recently found that song on Bandcamp and, browsing through the credits, I see so many musicians who became deeply embroidered into my New York story. I was even reminded that I played synthesizer on it! Another Swiss guy, Fa Ventilato, who was an eccentric and highly sought-after East Village drummer, also played on that song. Dorit Chrysler (from Graz in Austria), who is now one of the foremost theremin players in the world, gave a spoken word performance through a telephone. She actually called the studio from a landline and I recorded it. Her story, written by Frank Heer, was about seeing a really hot guy riding a horse! Musical wunderkind, Nikko Weidemann from Berlin, played Wurlitzer electric piano and, soon after, would play a life-changing role on my musical journey. In fact, of the eight musicians listed on *Did You See Me Riding On That Horse?*, seven either worked with me throughout my New York days, played on *Absinthee* songs, or became my studio partners.

Another Swiss writer, called Roman Game, came in next to record a song with me using many of the same players as *Bingo Palace*. Then, Nikko Weidemann himself entered the studio to make demos for his upcoming album. Nikko had arrived in New York from Berlin, after spending time living in London. He is one of the characters I remember talking with most through those long rooftop party nights. He is a very gifted songwriter, singer, pianist and guitarist. Usually, people specialize in either keyboards or guitar but some rare individuals, like Nikko, can play both ridiculously well. Legend has it that the great Frank Zappa himself once asked Nikko to play for him on a German tour. After Nikko's fourth recording session at Chateau Relaxo, he looked at me and said,

"I know an amazing record producer in Berlin and he would love this place. I'm gonna write him and tell him about you. You two are going to get along great."

These were prophetic, far-reaching words but, at the time, I was just excited to meet a German record producer and possibly sell more studio time!

During that uplifting summer of 1999 there was one highly memorable, warm weather rooftop party. Our hip, European nightlife crew threw a birthday party for... ME! I dressed up a little extra-cool and was speaking with Anne when a beautiful, sexy, (you guessed it) Swiss actress/singer named Claudi Sisti came right up to us and introduced herself. She was very bubbly and sweet and, in the course of our first conversation, mentioned to me that she was really into drum 'n' bass. This was a form of music featuring super rapid drumbeats with lightning fast hi-hat patterns that was taking over the New York club scene. At an earlier rooftop party, one of the only other Americans there, Trixie Reiss, introduced me to drum 'n' bass via the album, *Learning Curve* by *DJ Rap*. I actually loved those sounds and bought the CD immediately. Trixie also introduced me to her German boyfriend, En Esch, from industrial band *KMFDM*. He is a unique, captivating character, who wound up playing drums with *Absinthee* a year later.

Back to the lovely Claudi. She was so much fun, with her laughter and charming Swiss accent, that the next day I walked into the studio with the idea to make a few instrumental drum 'n' bass tracks. Then, I would casually invite Claudi Sisti down to pick one or more to sing on. I studied the *DJ Rap* album, trying my best to use drum loops from a CD ROM, layered with drum machines and keyboards. Those tracks were far from perfect but, by the end of the day, I had three slightly unsteady songs ready to go.

The next day I called up Claudi, who said she'd be thrilled to come over to the studio and try some singing. She arrived wearing a white leotard top, breathless and sweating from rollerblading down from midtown, among the taxis and cars on the street. Very brave woman! I was smiling to have her there in the dimly lit, air-conditioned basement, on that boiling hot New York summer day. She brought some lyrics she had in a notebook and sang on two of the songs. Those drum 'n' bass songs weren't really my best compositions, but that day was very enjoyable. It was a good exercise for me to dip into a new musical genre.

7: Enter Moses Schneider

Nikko Weidemann did indeed tell his Berlin music producer friend to check me out. On July 4th, 1999, Moses Schneider landed in New York and headed straight to Chateau Relaxo to investigate. Moses was very cool-looking with shaggy hair and rays of light beaming out of his dark brown eyes.

When he saw the studio, he smiled immediately, in a genuine, warm way and, as he spoke, he moved his arms quickly, painting pictures in the air. I got the impression that Moses was highly animated and naturally wired. It was clear that he already knew every piece of equipment in our studio, so I decided to play him my best recordings, hoping to really impress him with my brilliant style. He smiled as I played these songs, but I sensed the smile was intended to be polite.

Then he said, "Here's what I've been doing in Berlin" and proceeded to blow my mind with song after song.

"What's that grinding sound?" I asked.

"Oh, that's me playing a slowed-down bass guitar in 7/8 timing."

"Is that a real orchestra?" I asked. Of course, it was!

"Wow, Moses, what is THAT?"

"It's my partner Benson, playing keyboards with one hand while playing the drums."

I'd really never heard anything like a Moses Schneider production and, within the first hour of his visit, I was totally impressed, captivated by his imagination and conceptualization of music. I quickly called him, "the Albert Einstein of music production".

His Fouth of July visit coincided with big USA birthday celebrations. Anne's parents, Manny and Joe, happened to be in town too, so we all got together to walk around downtown Manhattan, watching the fireworks over the East River. It was hot and sticky, as summer always is there, but we all had a wonderful night together. After the festivities, I wanted Moses to come

44

around to my apartment on 7th Street, to 'pick his brain' about a few things. He was up for it, so we walked back from Anne's place up on 16th Street.

While we were walking down 3rd Avenue, we witnessed a really bizarre sight that shook us both. A shouting man was flailing his arms around on the sidewalk across the road, as some paramedics were putting him on a stretcher, then loading him into an ambulance. It was hard to tell if the guy was having a medical emergency, overdosing on drugs or just going crazy. The red light was flashing and the ambulance started pulling away. Suddenly, the back door flew open and the guy jumped out, running straight towards the middle of 3rd Avenue where he was promptly hit by a car. The paramedics rushed over to grab him from the street and loaded him back into the ambulance. Moses and I thought about that silently for a few minutes, looking at each other and shaking our heads.

Back at my apartment, my plan was to play Moses a few more of my songs, both solo and with *Absinthee*, asking for his observations and critique. I told him that I'd always been my own biggest fan and, though I thought my music was really quite ingenious, sadly, not many others shared my lofty opinion. I had presented my songs and the music of *Absinthee* for years but, so far, no one had ever wanted to sign us. Of the people I had shown my music to, it was rare to see them get excited (though I often saw looks of bewilderment and confusion). He sat patiently, listening to my greatest works from Seattle and New York, smiling a little bit here and there.

When I was done, I asked him what he thought.

He pondered for a minute and said, "I have a challenge for you."

I thought, "What-the-fuck? I'm looking for answers, not a goddamn challenge!"

Moses continued, "For one year, don't use any reverb or echo on any of your productions, ok?"

I was irritated, and shot back, "Well, how are you supposed to make drums sound huge, like the Grand Canyon, or guitars flying through space WITHOUT ECHO OR REVERB?"

He smiled wide saying, "Well, just try. Experiment with hard compression and ambient microphones and let's see what happens."

Before he left my place, Moses told me that he would bring his own band, *Van Der Meer*, signed on Polydor Records in Germany, over to Chateau Relaxo. They would arrive by the end of the month and book an entire week to record their singer, Susie van der Meer. This sounded both great and unusual to me. I'd never rented the studio for an entire week before, and yet, I wouldn't be the one doing the engineering or producing. All in all, I was excited for the upcoming opportunity to learn from Moses and watch him in action.

As promised, by the end of July, *Van Der Meer* came to Manhattan. I was introduced to singer, Susie, and drummer, Benson Lauber. Moses brought his favorite piece of equipment from Berlin, the Manley Voxbox, for Susie to sing through. Our procedure for the week was to arrive in the morning, set up Susie with a new song, adjust the mic sound and then just leave her alone for three hours to work by herself.

Moses, Benson and I would sit out on the front steps in the sunshine, watching the bustling city street scene on Ludlow & Grand. Sometimes we went for short walks, the two of them constantly rolling joints of marijuana mixed with tobacco—Euro-style. I rolled my eyes, as I didn't have much patience for pot-smoking, beer drinking or any other recreational drug use. I certainly DID have an awesome respect for Moses and Ben's recording techniques and musical expertise.

It was a wonderful week together and all three *Van Der Meer* band members became friends of mine. We had many great talks about the music business, songwriting, sound and production, while Susie was busy singing downstairs. After the vocal tracks were all recorded, Moses told me he would bring other German bands to Chateau Relaxo, as he loved the idea that their fans would see "recorded in New York" in the credits on his CDs.

Moses, like the others in my close circle of European friends, fell in love with New York and wanted to be part of that buzzing, creative whirlwind as often as possible.

8: A Brush with Fame

On a windy morning with dappled sunshine peeking down on the East Village, I walked my daily route down to Ludlow & Grand. I unlocked the studio and began working on new *Absinthee* songs: programming MIDI sequences with the Kurzweil sampler, making echoed space-cat sounds and playing distorted wah-wah pedal bass parts underneath it all. The day was going super well and, after burning through my creative energy, I felt the demanding pangs of hunger. I usually stopped at the fruit and vegetable market next to Niagara Bar on Avenue A on my way to Chateau Relaxo because I preferred having my lunch in our moody basement control room. My mind was deep in ideas about how to finish some new songs when our landline rang.

Our phone at the studio NEVER rang. I only used it to call Anne, asking her to come down to work with me or, in the older days when I needed help, to Scott Clark while he was at Scholastic. I was therefore surprised when I answered the phone and heard a guy with an English accent on the line.

"Can I book time in your studio?" he asks.

"Yes, of course. When do you want to come in?" I reply.

Him: "Right now, well, in 30 minutes."

Me: "Whoa really? What do you want to do?"

Him: "I've got a cassette tape and I want to do some singing. It won't take long!"

Me (thinking to myself): "Man, I hope this DOESN'T take too long, I wanna get back to my songs and, wow, he must be a drug addict or something—there are so many in this neighborhood! This poor guy is so low-budget that he's gonna sing over an old cassette tape!"

But, what I actually say is: "Ok that's cool. An hour will cost you $25 and what's your name?"

He tells me his name is Ian and that he'll be over in half an hour.

This is exactly what happens next, as the action unfolds:

I want to save as much time as possible so, while I'm there eating my lunch, I close my Logic session in order to create a new one. I make a blank session, naming it "Ian's Song". I also put a good microphone and headphones in the live room, while listening for the doorbell.

It rings right on time and I press the buzzer, waiting at the studio door for him to come downstairs. This guy Ian looks kind of cool, with rocker-style longish hair and a brown leather coat, but I'm still a little worried that it's some druggie guy from the neighborhood, so I'd better keep an eye on my equipment. He has brought along a striking-looking woman with long brownish-blonde hair, wearing a fashionable grey wool Mexican poncho.

Ian says, "Hi, nice to meet you. This is Fabiola."

As we walk through the small, cramped live room filled with drums and a few guitar amps, lit with a dim red party bulb, he comments, "Looks like a massage parlor!"

I laugh a little and bring them both into the control room. He hands me his cassette tape, and it's labeled *808 State* (great electronic Manchester band, part of a truly revolutionary wave of music).

I'm thinking, "This guy is really struggling. He can't even afford a new tape to make his own music on, he's recording over a hissy old used one!"

I pop the cassette tape into the studio tape deck, transferring the instrumental onto the computer so he can do his vocals. I DO notice that the song sounds remarkably well made, actually excellent. I point to the classic Neumann mic out in the live room and I ask if he's ready to go out there and sing.

He comes back with, "Do you have an SM57? And, if you don't mind, I'd rather stand in here with you."

I think, "Man he really must be a newcomer because that's a great mic out there and SM57 is THE most common mic, even the worst practice rooms have them."

But, of course, I set up the SM57 and sit down at the computer with him four feet behind me. Within one minute I have a decent vocal sound ready. Then I work for another minute, adjusting his headphones so that the music tracks and microphone channel from the computer are balanced in his ears (I'm also wearing headphones).

Me: "Ready?"

Ian: "Yeah."

I push record and sit back for take number one. He starts singing and within fifteen seconds I notice that his voice sounds eerily familiar to me. In fact, he's singing pretty damn well. Thirty seconds in and I'm desperately trying to figure out where I know that voice from. I'm staring at the computer screen, where the Logic session is labeled "Ian's Song" and it clicks—really hard.

My mind: "I think this is IAN BROWN from the *fucking STONE ROSES!!*"

The song is over in four minutes. I remove my headphones and swivel around in my chair asking, "Are you Ian Brown from *The Stone Roses??*"

He says "Yeah, I'm Ian Brown but *The Stone Roses* have been split up for a while."

I proceed to ask him how the first take went and he replies that it was perfect, then he asks me if he could double it.

So, he sings once more, just as perfectly as the first take and so the entire session is finished 35 minutes after he and Fabiola walked in. He wants me to burn the song on a CD and tells me that this is a demo because he is on the way to England to record with *808 State* and just wants to show them his ideas.

I ask him how he found out about our studio and he says he just looked in the phonebook for the closest studio to his apartment, so he could get over to JFK airport immediately afterwards. I had NO idea that we were even IN the phonebook.

He tells me that I am very fast and a good engineer, handing me a crisp fifty-dollar bill. Major event, well paid—I went straight back to my own music with an unexpected $50 in my pocket.

9: The Jimmy Goodman Story

This tale shows how the beginning tied in with the end, which then created a new beginning. Cool, huh?

Ms. Pamela Laws, from San Francisco, had been my first official paying client in New York City for what had now become my job, recording and producing musical artists. She worked on six songs with me and, for one of these, she brought along a hip, stylish musician named Jimmy Goodman, to program beats on his Akai MPC60—THE hot drum machine for hip-hop. Jimmy also played vibraphone, an instrument that's rarely seen in studios nowadays. He'd regularly been playing jazz and swing, but was also well versed in hip-hop, rock and electronic music. We got along well and he really liked the studio, returning with his own band *Mink* to record a potential hit song he'd written called *Paris Has Turned Black and Blue*. During these sessions he was buzzing with energy, telling many New York stories involving music legends he'd worked with and describing a cast of talented, colorful characters.

Being in a basement, right around the corner from Chinatown, with its seafood, meat and vegetable markets, meant that we would often see well-fed rats scampering around. Also, we had this really strange portable air conditioner set up in the storage area, adjacent to our control room, which was directly under the Ludlow Street sidewalk. Scott Clark called that thing "Pinguino", which may have been the brand name. It had a dreadful looking plastic hose that attached to the wall with a wire, possibly aiming at a vent in the ceiling. Pinguino made an annoying whirring sound and dripped water into a plastic bucket that had to be emptied every few hours. It made the air downstairs safer to breathe and, lord knows, we would have fried in the sweltering summer heat if that machine wasn't there.

As fate would have it, sometime in early August, Scott announced that the owner of our building had asked us to leave so that he could convert the basement into retail space, thus charging higher rent. This news really bummed me out! Here I was, just starting to get into my groove producing music, recording bands for money (never saving any, but comfortably paying my rent and having fun), yet we now had to go. I felt devastated, having no idea what my next move was gonna be other than back to square one. My only thought was to phone everyone that had been dropping by to work with me at the studio, to inform them that, if they wanted to finish their projects or do any extra recording, they only had one month before we moved out. Several people put in reservations for time.

When I called Jimmy Goodman, he told me that he didn't have any projects per se but asked me why Chateau Relaxo was closing. I told him our sad tale of being evicted and that I had no idea whatsoever what I would be doing after that.

He called me back a few days later proposing that he would become my new studio partner and we could look for a new space, in a good location, together. He said he would contribute some money towards renting a new studio and, perhaps, we could both take out loans to get started with equipment and to secure a lease. Jimmy told me that he'd like to watch me work for a while, as he was interested in starting his own career as a recording engineer/producer.

Well, to me this sounded like a great solution, even though I didn't think I was likely to be a good candidate for convincing a bank to loan me money!

I also wrote to Moses Schneider in Berlin, at his Transporterraum Studio, and told him that plans to bring more German bands over to New York would have to be put on hold. He generously offered that, if I found a new location, he would send me some excellent recording equipment directly from his studio and invest some money as well. He was very encouraging and let me know that he fully intended to continue our collaboration.

So it came to pass that Jimmy Goodman and I began scouring *The Village Voice* for a place that we could start our new recording studio. He found the contact number for a space at 154 East 2nd Street. Jimmy and I bolted over there to meet the building manager, one Rick Robinson.

He took us down in a scary-looking old freight elevator (with eerie scraping sounds, just like in my own industrial music!) to a dark basement. It was a massive space, lit by a couple of dangling lightbulbs and stacked high with dusty, disused furniture. There were tables, chairs and boxes as far as the eye could strain to see down there, in that dim light. Rick was also a musician and showed us his small room on the second floor, displaying some rare keyboards (Voyetra!) and a few pieces of recording equipment. There was a well-known professional studio on the fourth floor called Dangerous, but the basement had been a neglected storage area for over fifty years.

Rick sectioned out an area that could be turned into our studio's 200 sq. ft. control room and 450 sq. ft. live room. The section of the basement that we were offered was towards the back wall, under the sidewalk of Avenue A and directly beneath a methadone clinic. There was a strange narrow, rusted pipe coming down from the ceiling and I wondered if it was some kind of methadone drip feed from the clinic. I winced, remembering a visit to a different methadone clinic from my earlier life in New York.

If we were interested in renting the space, we'd have to haul out all the furniture and build soundproof walls. The rent was set at $2,000 a month and, when I heard that amount (knowing that to start with I'd be the only one engineering sessions, thereby bringing in the rent), I told Rick exactly this:

"We'll rent your place, but I promise you that we are going to have to make as much noise as a jet airplane taking off, 24 hours per day, 7 days a week, to pay that rent."

I wonder if he was just focusing on the extra money coming in, because he just smiled and nodded his head, "OK."

I asked Moses exactly what equipment he was willing to ship to us from Berlin, then began drawing up plans for the other recording gear we would need. I also started researching which Apple Mac computer and Pro Tools system was the latest and greatest. In the end, I calculated that we needed $20,000 for equipment and construction before we could open the doors and start our business. Jimmy didn't flinch, telling me that he was confident he could get his half of the money pretty quickly.

One of the reasons I desired this new, bigger studio was to have a super-plush rehearsal space for *Absinthee*, right in the middle of the coolest neighborhood in New York.

My next phone call was to Manny Hadlock over at Bear Creek in Woodinville, Washington. She was pleased to hear that I had rescued myself from the edges of going broke by finding musicians to record at Chateau Relaxo. She was also glad that Anne and I were playing shows and continuing to write songs together. Manny agreed to co-sign a $10,000 loan from her bank that I would be responsible for repaying. She graciously offered her decorating skills and her husband Joe's experienced help in designing and constructing the walls, windows and sound insulation we would need to have a great, working studio.

10: Transporterraum NYC is Born

In November 1999, Scott Clark and I said goodbye to Chateau Relaxo. I moved my keyboards and guitars into Philippo's apartment that I was still subletting, while Scott made preparations to ship his entire studio to England.

Jimmy and I spent a day moving the old dusty furniture out of our area in that 2nd Street basement. We discovered 100-year-old iron radiators laying in the dust and had to hire a special moving service to come carry those heavy things away. Digging more through the piles we found a massive wooden table. Wiping away a bit of the dust we realized it was beautiful dark wood with a glossy, shiny finish. We both agreed that this would make a real statement as the main work surface in our studio, rather than the usual 'audio-technology'-looking contraptions that may have been more practical, but far less stylee, for SURE.

Next came the very strange job of shoveling DIRT out from beneath the Avenue A sidewalk. It was weird to see so much organic earth gathered in a basement in the East Village. It was also sweaty, laborious work removing those mounds of dirt from the area we had designated as the future storage area for drum kits, cables, tools and instrument cases, so they wouldn't clutter up the control room. A few days later, we were ready for the next big steps.

Anne's father, Joe Hadlock, is an amazing man. A tremendous piano player who, along with Manny, made Bear Creek Studio one of the best equipped and most beautiful-sounding studios in the world. Aesthetically, the wide-open classic barn structure and its interior decor create a comforting, creative bubble, encouraging artists to do their best work. Joe earned a fortune early in his career producing hilarious soundtracks for Rainier Beer television ads and his roots go back to the real beginnings of Seattle's recording studio culture. He's usually a pretty quiet guy, except when he sings and plays the piano or mows the pastures, riding atop his noisy red tractor. Having taken a keen interest in our new studio project, Joe stepped off a plane from Seattle carrying a table-saw and a heavy toolbox! After a taxi ride, he arrived to our recently cleared out basement and we helped him bring down his construction equipment.

A truckload of lumber (2x4s and 4x4s), loads of sheet rock, tape, nails and plaster would soon become walls. Large flat particle boards and rolls of Rockwool (aptly named in this case) were going to be used for sound insulation and to make acoustic baffles. Then came weeks of cutting, sawing, nailing, gluing, stapling, mudding and painting.

Prior to this, hardly anyone had ever seen Gordon Raphael up on a ladder wearing a dust-mask, drilling holes or pounding nails. My gentle soul was much more commonly seen playing scales on an upright piano, eating cookies, messing with knobs on a synthesizer, going out to the movies, or painting my fingernails in Day-Glo colors. There exists at least one photo of me doing that semi-manly construction work in the basement, and I shall dig it out as proof. Yes, it's also true that Jimmy and Joe would roll their eyes and shake their head watching the delicate (read: slow and/or inconsistent) way I performed the jobs assigned to me.

Walls did appear and there was a rectangular hole between the control-room-to-be and the live-room-to-be, where a professional-looking, double glazed, soundproof window was going to be installed. It was starting to look very much like the skeleton of a cool music studio, in formation. At this point, Manny and Anne stepped up to lead the vibe-creation and visual design phase. Their contribution was maximal, really creating the impression and atmosphere that everyone who ever recorded, rehearsed or produced music there will remember. This is how it went down:

Having measured all the areas within our studio, Anne and Manny searched all over downtown NYC looking for yards and yards of special, rich purple velvet. Then they selected red and purple paint, royal blue paint, silver paint and bold leopard print fabric. They sewed and sewed at Anne's apartment while Jimmy, Joe and I did the grunty, sweaty, wall building and insulation. Buckets of paint and brushes were delivered, so we all got busy making stunning purple and red walls in the live room, saving the royal blue for the control room. Then Anne ceremoniously threw handfuls of artist-grade glitter onto the wet paint, elevating the whole feel of the place to a psychedelic fairyland. Two thick studio doors were hung and subsequently painted shiny silver with red glitter window frames. Manny surprised us all when she arrived carrying an old, restored farm window, with eight rectangular glass panes. This was an unusual choice for a studio window, but when we painted the frame matte black and set it into the wall, it was visually spectacular.

After all the paint dried, Anne and Manny brought in their handmade purple velvet cushions and made a bohemian, comfortable couch out of a cement ledge that had been conveniently built into that basement when the building was erected in the 19th Century. The thick purple velvet draperies they hung next were made not only to cover the trashed brick walls that we'd be facing in the control room, but also served as excellent sound absorbers, helping our studio speakers sound more accurate and focused.

Christmas was only a few weeks away and we hoped to be open for music and business magically as the old century passed and a new one began. There were a few small jobs left, so we all helped in constructing two large sound-baffles that could be moved around in the live room; yes, the faux fur leopard print one and the purple velvet one. The wood frames for those were dutifully painted shiny silver to match our control room door and the studio entrance door which separated our place from the bombed out, dirty mess that filled the rest of that big basement.

Other cloud-like baffles were hung from the ceiling above the drums area and in the control room over the shiny wood work table, at an angle, so that our speakers' loud sounds wouldn't bounce off the ceiling and make distracting 'reflections'.

The last pleasing detail was a high wooden bookshelf, painted matte black, that Joe designed to go right over the couch in the control room, all the way up to the ceiling. This would be loaded with books, an old microscope my grandfather had left me, dolls, lamps and other items whose primary function was to further deflect sounds from the speakers, for clarity. It also gave a cool artistic and homey finish to the studio that we chose to call, Transporterraum NYC, in honor of Moses's studio of the same name in Kreuzberg, Berlin.

Here are the words from great music philosopher and producer Moses Schneider, whom I have called "The Albert Einstein of music production", in humorous contrast to my *Three Stooges* approach:

"Yes. Transporterraum is from *Star Trek*.[6] I have been a Trekkie for almost my entire life. Transporterraum means everything is possible, you can beam yourself into another dimension. I love that the crew must shout the order, "Energy!" before you will be dematerialized."

The name was indeed a tribute to him because we were thankful for the huge boost to our mood and confidence that came when he offered to help us AND bring German bands over to record.

Once the construction phase was complete and there was no more dirt, sawdust, Rockwool scraps or paint flying around, it was time to install the audio gear. Moses's shipment had cleared U.S. customs and arrived exactly when we needed it. All of that fabulous recording equipment that Jimmy and I had ordered was in boxes about to be unpacked.

One more hero landed at JFK airport to assist us—a former Bear Creek employee who'd been a good friend to me during our first *Absinthee* album session, Mr. Don Farwell. He flew seven hours across the USA and then sat in a corner for ONE WEEK, soldering hundreds of tiny wires into our Neutrik patch-bay so that every microphone, preamp, EQ and compressor could be quickly and flexibly connected.[7] Don did his soldering work

---

[6] Moses is, of course, referring to the original *Star Trek* series (1966-69).
[7] An EQ or Equalizer is a piece of musical equipment that alters the frequencies of any sound, part or melody. Imagine a highly detailed, scientific version of treble and bass controllers found on car radios,

precisely and steadfastly for eight hours a day, breathing in small plumes of smoke from the tin and lead that lies at the heart of every piece of electronic machinery.

Moses had shipped us a 32-channel Soundcraft Ghost mixing console that he'd been using for many years. He also threw in an SPL GoldMike tube preamp (made with love in Germany) and a sky blue (Danish) Lydkraft Tube-Tech Equalizer, which I soon fell in love with for thumping drum sounds.

From our side, Jimmy and I purchased a new state-of-the-art Apple G4 computer, a Pro Tools Mix Plus system, an 888/24 audio converter, Emagic Logic software, two super-hot Neve 1272 preamps, a host of software effects plug-ins, four sturdy microphones (our friend Chad Swahnberg augmented our collection by loaning us some of his beautiful Beyer Dynamic mics) and the thing I had really learned to love at Chateau Relaxo, the Avalon 737 SP tube pre-amp/EQ/compressor. That was the entire gear list for the studio, and, with those pieces, I was convinced that we could become what Chad had envisioned for us: a giantkiller studio!

One last note about this technological arrangement: Logic and Pro Tools were not yet authorized to work on the new G4 computers, but my former partner and computer genius, Scott Clark, fiddled about with preferences and extensions, ensuring that our system was completely stable and bullet-proof.

---

televisions or home stereo systems. A preamp (preamplifier) is what a microphone plugs into to get it loud enough to record. Good ones can cost between $500 and $4,000 per channel, and these can add a lot of magic to the sound. A compressor helps the volume level of a sound stay steady. When a vocalist suddenly jumps up in volume, the compressor can gently or harshly press back down so the overall presentation is smoother.

11: Opening the Doors

Jimmy printed up some really nice blue business cards, some with my name on them and some with his, featuring a sleek, modern-looking Transporterraum NYC logo. We put the studio name on our building's buzzer.

Our entryway on East 2nd Street was an eyesore, layered with a decade's worth of jumbled graffiti tags, garbage piles and the crowning touch; a continuously overflowing, bright green dumpster. We installed a landline with modem for 'dial-up' internet and I dutifully bought myself a Nokia cell phone.

On the first working day of the golden year 2000, we opened for business. I really don't remember who our first customer was, but everything was written on a calendar made out of thick card stock, that I drew each month in permanent marker. (I possessed that entire pile of calendars until one magical day in 2008 when I chose not to pay for my Bedrock storage unit on the West Side and everything disappeared).

Jimmy Goodman contacted all his musician and producer friends, trying to round them up to come work in our new underground lair. His calls yielded results, for I was consistently and happily working away, starting from our very first week.

One of our early clients was the friendly and sweet dance music producer, Louie Balo, who was a good friend of Jimmy's. He was active in a long-running Sunday afternoon dance club called The Tea Party. Louie hired me for long days of engineering/mixing and brought in an amazing singer, Sheila Brody (aka Amuka), who regularly performed with George Clinton's *P-Funk*.

It was my first experience working with a dance music producer and those sessions were complex and difficult. He used five different kick drums, four hi-hats and three flavors of tambourine, among those 64 audio tracks in Logic's 'Arrange' window. I always tell people that when Louie said, "please make tambourine number three louder," it would take one minute of complete eye strain to even locate the correct track!

The first full album project I worked on at Transporterraum was another project Jimmy brought in, *The Scarlet Dukes*. He actually played in this band, which combined early rock 'n' roll and swing music, resulting in jazzy party songs featuring dirty saxophone along with Jimmy's great vibraphone playing. This was really the first time I sat and engineered an entire album's worth of songs, learning exactly how much patience, concentration and time it took. I also became proficient at keeping twelve songs' worth of digital information safe, copied and backed up reliably, so every chance NOT to lose something important would be taken.

Album number two followed immediately, again thanks to Jimmy, who invited his other band, *Mad Juana*, to record with me. *Mad Juana*'s head honcho was none other than Sami Yaffa, bassist extraordinaire from *Hanoi Rocks*, the first band from Finland ever to gain worldwide popularity. *Hanoi Rocks*, with their glamorous lead singer Michael Monroe, were the darlings of rock magazines back in the 80s and I often saw Michael holding court while walking down St. Marks Place. *Hanoi Rocks* also had an unwanted spotlight thrust upon them in December 1984 when their drummer, Razzle, tragically died in a car accident involving *Mötley Crüe*'s Tommy Lee, while they were both drunk.

Sami and I made a good team and he must have appreciated my studio skills, because he came back to me when we completed *Mad Juana*'s album, proposing that we work together with a band from Mallorca. I hadn't heard of Mallorca yet, but he described this beautiful island in the Balearic Sea, with pristine wild beaches, where he had lived for a while. He had met the band, *Satellites*, when they were teenagers, just beginning their musical journey. I wondered what kind of music would come from that small island in the sea and prepared to do my best work ever.

By this time, I really knew how to use the Transporterraum studio as a finely tuned rock and roll instrument!

A funny thing happened on the very day I met *Satellites*. I'd been developing a new concept which was to prepare the studio completely BEFORE the bands arrived, sparing them the boring, unpretty set-up time, stringing microphones and cables. Usually, when a band arrives in a studio, they are very excited to play and record (barring a few horrible hangovers), yet in most studios they are made to sit for HOURS while all the microphones and preamps are plugged in. And almost always, lo-and-behold: "One cable that worked last week doesn't exactly work this week."

So, the musicians and their guests are forced to watch the engineer bend down, crawling under the mixing console with his hairy butt-crack exposed, while taking up their time and money (even worse, their valuable enthusiasm and energy) just trying to get the equipment to function properly.

The 'Gordon Raphael super-hero technique' is to spend a couple hours on my own, doing that stuff the night before. I can make a party of it, blasting my favorite music through the speakers, enjoying the fact that there's no one around as I set up and test all the mics. The final step before I go home is to make a new session on the computer, fully labeled with all the instruments that will be recorded.

When the band walks in the next day, they put their coats down, set up their own amps, instruments and pedals and then I ask them to start playing as soon as they finish their bagels and coffee. Every band looks shocked at this, every time—and I enjoy seeing the surprise on their faces. When the first song gets recorded before noon, the psychological energy boost the band gets, realizing how easy and doable their project is going to be, is priceless.

That day, I arrived at Transporterraum NYC at 10 am. *Satellites* were set to enter the room at 11. I vacuumed the rugs, set the lighting just right and turned on all the equipment. As a last thought, I got the big feather duster out of the storage area, deciding to give the Soundcraft Ghost mixing console, the heart of the studio that sends all the sounds to the speakers, a once over. After that last little shine on the studio, I went to play a John McLaughlin CD through the speakers just to set a mood.

Much to my dismay, NOTHING was coming out. No sound, NADA!

"What the fuck?!" I said out loud.

I started pushing every button on that goddamn mixer and turning every knob but nothing worked. TOTAL panic.

Me = SWEATING. The band was to arrive in thirty minutes and I had no sound available in the studio. I called upstairs to our landlord Rick and he agreed to lend me his (sonically inferior) Mackie mixer.

As the band walked in, I'm meeting them for the first time looking like a speed-freak on a bad coke comedown, I'm yanking every wire (oh, about twenty cables!) from the Soundcraft and re-plugging them into that shitty Mackie. The inside of my mind was yelling,

"Hey, we're a great new studio with a Mackie mixer at the heart...gaaaah!!!"

After that catastrophe, the day went OK, but I was shook up. When I came to the studio early the next morning to inspect the Soundcraft Ghost more calmly and carefully, I could see that one tiny red 'solo' button had been accidentally pushed in by the feather duster and, when I pushed it out again, everything worked fine.

From the first notes of *Satellites* playing in our live room, I was falling in LOVE with their music. The purest beauty, like birds flying over an island sunrise, then suddenly being attacked with a mental breakdown of ferocity and unbalanced power. The tension they built was like a lightning storm over dark, choppy waves on the open sea at night. The two guitars of Jordi and Michael combined with a mystical alchemy, their sound was transportive and visceral. We recorded all the instrumental parts first, so I still had no idea what the songs were actually gonna feel like once the vocals were added.

I became instant friends with the band as they could tell I was completely involved in their music and they, in turn, loved the sounds that were playing back from the recordings. In his role as producer, Sami Yaffa was very relaxed and cheerful throughout the sessions, allowing me to get on with whatever ideas I had, while he focused on Puter, the bassist, who looked up to Sami as the veritable god of BASS.

When Jordi stepped into the live room to sing through our Audio-Technica mic, I got what I considered to be a very cool sound for him, noticing that he was going to sing quietly at the beginning of the songs, then howl and scream intensely later on. That's never easy to engineer, as a mic setting that works perfectly for quiet singing will often become overloaded, breaking down with nasty results once the screaming starts.

The moment Jordi started singing, I thought he was phenomenal both in his poetry and his vocal tone. Some of my favorite bands are European, for whom English is their second or third language. When they sing in English their special accents make the phrases sound extra dramatic and romantic. In addition to his intriguing accent and the completely strange subject matter contained in his lyrics, he would sometimes sing in the Mallorquín dialect spoken on their island.

After the first take, which I was so impressed with, Jordi came bounding back into the studio to listen, wearing a mischievous grin on his face.

He said, "So?"

I replied, "Wow, amazing—I would use that whole performance as a lead vocal, except there were TWO notes that I think you should sing again."

Well, he looked at me with a "What the fuck are you talking about dude?" in his eyes, so I played him the track.

There was all of this sweet, smooth singing and then came that storm of pushing his voice high, breaking and screaming. Those leaping, soaring parts of the melody were very difficult and tricky for sure. When I showed him the two small spots where I thought he slightly missed the notes, he said (and I will never forget),

"Gordon, listen, you take big jumps in life, sometimes you make it and sometimes you don't! This one is fine, just leave it and let's go on to the next song."

That first song is called *I Bet* and it exists out there in the world somewhere.

Satellites finished their album in two weeks and we celebrated by watching them play a small, cool show at Lakeside Lounge, a bit further down Avenue A. They invited Anne and I to stay with them if we ever wanted to visit Mallorca, promising to take us to beautiful beaches and tall cliffs with wild ocean views. Before they left New York we discussed what to name the new album. Everyone thought for a moment and, after considering what their music sounded like, I blurted out,

"Our Very Bright Darkness."

They laughed because it rang true and then chose it as their album title.

I'm extremely proud of *Our Very Bright Darkness* and it is discoverable on modern streaming platforms; Sami Yaffa is credited as producer while I am designated—Space Pilot.

12: In Between Days

In between short one-day jobs and longer album projects there was plenty of time for Anne and me to rehearse with *Absinthee*. By now we were a mixed-up melting pot crew, as one would hope when choosing to plant oneself in the Big Apple.

Our bassist, Benjamin, was French; Peter (Piotr) our power drummer, direct from Poland; our second drummer, En Esch, was German and our frantic metal-tinged guitarist, Yuval, was an Israeli. We set up our instruments and amps at Transporterraum a few days before the studio officially opened for business. Something happened during that first rehearsal which was a very bad omen for things that would occur later.

We were rockin' out, feeling charged up to be in such an aesthetically pleasing and comfortable space, located in such a happenin' area of the city, especially for ROCK culture. My big keyboard rig was positioned near the studio's front door and we were about an hour into our band practice. I glanced for a moment at that silver door to behold a most unwelcome sight.

Our landlord, Rick, had pressed his bearded face up to the small rectangular window. He had a GRUMPY frown and was shaking his head. As I'm rocking-the-fuck out on my Les Paul, distorted heavily by the RAT fuzzbox, deep into an *Absinthee* song with Anne singing her heart out, Rick's out there, hand signaling me through the window to "TURN IT DOWN!"

He was even mouthing the words, "Too.... loud."

"FUCK YOU" was the instant, angry thought going through my head.

He slunk off but, from the first day we ever played music in our new studio, there was a creepy shadow and I felt concerned for our future.

Moses Schneider crossed the Atlantic again just as he'd promised, bringing with him a major label signed band from Stuttgart called *Stone the Crow*. I was hired to be his assistant and this would be the first time I would closely observe his production magic with a full band. When *Van Der Meer* came over to Chateau Relaxo, he was only setting up one microphone for Susie and then letting her sing on her own. But now I was going to be with Moses for two weeks straight (well, I was straight and he was stoned, haha!).

I remember when I first met this Berlin mastermind and asked him, "How do you produce a song?"

His answer, both cryptic and perfect, was: "Well, first I look for the secret of the song, and only after I discover that, come the ideas for producing!"

I was puzzled when I saw him drop to a push-up position on the floor, lying prone in front of the drummer while the bassist and drums were playing together. He was checking to see if the kick drum was in tune with the bass. I'd never heard of anyone doing that before and certainly had never done it myself. He then showed me that every microphone has a special frequency where it resonates, adding an atonal color which can fight the key of the song. To combat this, he used a razor-sharp EQ curve to remove that unwanted part of the sound from each mic.[8] Then he just did weird stuff, like wrap a microphone in wadded-up newspaper before sticking it between the hi-hat cymbals. This created a destructive, grinding sound every time the drummer smacked them with his sticks.

Benson Lauber had also come from Berlin to work with *Stone the Crow* and his job was to continuously edit the drum tracks on a separate computer, throughout the sessions. Those two weeks with Moses and Ben were eye-opening, inspiring me to keep pushing further and to use more of my imagination to keep the recording process fresh.

---

[8] An example of this would be using a software equalizer to select the very specific frequency 16 kHz. This is a sound that vibrates at 16,000 cycles per second and is up in the highest octave that humans can hear, like a shrill whistling sound. Once selected, the equalizer can make that specific frequency much quieter, or even seem to disappear completely.

By mid-2000, Transporterraum NYC was busy full time. This was exactly what we had gambled on and hoped for. Jimmy started recording his own projects and we met another very talented engineer/producer/musician named Quentin Jennings, who also booked the studio, bringing us extra income. We were charging $400 per day, splitting this evenly between the studio (covering rent, new equipment and repairs) and whoever engineered the session.

Having Jimmy and Quentin working meant that I could enjoy some days off and the studio would still be getting paid. Usually I worked ten-hour shifts, four to six days a week. I never worked with an assistant engineer. Ever since the Chateau Relaxo days it had been just me in the studio with the musicians, except when a guest producer, like Moses, would come along.

On nights off I would go out with Anne, our band members or Chad. We'd head down to the nearby Ludlow Street strip hitting Luna Lounge, Mercury Lounge or one of the many dive bars in the neighborhood. I enjoyed handing out my little blue business cards, walking up to bands I liked right after they played to tell them about Transporterraum studio and what great sounds we could get. Sometimes that worked but it didn't always bring me jobs.

Two cool Seattle producers came to visit, bringing in very interesting projects. Layng Martine III, who had hired me to play keyboards on one of his recording sessions during the early *Absinthee* days, brought David Schools from *Widespread Panic*. David's new group was called *SLANG* and we collaborated on their album, *The Bellwether Project*. I engineered on that album and also played two of my favorite synthesizers, Arp Odyssey and Micro Moog.

Anne's brother, Ryan Hadlock, then brought the legendary *Fugazi* guitarist, Guy Picciotto and tremendous band, *Blonde Redhead*, to record Italian and French vocals for three tracks on their EP, *Mélodie Citronique*. Guy and Ryan had been producing

Blonde Redhead's album, *Melody of Certain Damaged Lemons*, over at Bear Creek but decided to come to New York for these songs.

Absinthee was getting some minor bookings at rock bars here and there. The furthest afield we went was driving to the great city of Baltimore for a one-off club show. I thought our band was amazing and thoroughly enjoyed playing my keyboards and guitar parts, but things were not blowing up, shall we say. There had been a noticeable downshift in the popularity of rock music going on in New York. What was coming up was drum 'n' bass, jungle and that ever present acid-jazz lounge music featuring DJs wearing backwards baseball hats and thick gold chains. *Destiny's Child*, Christina Aguilera, Enrique Iglesias, NSYNC and Aliyah were topping the US charts. The once powerful influence of Seattle's grunge scene was no longer evident.

The dot-com explosion, which had jumped up the year before in the form of new web-based businesses hosting gigantic loft parties in the East Village, replete with open bars, arty decor and DJs, was still continuing to grow. Somehow, I landed two well-paying jobs from that—writing electronic music for an exercise and yoga website.

Summer 2000 was mostly spent working down in our dark, cool basement. This was far preferable to the sweaty, sticky feeling of Manhattan's bus-fume smelling air in July. Anne and I took a trip to Spain in August. We started in Madrid for a week, exploring art museums and the city. We both share a fascination with 15th Century Flemish artist, Hieronymus Bosch, and the Prado Museum houses a fabulous collection of his bizarre paintings. We loved the sprawling El Retiro Park but had a hard time finding vegetarian food. We also felt the patriarchal male dominant culture all around us, especially in the form of catcalls and comments towards Anne and her blonde hair.

Next, we visited Jordi, Puter, Michael and Joan Antoni—the *Satellites!* We took them up on their offer and flew into Palma de Mallorca, where they met us at the airport. The six of us piled into their small car, heading straight out to a beautiful beach in the

69

late afternoon sun. It was still warm but with a lovely fresh breeze. We all squished OUT of the car and walked along a trail down to the water. Standing in a circle, we were smiling, talking and generally feeling amazing, when one of the boys took from his pocket a small plastic bag, rolling papers and a plastic lighter. Now I already knew that *Satellites* were stoners, since they were smoking weed constantly during those *Our Very Bright Darkness* sessions. Ever since quitting nine years before, I had a zero-tolerance policy. This meant,

"NO, you may not smoke weed in my studio, if you wanna do that shit, get out of my sight and smell, just go outside on the street!"

Everyone I knew either drank alcohol or smoked pot, usually both, but I just couldn't stand the smell or the idea of it. After all, I was the one who used to continuously smoke pot, day and night from the time I was fourteen till my heroin habit replaced it at age thirty-one. I was just about to say something rude and bossy to Puter, to tell him to get it away from me and out of my face, when I noticed it wasn't marijuana. It was in fact smooth, blondish-brown HASHISH.

13: Opening Pandora's Box

I decided to hold my tongue. I refrained from any snarky comments to Puter as he first toasted the hashish with his lighter, then crumbled it into a pile of loose tobacco in the palm of his hand.

I was participating in conversation with Anne and the *Satellites* boys, but all eyes saw me glance over at Puter as he lit his skillfully rolled joint. I'm sure they all wondered why I wasn't being snappy like I was back in New York.

As we talked, I watched the hash-joint going slowly around the circle and smelled the heady, intoxicating aroma which instantly brought euphoric, highly charged memories flooding back to me. I recalled happy times, laughing, while my parents were out, placing two dinner knives together on red-hot electric stove burners, then pressing golden Afghani hash between the blades.

My best friend and I would take turns inhaling giant lungfuls of the fragrant smoke until we just couldn't take anymore. Then we'd be rolling hysterically on the floor, a feeling like floating, tripping on how the whole universe suddenly made perfect sense. These were memories from my senior year in high school, for soon after that hashish disappeared from the Seattle area, replaced by progressively stronger strains of genetically mutated, hydroponically grown, expensive marijuana.

All too familiar were the gears and mechanisms spinning in my brain now, ignited by this recall of past delights. Fierce curiosity swirled around my eyes as we stood there in that first hour, first day of our Mallorca visit.

When the joint reached around the circle to me, Anne quickly moved to hand it past me to Michael on the other side. My voice spoke up,

"Hey! I want to try that."

"Fuck you, Gordon, you don't smoke" replied Jordi.

But I DID grab that porro (that's what they call it on the island) and took a deep inhale. In fact, I instantly resorted back to my inner addict nature and kept it to myself until I'd had at least three good hits, already feeling the effects.

Glancing to my left I saw Anne looking shocked, noticing sadness in her eyes too. It was as if I'd pulled the rug out from under her, since I was the one person she knew who DIDN'T get high. She had grown to rely on me for that and now I had just taken a giant step backwards.

During my first incarnation as a head,[9] stoner, waster, I managed a nearly twenty-year drug habit with NO MONEY. I never had a job, no cash of my own and yet I was able to get high and stay that way every single day. My inner 'get-high-artist' aka addict had figured out endless ways to convince friends, acquaintances and total strangers to offer me some of whatever they were having that I wanted and craved.

Now I was standing in Mallorca as a working producer and New York studio owner, not rich, but I did have money in my pocket and some to spare. I asked the group (five minutes after the first porro),

"Um, can you guys get me a large chunk of that hash? That was really nice and I'd like to have some of my own for the rest of the trip."

Fast as that, simple as that.

Our holiday in Mallorca flew by with great swimming, talking, sightseeing and me smoking myself into some semi-dream-state just like ALWAYS, it seemed. My nine years of sobriety now appeared to be one abstract detail in someone else's life.

Flying in the plane back to New York I was deep in thought, having a serious talk with myself. I knew that last time I started my heroin habit in Spokane, Washington on a Christmas vacation and promised myself it would not follow me back to our apartment on 2nd Avenue. My strong resolve only lasted about

---

[9] In high school, weed smokers out at the big tree were "heads" or "stoners", as opposed to the football (not soccer) players who were "jocks". Head, from the term "acid head", applied to habitual users of the drug LSD.

three days before I started coming home with little white stamp-bags filled with China White (at least that's what we hoped it was) and chemically stepped-on cocaine.[10] Things turned bad, bad, bad from then on and I didn't want to repeat that with possibly worse consequences THIS time around. I called on every strength inside me that remembered drug-treatment and my nine years without drugs, making a promise to myself to get back on that good track.

---

[10] In the 1980s, the term 'China White' was used to distinguish white powdered heroin coming into Manhattan from South-East Asia from the brown tar heroin widely available on the West Coast coming in via Mexico.

14: Snapped Back, Doing Well

Got back and smiled while entering the ever-distasteful, graffiti-covered front doorway of 154 East 2nd Street, home of Transporterraum NYC. Down the paint-peeling stairway (the bathroom was also quite yucky but not completely horrible) and into the basement where I noticed a tiny new studio had been built right near the stairs. There was also lumber and construction dust in front of my studio, where another medium-sized room was being built.

I met two new basement neighbors, Didi Gutman and Fab DuPont, who were studio partners. Didi is a world-class keyboard player, composer and producer originally from Argentina. Fab was already a talented producer back then and today he is world-renowned. My new neighbors were both genuinely nice and smart, we never had any trouble sharing the basement or our equipment.

I checked in with Jimmy Goodman and he showed me the bookings for September and October. I blocked out the available open days to begin work on our second *Absinthee* album, excited to record that cast of characters we'd been gigging with for a while.

My friend Philippo Scrooge called from Seattle informing me that he'd be returning to New York in one month and wanted his apartment back. He offered that I could sleep on the couch near the front windows that overlooked the fire escape and Tompkins Square Park, until I found a new place. I was a bit bummed out as I liked having his place to myself and especially living right next to that park which was the only place full of trees in the East Village. I decided to deal with it later, for now I wanted to concentrate on my music.

The new *Absinthee* songs turned out really well. It was great to be in control of every sound, inventing crazy orchestrations which by now was truly my forte. Anne showed me a piece called *Mary's Song* that she'd written with a Seattle guitarist long ago, before we met. It was a story about chaotic upheavals with a former roommate and girlfriend. *Mary's Song* begins harmoniously, sweetly, with soft poetry but, just when you feel serenely safe, the lyrics explode into a massive rage, utter insanity while the music brings an onslaught from the lowest possible tone to the highest piercing screams.

In the middle of these sessions Anne introduced me to a very striking-looking young musician from London named Julien Davis. He had tiger-striped hair so we called him, Tiger Boy. Already having a soft spot for all things related to British music, I was pleased to meet him and chat. I soon offered to record a few of his songs for free, simply for the pleasure of having him around. Tiger Boy informed me, sadly, that rock music in London was really closing down. He said it was getting harder and harder to find good places to play and that live music venues were rapidly going out of business. This confirmed what I'd been feeling in New York but it was particularly miserable to consider a Great Britain that didn't rock anymore.

Almost all of my childhood music heroes were British, from *The Animals*, *The Beatles*, *The Rolling Stones* and *Yes* to *The Psychedelic Furs*, *Bauhaus*, *Joy Division*, Bowie, *Siouxsie and the Banshees*; those sounds truly made me who I am today. Again, it was England that saw the value and promise of Jimi Hendrix when no one else did and England who kickstarted the grunge movement by being the first to write about and support the original wave of Sub Pop bands when they crossed the Atlantic to tour.

While we were mixing the new *Absinthee* album, I was talking with our dashing bassist, Benjamin. He told me that he'd met a cool young woman (he started many of our discussions with those words!) named Kerri Black, who was promoting shows downtown. He added that she had excellent taste in music and could possibly help us, as well. That's all I needed to hear, so I asked him to invite her over to one of our rehearsals. I wanted to play her a few songs, show off our new recordings and introduce her to Anne. A few days later, Kerri Black came over and that's exactly what we did. She was intelligent and focused but, luckily, also friendly.

Kerri invited us to come to a party she was throwing that same week at Luna Lounge so we could see her in action. She gave us a flyer and mentioned that one of the bands on the bill was quite cool and might even be looking for a producer to record some decent demos.

Luna Lounge had been one of our main spots ever since moving to NYC and, of course, we played our very first show there as *Absinthee*, around Anne's 20th birthday. They usually had three bands playing per night with low or free admission.

Because we'd been going there so often, I'd already seen at least twenty bands I liked. I was always looking for bands that were innovative, played well together and gave unique, shocking performances. When we walked into Kerri's party there was a band onstage called *Come On*. Halfway through their first song I was already going kind of crazy for them. They had everything I enjoyed; really well-crafted songs, powerful guitar playing and vocal harmonies like the 60s British Invasion bands that I listened to. Every song they played was cool so I was eager to speak with them after their set, to hand them my business card. I wanted to tell them,

"I have a studio nearby, just down Avenue A. We can make great sounding demos, really cheap."

And so, I did.

The live music room at Luna Lounge held about a hundred people and, on this night, there were only about forty. Not so packed and I was honestly a little disappointed seeing that. While the second band was setting up, I hung out with Anne and Benjamin, walking over to say "hi" to Kerri Black. After the break, a loud insistent guitar riff started up over a bouncy beat, so I looked towards the small stage to watch the next band.

Kerri told me that they were called *The Strokes*. I immediately noticed that they were very stylish and young. One guy with dark curly hair was wearing a pretty sharp-looking suit and the drummer had a green T-shirt, also with very curly hair that flew into his face every time he smacked his snare drum. In fact, on closer look, he was forcefully throwing his head down with a SNAP each time he hit the snare—it really looked like he was going to break his own neck. I couldn't look away from that drummer, like watching an accident about to happen.

I glanced at the other guitarist who was tall and not wearing a suit as he stood in a wide-legged stance in extremely tight jeans. He looked like he was really trying to be cool. The guy who was singing presented himself like he was also 'so cool', but I couldn't really hear his voice that well and kept looking back at the drummer to see if he'd hurt himself yet.

I'm sorry to say but I wasn't that impressed with this second band, yet, when they finished, I saw the two guitarists step back onto the stage to collect their pedals. I went straight up to them and said,

"Hi, I have a studio very close by and I can make great sounding demos for cheap."

The guitarist from the second band, wearing the suit, asked me how much that would be, so I told him $200 per song, then handed him my blue business card.

As I turned to walk away, he shouted, "Hey, let me write my number down in case I lose your card."

He wrote 777-9299 and put the name Albert over it. I still have that Kerri Black business card with Albert's name and number written on the back of it.

Absinthee (bold Anne and timid me): first band photo in Seattle, by Charlie Hoselton. Note how mannequins have always been in my life!

Brian Phraner with his Hagstrom bass. This mystical figure had the patience to help me become a better musician. He inspired me with his Medusa songs to learn how to record and produce.

Mental Mannequin: (L-R) Mike, Tor, Barbie, Me, Ben and Pony. This was the first band that played my songs and allowed me to sing in front of an audience. Photo by Kelly Gordon Mercier at Sea-Tac Airport.

Scene from our church/studio after it burnt down. One forlorn destroyed drumset. There's also a photo of my hammond M3 organ in this state, with its ghostly wires still reaching towards the wall. Photo by Kelly Gordon Mercier.

Chateau Relaxo. Possibly one of the only photos of its interior in existence. I am with Stormy Lee Rollins, a friend from Seattle, recording her spoken word album, Girl.

Musician Susie van der Meer and the fabulous producer Moses Schneider at breakfast. Hannibal Bar Cafe, Kreuzberg Berlin.

The gorgeous wood room at Bear Creek Studios. Steinway piano, Fender Rhodes and antique wooden pump organ in the background. This room is phenomenal for warm intimate musical sounds, even with a loud rock band playing in it.

Yeah, me trying to look busy building the control room wall at Transporterraum NYC, much to the dismay and delight of Joe Hadlock and Jimmy Goodman. Photo by Anne Hadlock.

My musical partner Anne Hadlock in the control room of Transporterraum NYC. We recorded an album of our Absinthee music there, shortly before The Strokes entered our lives at Luna Lounge.

Eerie empty control room of Transporterraum NYC. This humble/glittering basement studio became a vortex for rock 'n roll and was usually as loud as a jet airplane taking off from noon till 2am every day. Good for the ears.

Carole (aka Miko) and Manny Hadlock during a Christmas holiday at Bear Creek Studios. Anne and our friend Jayna were busy making paintings just out of frame, while Joe Hadlock played melodiously on his Fender Rhodes.

Gordon Raphael (Space Pilot) recording with Satellites *at Transporterraum NYC. The resulting album,* Our Very Bright Darkness, *is a wonderful masterpiece. Mallorcan intensity produced in Manhattan.*

Sky Cries Mary. *Our tribal space rock band. Photo by the illustrious Karen Moskowitz, thank U! (L-R) Me, Roderick, Joe Bass, Loren, Anisa, Ben, DJ Fallout.*

Colour Twigs, *one of my best musical projects ever. (L-R) Me, Michael Davidson, Tor Midtskog, Photo by the light wizard, Cam Garrett.*

Medusa *bandmates outside Paramount Theatre in Seattle. (L-R) Don Freeborn, Bruce Main and me. I'm holding a telescope and a copy of the* Bhagavad Gita, *strange! A very windy day.*

Debe Lazo and I. We went through many ordeals together. Here we are shown at our very own intervention! Yes, we walked into my sister Lisa's apartment to be unexpectedly greeted by Debe's entire family and mine. It was a trap and we were extremely well dressed for it. In the end, she went to rehab in Spokane and I went to rehab in Port Angeles. Happily, we are both still showing up for life each day with great energy and enthusiasm. It works when you work it.

15: Those Demos

I worked for the next couple of days, waiting and hoping that
Come On (the band I dug from Luna Lounge) was gonna call me.
Instead, I got a call from Albert who asked if he could come by
and see the studio.

The very next day he dropped in for a visit in the same suit
he'd been wearing onstage, but with a different tie. He was
incredibly friendly with a charming smile. After he looked around
at the red and purple glitter walls, taking in the old ripped-up
guitar amps, matte black farm window, purple velvet couch with
matching draperies and the black bookshelf with my grandpa's
old microscope on it, he nodded his head.

"You wouldn't believe the studios we've been in so far," he
said, "They're so sterile and corporate, like all they want to do is
record TV commercials. It's hard for us to feel comfortable in a
place like that."

Albert then told me that *The Strokes* wanted to make some
high-quality demos so they could hopefully book some better
shows. They'd been playing gigs at Spiral, Arlene's Grocery and
Luna Lounge and were ready to move on. He asked if he could
hear something I'd recorded, so I played him *Satellites* and
Absinthee songs. Albert liked what he heard and enquired about
the cost for three songs to be produced over an upcoming three-
day weekend. I gave him the $200 a day deal which he thought
sounded fair and then Albert ran off to tell the band.

Soon after, he phoned me back to confirm that *The Strokes*
would indeed come in and have me produce three demos.[11] He
asked if it would be OK if they paid me the first half when we

---

[11] Typically, a demo is a fairly quick, rough version of a song that will be
developed in a more refined, polished and powerful form later; usually
with more time involved and a much higher budget, provided by a
record company.

finished recording and the second half a few weeks later, after they'd had enough gigs to cover it.

I said, "Sure!" and blocked out that weekend in late September on our calendar, in black permanent marker.

I had an extra reason to happy about this booking; I'd been invited to Seattle for the *Sky Cries Mary* 'demise party' on October 6th. They had stayed together for four years after I'd left the band and now were officially breaking up. The $600 payment from *The Strokes* would cover my plane ticket and I'd stay a few extra days to visit family and friends.

Around noon on demo day one, the musicians from *The Strokes* rang my buzzer. Albert led them through the silver door with the small red-glitter window. I was in the control room opening up a new Logic session on the G-4 computer, double-checking that everything was in order.

Their drummer, Fabrizio, bounced in energetically with a big smile, carrying his cymbals and snare drum. Albert introduced me to the tall guitarist, Nick Valensi. They both headed out to the live room, laughing and joking around with each other while setting up identical Fender Hot Rod Deville amps and identical Jekyll & Hyde overdrive boxes. Bassist Nikolai walked in calmly and quietly, with a gentle smile. I didn't recognize the last person through the door.

He wasn't smiling and didn't have an instrument in his hands. He only carried a brown paper shopping bag and, while everyone else got busy setting up amps, drums and instruments, this guy just sat out in the live room against a wall. I figured he was a friend of theirs they'd brought along to hang out with them in the studio. He reached in the bag and pulled out a six-pack of beer. This person eventually walked into the control room and, with a kind, yet serious look on his face, introduced himself as Julian, the singer. He asked me if it would be ok if they brought someone else to the session as well. They invited JP Bowersock, who was a mentor to *The Strokes*. The band felt secure having him there to help and consult, his presence also made them feel more relaxed in their new environment, Transporterraum.

JP was a big guy with a powerful voice. He shook my hand, smiling warmly, yet I really had no idea what to expect from him or how our communication would be. I wondered if our roles would combine or clash during the production. But now it looked like everyone was present and we were ready to begin.

I placed microphones around the room where I thought they should go and then asked if everyone would join me in the control room. I had one big question,

"OK, so what kind of sound are we going for?"

I wanted to know how they envisioned their sound so I could do my best to give them something they liked by the end of the weekend.

Fabrizio spoke first, "You know what everyone is doing these days? Well, that's what we don't want to do!"

FINE, that gave me an instant vision.

What everyone was "doing these days" was to carefully and meticulously cut the drums to a click track, edit the human feeling out of them and then proceed to fill up 64 channels with musical parts—because this was the first time in history that we could do that! Up 'til recently, only musicians on the level of Michael Jackson or the *London Philharmonic Orchestra* could afford to link two Sony digital tape machines together to achieve 48 tracks, everyone else had to make do with 16 or 24. Anyone who owned Pro Tools could now stack 64 tracks and OH! they certainly were doing that.

"Anything else?" I asked.

Julian spoke the first of several cryptic, poetic ciphers that I would hear from him. "Imagine you're in a spaceship and you travel to the future where you discover a great band from the past that you really love."

"Ok, Julian, right..." I trailed off, needing to think about that one, not getting an instant clear picture in my mind. It dawned on me that he was describing a symbolic dichotomy of something that might be considered old and new at the same time!

I got a simple vision and came up with a plan. For me, the furthest thing from what was happening around me in other New York studios would be to send the musicians into the live room and have them just play their songs! I wanted this done in a live, all-at-the-same-time kind of way, with all the amps blaring and bleeding into each other.

"Can I sing with the band?" asked Julian.

I hadn't considered that because I imagined needing all available eight inputs for the instruments and was afraid the band would play too loud, drowning out the singing anyway. But, since he asked, I thought we could give it a try.

I ran his vocal through a small (shitty sounding) Peavy keyboard amp that I used with *Absinthee* and then mic'd that amp using the Audio-Technica condenser.

They ran through a song called *The Modern Age* one time and came in to hear what the recording sounded like. Generally, they were quite happy with the all-at-once-in-the-basement sound, but Julian shook his head saying,

"I don't want to sing with the band. Let's do it afterwards."

That worked fine for me and I was glad he wanted it that way. I usually like to record the singer separately so we can concentrate hard on every line and each expression. I consider the singing and the story within the lyrics to be the central theme of every song (that has vocals/words). In a painting, the singer would be the main subject while the instruments provide a wondrous background.

They plugged back into *The Modern Age*, working on it for a few hours to get the playing and performance exactly right. The amount of time they spent was a big point in their favor, because they were already so focused on the details, refusing to let even the smallest thing that sounded like a mistake make it onto the final version.

JP sat calmly on the couch quietly observing the proceedings but, when he had an idea or suggestion, his voice was clear and direct. Sometimes the guys would ask him which pickup on the guitar to use or if the distortion pedal was set correctly. Sometimes JP would holler over to me from the couch,

"Hey Gordon, why don't you boost a little 12k on Albert's guitar to brighten it up a bit?"

I would hear this type of comment many times from him in the coming days but, truth be told, I never learned the correspondence between frequency numbers and sounds, so if I heard the word "brighten" in there, I would add some treble on the EQ and that seemed to satisfy JP.

I really liked the instrumental parts for *The Modern Age* and wondered what the final result would sound like once the lyrics and vocal melody were added. I thought the rhythmic interplay between the two guitars was irresistible, building great tension, while Fab's drumming threw in relentless, youthful energy, driving the beat forward. Oh yes, and I completely flipped out when I heard Nick Valensi's CRAZY guitar solo for this song. I watched in amazement as he played it and that was the precise moment that he captured my respect and admiration for his wild, dangerous guitar abilities.

I noticed how well-rehearsed the band was during the recording of the first song and their level of precision was new to me. I've worked with many excellent musicians before but most of them weren't that bothered if things were kind of loose or some small accidents happened. They'd say,

"Well, that's rock 'n' roll. It's not supposed to be rocket science!"

I observed something else that was fascinating about *The Strokes*. When one of them needed to point out an error or if they had a disagreement; they spoke directly and honestly with each other. They would say what was on their mind but never discourage each other with put-downs or passive aggressive behavior. Right off the bat I was really impressed with their demeanor and communication with each other in the studio. I remember thinking, "I wish some other people I knew could see this and learn from it."

While the instrumentalists were out in the live room playing, Julian and JP were behind me discussing things on the control room couch, over multiple beers. Julian was also leafing through notebook papers, jotting down ideas and fine-tuning his lyrics.

Late in the day, the band began a second song called *Last Nite*, but didn't achieve a perfect, complete version. Something about the beat of that song reminded me of Iggy Pop's second solo album and something about *The Modern Age* reminded me of *The Velvet Underground*.

I considered those connections and became quite puzzled. I mean, people from my generation knew Iggy's music and also *The Velvet Underground* but, believe me, these were not highly discussed topics in the year 2000! So, how did these young musicians discover those bands and why were they inspired enough to carry echoes from that era in their own songs?

Of course, nowadays Iggy is a festival favorite, universally revered as a treasured performer but, when *The Stooges'* albums were originally released, it was a small, niche audience that cared about them (emotionally impacted rebels with a penchant for drugs?). Same story with *The Velvet Underground*. These two bands were railing against everything in mainstream music AND the counterculture, which is why they were unpopular and unloved... until much later.

Both emerged as the U.S. was entering the FLOWER POWER, peace & love generation, so music was either urging political change, revolution or simply offering a 'beautiful experience'. The mean, rough, dirty sounds and stories that *The Velvet Underground* and *The Stooges* told had NOTHING to do with those things! The poetry of *The Door*'s Jim Morrison and certain depressive lyrics from Jimi Hendrix could be examples of dark, heavy energy that was also permeating the spiritual atmosphere in the 1960s. There were certainly dark currents with the war in Vietnam and the sudden flooding of youth culture with heroin, cocaine, barbiturates and amphetamines. Somehow, *The Doors* and Hendrix ticked enough boxes with the fans that they were at the top of the popularity charts, whereas Iggy was dropped from his label and *The Velvet Underground* were shunned for being too avant-garde.

I felt kind of sad for the diligent and highly focused members of *The Strokes*. They were right in front of me making innovative guitar rock in the year 2000, when it was all but certified that this form of entertainment? art? cultural expression? was now past its sell-by date. People just weren't that interested in it anymore. I'd even read an article in *The Village Voice* with a drawing of a gravestone in the shape of an ELECTRIC GUITAR, rejoicing in the fact that finally the old man, 'rock music' had died! It mentioned that since Elvis put rock 'n' roll into mainstream cultural consciousness back in 1957, this style of music had been a thriving, powerful influence for more years than any other genre in history. But now, having finally run its course, it was being buried.

The Strokes and JP seemed satisfied with our progress on day one so, with everyone's energy dwindling, it was time to go home.

On day two *The Strokes* performed live guitars, bass and drums for two songs, *Last Nite* and *Barely Legal*. On the early takes of *Last Nite*, I learned that Albert Hammond Jr. was not only a rhythm guitarist. He stepped up with a wonderful guitar solo that took the song to a much higher level. There was an enthusiastic spirit among the musicians. They were hyper-focused, generating sparks of rock 'n' roll electricity all afternoon.

Now that they were in my studio, where I could hear the instruments more clearly, I liked the band's sound very much. When I first saw them play at Luna Lounge it hadn't dawned on me yet how serious they really were nor how well the songs had been put together.

I was excited to hear what Julian's contribution as a singer was going to be and curious to know what mood and atmosphere would end up on the final versions of these demos. Julian had been in the control room so far, sitting next to JP and occasionally going out to the other band members to discuss sections that hadn't been performed correctly yet. Again, there was great attention to detail in how the parts were played, how their sounds were and maintaining steady tempos.

By late afternoon, the music tracks were finished and it was time for Julian to sing. I will never forget his attitude when this moment came. Most of the singers I'd ever worked with (including me) are just itching and twitching to run out and sing their parts. It's as if they'd been waiting impatiently for hours or days as their bandmates struggle, slog and sweat getting their parts right. When the instrumentalists FINALLY make it through the song, a singer will usually leap from their seats to prance, dance, jog or sprint out to the live room, grabbing their beloved microphone to show the entire WORLD what they can do! Most singers are proud, eagerly taking sports towels (for their sweaty brows to-be), Evian bottles, bottles of wine, photos of their favorite rockstars, scarves, whatever, out to the vocal mic, with all eyes on them, the STAR, the center of attention.

"Ok, Julian, your turn. Are you ready to go out there and do your vocals?" I asked, watching his face.

His reply?

"Oh... you mean now? Right now... I have to?" He looked concerned and a bit forlorn as he grabbed those pages with words written down and slowly, solemnly, moved through the silver control room door.

I went out after him to adjust the mic height to 'exactly where his mouth would be', and asked him what kind of voice sound he wanted.

He told me that he wasn't sure yet but to use my best judgement.

I then had a GREAT idea. The music I had been listening to all through the 90s, which had, in fact, influenced the sound of my own writing for *Absinthee*, was industrial music. The leaders in that field were *Skinny Puppy* (from Vancouver B.C.), *Front Line Assembly*, *Laibach* and *Chris & Cosey*. One of the features of this music that I liked the best was that they DISTORTED the living hell out of the vocals.

I thought this would be interesting to try on *The Strokes*, especially since they were the furthest thing from industrial music, which was mostly drum machine and synthesizer based. I had the Audio-Technica mic running into the Avalon preamp and turned the input gain up full, to 10!

Julian sang *The Modern Age* one time and walked in slowly to check the sound. After I played back his performance I asked,

"How do you like that, Julian?"

"I don't like it at all. That's an ugly sound!" came the response.

I felt a bit deflated but he came back with,

"Hey, you know how your favorite jeans, they're not brand new, but they don't have holes in them either?"

"Oh... uh, right" I said, considering his second riddle, thinking "What the fuck?"

But, after a moment his mysterious message actually made sense to me. Ok, shiny new jeans are stiff and uncomfortable, but after you wash them a few times and wear them for a while, they start to feel great! I translated that further,

"Hmmm, maybe if I turn the input up to 5 instead of 10, I will still get a warm, comfortable overdrive, but it won't sound like NUCLEAR DEVASTATION!"

Out he went for a second try and this time when he came back, he and everyone in the room, including the very particular and intelligent JP, loved the sound.

That was great. I enjoyed feeling their approval and was also pleased that it didn't take too long to find our way forward. It only took a few takes to complete the singing on *The Modern Age*, but we spent some time listening to each of his recorded performances. Then we made a vocal comp (compilation) track by editing the best parts and phrases from each of these.

I instantly liked the lyrics on this one. Julian's voice throughout the song was killer, just perfect for my musical tastes and I really liked the way he made it sound like someone telling an old story from their life:

"*Stop to pretend, stop pretending*
It seems this game is simply never-ending"

Great lyrics indeed.

Then he wanted to sing on *Last Nite*, which again didn't take long at all. Although Julian was never jumping around or acting super-excited, he sang incredibly well with a powerful voice and a roar that just hits you in the face. *Last Nite* was a perfect combination of infectious groove, catchy vocal melody and those lyrics rocked my world right away:

"*Oh, people, they don't understand*
No, girlfriends, they don't understand
In spaceships, they won't understand
And me, I ain't ever gonna understand"

I've always been a big sci-fi fan, growing up in the age of rocket-ships and moon landings, so to hear a reference to spaceships in Julian's crooning delivery, brought a big smile to my face. I did puzzle about what kind of self-aware mentality it would take to write those confessional words, "I ain't never gonna understand."

We started recording vocals on *Barely Legal* late that night but stopped after Julian said that he wanted to work on the lyrics a bit more.

On the last day, we had one song to sing and all of them to mix, honoring the three-day, three song deal. We spent the first two hours working on the vocal parts for *Barely Legal*, which went steadily ahead with great performances on each take. There was, however, one line missing in the lyrics, which troubled Julian. I offered to take a look and he showed me his page of handwriting.

"I never show up on weekdays..." and then a blank.

We each made a few attempts to fill that empty space, and then I shot back,

"That's something that you learned yesterday" and he smiled, jotting it down.

That was the first and last time I ever got involved with his words and it still makes me happy every time I hear that song.

Interestingly, after these sessions were done, I found his pages of lyrics tucked into the black bookcase, behind the studio couch. I kept them, but maybe I'll give them back one day.

After *Barely Legal*'s vocals were finished, we checked all three songs to make sure there were no suspicious parts or missed crossfades. With digital audio one must crossfade every time two different regions of audio are next to each other, or else you'll hear an annoying high-pitched click. Sometimes I would miss one of these but Fabrizio would always catch them and point them out to me. Finally, each song was organized and now ready for mixing.

I was cultivating a very efficient style of production where I tried to mix everything the way I thought it should sound, as we went along. This meant getting the tones and balances right from the very beginning of first soundcheck. I believe in this method because it allows artists to clearly hear what they are getting, what's working, what needs to be tried again or thrown away. So it was with *The Strokes*' three demo songs.

I've always been well served by this approach when it comes time for the big final mix because, in my view, most of the important work is already done. I never have to wonder how to blend the parts or make them sound good—they pretty much already sound great. When all the instruments and singing are done, the final mixing starts from that level, then we can spend our time hyper-detailing, until every note is balanced in accordance with the band's wishes.

I never want to put all the faders down to zero and start fresh with a song's mix. That's exactly what we used to do when we worked on tape, back in the day, because it was the only option.

UP ON A HILL
IS WHERE LE BEGIN
THIS LITTLE STORY
A LONG TIME FROM NOW...

STOP TO PRETEND
STOP PRETENDING
IT SEEMS. THIS GAME IS SIMPLY
NEVER-ENDING.
JUST
IN THE SUN, SUN HAVING FUN
IT'S IN MY BLOOD
I JUST CAN'T HELP IT
DON'T WANT YOU TO SAY NO
LET ME GO

LEAVIN JUST IN TIME
STAY THERE FOR A WHILE
ROLLING IN THE OCEAN
TRYIN TO CATCH HER EYE
WORK HARD AND SAY IT'S EASY
DO IT JUST TO PLEASE ME

The Modern Age *lyric sheet in Julian's handwriting, left behind in Transporterraum after recording the 'demo'.*

97

It used to take four people (eight hands!) to rehearse the ballet-like movements on the mixing console to get a really fabulous mix. That's what it took to keep up with all the volume changes and to make sure the effects parts would come in and out at the right times. If there was a sudden loud word, you'd have to reach up and duck the slider to a lower position (marked with felt pen on masking tape stuck to the console). If a single drum hit needed a huge reverberation, you'd press a red auxiliary button on the exact beat and then release it again immediately afterwards. Since the advent of computerized recording, all of these details can be manipulated one at a time and preserved forever once you create (and safely back-up) the information.

In the first moments of *The Strokes* mix, I heard two questions from Julian that I'd never heard in my entire life of recording music. The first shock arrived as,

"Hey, why do the drums have to be so loud? Can you turn them down?"

This broke my mind, because for YEARS I'd been working, studying, experimenting and sweating TO MAKE DRUMS BIG! It's really hard to make giant drum sounds when there's loud guitars, doubled or tripled guitars, screaming vocals, plus keyboard layers. In most rock music, a mixer really has to labor scientifically to make the kick drum cut clearly through the noise.

Sighing, I turned the drums down and, yeah, I was surprised, it did sound cooler with way more swing, like an old-fashioned record. Julian's next line was just as rare,

"Now can you take the bass out of the bass?"

This almost put my mind into a feedback loop. I mean, who doesn't want BOOMING, heavy bass? Wow, I just couldn't believe that he asked me to do that. I was quite confident in my ability to record big, fat bass sounds using the correct microphones and a direct box (no, I don't use direct boxes anymore), yet now the singer was asking me to attenuate that big bass sound! Naturally, I did as he requested and, once again, it sounded really cool and, refreshingly, fit much better with the new drum sounds.

What followed was a very long, shifting list of minuscule volume and EQ changes on all the instruments and then varying those changes for each section of the songs.

I often had three different musician's voices in my ears simultaneously telling me to try this or undo that. JP sat on the couch with his classic,

"Hey Gordon, why don't you cut the 100 hertz on Nikolai's bass and boost the kick drum at 1k?"

I'd nod and move some sliders on the Filterbank EQ while Albert informed me,

"I played the beginning notes of that verse too quietly. Can you raise them a bit?"

And thus progressed a delightfully intense six hours in the studio on a Sunday. Julian had many finely tuned comments and requests, but so did all the other band members. What was really COOL was that guitarist Nick might make suggestions about a drum part and drummer Fab would talk about the impact of a particular chorus. Clearly this was a band where everyone was aware and involved, they were very interested in the overview, not solely concerned about making their own parts perfect. It was good to note that they were in NO hurry to leave the studio to go party somewhere. Their priority was the music.

We all put in a huge amount of concentration and creative energy that weekend. I was feeling woozy and TIRED by the end of the third night. Luckily, we were nearly done and I knew we'd be able to leave soon. I was ready to go home and rest, looking forward to sleeping late the next day. We were putting the finishing touches on *Barely Legal*, which was sounding excellent to me. What followed was one of the most influential exchanges of dialogue in my entire career:

Julian: "Hey Gordon, can you turn my vocals up in the chorus a little bit?"

Gordon (thinking): "Goddamn it, we've been over this part so many times already!"

Gordon (out loud to Julian): "Hey, we've already worked on this part and I think the vocal volume is fine where we have it now. Let's leave it."

Julian (sighing): "Yeah, I expected you to say something like that. You recording guys always think that you know what's best! Will you at least humor me? Look, what's the smallest volume change possible in Logic?"

Gordon (condescendingly): "One tenth of a decibel, you would never even hear that."

Julian: "Well, turn it up one tenth of a decibel and, if it doesn't sound better, we're done and we can go home."

I pushed the voice on the chorus up by one tenth of a decibel, showing an exasperated, grumpy look on my face.

Then I pressed PLAY, anxious to hear the band say they couldn't really hear a difference, and we'd leave it where it was.

As we all listened back, I was faced with a BIG DILEMMA. The chorus did sound noticeably better to me, so—do I admit that to Julian, the band and JP, thus losing 'face', OR do I pretend there is no difference and let the song suffer because of that??

I told him he was absolutely right and Julian smiled a little. Those three songs were now finished and mixed.

It was late at night when *The Strokes* left the studio. After making info backups and switching off the studio equipment, I walked up the stairs, out into the peaceful, vibrant East Village night and headed down Avenue A, home to bed.

———————◆◆◆———————

Three days later, Julian called me up and asked if I wanted to go to a party up on a rooftop.

He picked me up in a classy old Mercedes, with its interior ripped to shreds. I remember being utterly terrified at the speed he was driving on those New York City streets. I supposed that having grown up there, he truly knew the roads well.

At the party there was only the band with a few of their friends. I saw Ryan Gentles and found out that we were on the roof of his apartment building. Ryan was a young musician too and he showed me a very sweet Fender Rhodes electric piano in his living room. He worked at Mercury Lounge in the booking office and had visited us several times during the demo recording, as he was just starting to manage *The Strokes*. That night, I also met Nikolai's brother Pierre and Cody Smyth, a photographer who seemed have known the band for years. The demo recordings were played on a boombox, over and over again out there on the rooftop, under a cloudy night sky illuminated by New York's city lights. It was a high-energy celebration, with great enthusiasm for what we had done together and a group of musicians determined to push it further.

On the last day of the month, *The Strokes* played a gig at Don Hill's for a party called TisWas, hosted by the very cool British DJ, Nick Marc. That show was sparsely attended but the band played very well. I really loved their music now that I was more familiar and involved with it. I witnessed something very unusual which took place after *The Strokes*'s final song. While the audience was clapping, Fabrizio Moretti jumped out from behind his drum set and made his way to the front of the stage. He intended to do a stage dive onto the small crowd gathered below him.

Making a show of it, he leaned forward, raised his arms like wings and then dove off the stage. That small crowd just stepped aside, leaving him to smack down rather abruptly, his chest hitting the hard concrete floor. He picked himself up looking startled and winded, then limped off towards the bar.

16: I Lick the Moog (Return to Familiar Territory)

Dear October 3rd in the year 2000:

I'm on my way, flying to Seattle for *Sky Cries Mary*'s demise party...

The last time I toured as a member of this band was after releasing our fourth album, *Moonbathing on Sleeping Leaves*. This was the record where we jumped from a small label, World Domination, and landed at a giant, Warner Bros. Records. When I decided to leave the group, it seemed like we were at a high point. We believed that being signed to a major record label was the perfect opportunity for reaching a wider audience and pushing our music further.

After I left, it became apparent that *Sky Cries Mary* was NOT being embraced, supported or loved by Warner Bros., and the band was quickly dropped from the roster. There were some harsh feelings between us after I made my exit from the group to concentrate on *Absinthee* but, after a while, we were back on warm, friendly terms.

This party was held at the spacious loft belonging to our guitarist, Michael Cozzi and his wife Karen Moskowitz, one of Seattle's top photographers. Members of the group, past and present, were there and since we had gone through many line-up changes over years, it was a big party. There was much love in the room as we all recognized and affirmed what a powerful combination we were together, remembering the tremendous waves of energy we'd been able to give and receive while sharing the stage.

No one was overly intoxicated, no outlandish behavior or spectacle went down that night but, for me, there were many levels of subtle emotion at play. First of all, I felt proud of myself for getting away from Seattle, my longstanding hometown, and making a stable and fairly successful go of living in New York now. I thought it was luxurious and elegant that I was able to produce a band in my studio and use the money to travel across the United States to be present with these close friends. It meant I valued our times together and respected the fact that when I joined *Sky Cries Mary*, I was freshly back in Seattle trying to find my way forward and, through this band, I had the opportunity to live and travel on an extremely powerful and creative path. It was indeed this special combination of people that attracted attention from audiences, which in turn provided us with a very enjoyable way of living.

In particular, there were two people in attendance at the demise party who I was pleased to see. Tor Midtskog, who had been one of my closest collaborators on my own music, was one of them. He had been in all my own original bands and had briefly played guitar in *Sky Cries Mary*, as well as an early version of *Absinthee*. The other person was Barb Ireland, who was 16 years old when she joined my band *Mental Mannequin* playing harp (yes, a real golden harp like a fairy) and electric organ. She had directed several of *Sky Cries Mary*'s best videos and it was an unexpected joy to see her that night.

I was happy, as always, to be back to Seattle even though it was only for a few days. I dropped in to say hello to my dad and his wife Gail, and also saw my two sisters Lisa and Cherron for our traditional breakfast in Belltown, at CJ's Cafe. My family was pleased to hear that I'd been doing well in New York and that my situation had improved considerably since the last time we were together, around Christmas '98.

Upon returning to Manhattan, I tried to adjust to living with Philippo in his studio apartment now that he was back. But, really, sleeping on his couch wasn't so comfortable and having the two of us in that tiny space felt quite cramped. I decided to stay at Transporterraum studio instead. Woah, what an idea! I would save $500 a month and since I was already working there most days, it seemed to make some kind of sense.

I joined a gym located in a basement on East 3rd Street, just one block away. It was really small and had a great bohemian spirit of the East Village vibe all the way through. THIS is where I planned to take a shower each day and even get a little exercise after breakfast, before the studio sessions began. Being in the Transporterraum basement with no light or windows was fabulous for sleeping at any time; it always felt midnight dark!

Great. So I woke up in the studio, hit a local cafe for breakfast and then went to the gym. I would appear for work at 11 am, fit and ready for a day of making music and recording. On my days off I'd go visit Anne at her apartment. We'd do photoshoots together for our new record or make promotional flyers for gigs. She was a visionary and prolific photographer, using only film and old cameras. Her style leaned heavily on 'cross processing', which intentionally developed the film using the wrong chemicals. This gave her pictures a supernatural look with exceptionally glowing greens, blues and yellows.

Thanks to Anne's photo obsession we have hundreds of images from those great days in New York. She was in a highly outgoing and social phase of her life and had a great collection of interesting friends, old and new. I always enjoyed the wild characters that I'd meet at her place or that she would bring out with us at night. Anne and I were very close and had wonderful times walking in Central Park enjoying the paths and ponds, the Alice in Wonderland sculpture and, of course, Strawberry Fields on the west side. Speaking of Fields, we also spent hours shopping at Patricia Field on 8th Street, where the most outrageous NY fashions were profusely on offer, along with gorgeous drag queens cutting hair and doing makeovers for clients in the front window. After shopping there, I never missed a chance to walk two blocks away and touch the curved brick wall that housed the magical Electric Lady Studio, built specifically for my hero, Jimi Hendrix. Of course, there was always a NEED to drop by Trash and Vaudeville to pick up Day-Glo rainbow-colored reptile-print trousers (to which I would then add green glitter), pink on black Johnny Thunders T-shirts and hot-pink metal studded wristbands—after all, we WERE representing East Village rock culture and were nothing but proud ambassadors.

One evening after I finished work, I left the studio to go find some dinner. As I stepped onto East 2nd Street, I saw David Bason walk right past me. Dave was a local musician that Sami Yaffa had brought down to the studio and I wound up recording a few of his songs.

While we were working, he mentioned that he'd recently started a job in the A&R department at RCA Records. I invited Dave down to Transporterraum on several occasions to play him my new songs, hoping he might like them enough to show them around at RCA.

On this particular evening, I ran up behind him, tapped him on the shoulder and said, "Hi!"

I knew he lived down the street from my studio and he was probably just coming home from the office. I asked Dave to come downstairs to check out the latest recordings—*The Strokes* three song demo. He agreed, smiling to himself about how I was always trying to show him SOMETHING if I had the chance!

Re-entering the studio, I flicked the lights back on, fired up the sound system and we both sat on the purple velvet couch as the song *The Modern Age* started. The look on his face told me that he was liking it a bit, but not actually feeling thrilled or 'into it'. Song two came on, *Last Nite*, and suddenly his look changed to super-serious at first, but then his face lit up brightly.

"Hey! Play the first song again!" he exclaimed.

So, of course I did.

On that second run though, when he heard *The Modern Age*, he said,

"This is great, wow! I love it."

And, after *Barely Legal* finished, he asked me to burn him a CD, telling me he'd take it to RCA the next day and see what he could do.

At the end of October, *Absinthee* played a Halloween show at Continental on 3rd Avenue and St. Marks Place which, for decades, had been my favorite street corner in the world.

I spent countless nights walking up and down St. Marks from 3rd Avenue to Avenue A, back and forth, just being hypnotized from staring at all the people. In the 80s and 90s those streets were a carnival of killer record shops, rock 'n' roll clothing boutiques and well-stocked thrift stores. Floating along the sidewalks was a sea of weirdos, misfits, bizarre outfits, junkies, thieves, drag queens and me with my head spinning, taking it all in.

On those nights, when I reached 3rd and St. Marks, I'd stand with my back on the payphone in front of the magazine shop, just watching the human parade—especially on weekend nights. I would almost always see Lenny Kaye (a real, live chunk of human rock history, revolutionary guitarist with Patti Smith) walking home towards his place. We knew each other a little bit from one Christmas with Debe Lazo back in Spokane, Washington. One time he even came down to hear songs at Transporterraum studio. I made a six-minute art film about *Absinthee*'s Halloween show at Continental (which one can still find on YouTube); Anne was a fairy called Tinkerbell that night, with cute transparent wings, a provocative white mini-dress, fishnets, high heels, a magic wand and her super-bleached-out hair. The little movie I made concentrates on the party that was happening in our dressing room, spotlighting the characters, who were our East Village friends at that time (including Sami Yaffa) in full effect.

Somewhere in November 2000, around three weeks after I'd handed those *Strokes* demos to Dave Bason, I'd just finished a recording session. After the musicians left, I was sitting alone in the empty control room which was now my home as well. It was only 7pm, but I had absolutely no idea what I wanted to do for the rest of the night. In that moment of void, I flashed on a small, poisonous idea that suddenly sprung up to loom quite BIG in my mind.

Over the past two years I had been approached by various Puerto Rican guys who were always hanging out on the corner of 1st Avenue, near 9th Street, saying,

"Hey, smoke, smoke?"

Of course, I'd walk quickly on by, paying them no mind, frowning to myself at the mere mention of "smoke".

From Halloween 1991 (my last time of getting high on drugs while living in Hollywood) until that week in Mallorca with Anne and *Satellites*, I had been steadfast, clad in armor and militantly AGAINST all forms of chemical intoxication. For the first few months in New York after our stoned holiday in Spain, I adhered strictly to my resolution to stay 'straight' and forget about it. But this night the bells were ringing louder as I pictured scoring some weed, then rushing off to Gem Spa for a pack of cigarettes, rolling papers and a lighter.

On went my coat, I checked my wallet for cash and then walked that exact route: from studio to 1st Avenue & 9th Street, to Gem Spa on 2nd & St. Marks and back.

That circle, from running upstairs until returning downstairs had taken around 40 minutes. I made sure to lock the front studio door, then entered the control room. For the very first time, but certainly NOT the last, I poured tobacco from a ripped-up cigarette along with crumpled up, sticky marijuana onto the classy, dark wood table in front of me.

Most citizens in the USA do not mix weed with tobacco. It's a Euro-thing which indeed had been taught to me by Swiss Sigmund back in old Seattle. I never could roll a professional-looking joint, I was far too impatient for that, but I always managed to craft something potent that burned fairly well, delivering the intended dose to my brain and body.

I smoked one, put on some music and rolled a second one an hour later. I figured that the smell would be gone by noon the next day when another music project was scheduled to begin. I certainly didn't want Anne or Jimmy to find out that I was smoking and, for the moment, I decided to be careful about that.

As December and its freezing North Atlantic weather moved in, the recording business was slowing down for the approach of the Christmas holidays. This meant I had plenty of time in the evenings to lock the studio door and get high. By now, I had a ritual of smoking joints and then turning on the studio equipment; plugging in my keyboards (including a Wurlitzer electric piano purchased from Zappa's former guitarist, Jeff Simmons, who was immortalized in cartoon form in the movie *200 Motels*), guitars and my Oberheim DMX drum machine. As my mind began spiraling in a haze towards the sky, I'd improvise textures and melodies on these instruments.

When one of these sounded "AMAZING" to me, I'd record it and then develop a song from that idea. Over the course of one month, I composed and recorded twenty-one songs. As always with my music, some of these rocked, some were psychedelic, there were many with singing and a few instrumentals. I had written many songs I really liked at Chateau Relaxo, some for Anne to sing and some for my own voice. Most of my time during the first year at Transporterraum NYC was split between recording bands (gettin' paid!) and rehearsing with *Absinthee*. In the midst of the pre-Christmas rush (shall we say?), it was all about finding my way back into the wild, fiery world of my own original music, with as few distractions or limitations as possible.

One of my best Gordon Raphael albums ever came out of this period, a thirteen-song collection entitled *I Lick the Moog*. I saved eight additional songs (discombobulated synthetic abstract experiments) for a separate album called *Electro-Weird Side*.

I had an incredibly joyous time locking that studio door, smoking pot & tobacco spliffs and journeying out, out, out into my own world of music. All of these songs were exhilarating, vastly fun to invent and record, but one has a particularly magical story around it.

One freezing cold night, the doorbell rang. I wasn't expecting anyone and answered,

"Hello. Studio."

It was a woman named Carla who had come by to visit the studio several times before, as she knew many musicians in the East Village. I always liked her and we had several very cool, short talks on those occasions. She came downstairs and said that she just wanted to say hello. Then she sat next to me on one of the studio chairs. I told her about the new songs I was working on and she told me about her work at a famous television network. She was super-extra friendly, looking into my eyes with a very nice feeling attached to that. Just when I was feeling a sweet rhythm developing between the two of us, the doorbell rang again and this time, it was Anne.

She floated down the stairs and when she came in and saw Carla, they immediately began talking with each other.

After a few minutes, Anne announced that she felt like hitting Mars Bar, right in the neighborhood, and asked if we'd like to come along. I felt somewhat sullen and chose to stay in the studio, while the two of them put on their winter coats and gloves and went out together.

That situation put me into a really intense mood, one that had been familiar to me many times before in my life, but here I was in a good studio and able to channel a whole bunch of anger, frustration and heartbreak into one new song. The minute after Anne and Carla left, I smoked yet another joint and got further high.

I had my SG guitar and I was thinking about *The Rolling Stones*, specifically songs where Keith Richards and Mick Jagger sing together. I thought of how broken and thin Keith's voice is and then Mick always sounds tough and powerful next to that.

My idea was to make a song where I could try and do both their voices and see what happened. I made a fat rock-beat on my drum machine and put seven heartfelt, nasty guitar chords over it. Then I played a monster (if I don't say so myself) bass line and tracked an off-beat Motown guitar plinky groove. For the chorus, I added mournful, lovelorn, distortion riffs and two rag-tag guitar solos. After the music seemed all killer and raging, I put on my headphones and within an hour had lyrics and two singing parts done, just as I had envisioned it. This whole song was VERY pleasing to me and I named it STRONG.

Synchronistically, mere moments after I finished that song (2am), I heard the fucking door-bell ring again.

"Hi, it's me"—Carla's voice.

She came back into the studio and sweetly asked me what I'd been doing. I didn't tell her "This song is about you," but I pressed play and she heard my song, *Strong*.

She told me she really liked it and was impressed. Then we just started kissing really hard, really long and very well. We made love on the purple velvet studio couch and that was incredible too. Right around 6am, she asked me if I wanted to come over to her apartment on the Lower East Side and get some sleep.

I said, "Yes."

17: Run-Ins & Residencies

In mid-December I went walking up my sacred path on St. Marks Place. It was a crisp, cold Saturday afternoon and who did I happen to see crossing the road, but Albert Hammond Jr. from *The Strokes*! He looked pleased to see me and I noticed he had just come out of a record store and was heading towards Kim's Video, another record store, carrying a small cardboard box.

"Hey, Albert, what's up?" I asked.

He said, "check these out!" as he reached into the box and pulled out a very nicely designed CD.

They had pressed their demos onto CDs and came up with a minimal, aesthetically pleasing cover; circles and spirals in orange and yellow with the words, "The Modern Age" and "The Strokes" printed over it. I thought it was very cool that they had taken the initiative to do that on their own. I also considered that Albert was being very brave, as trying to put your own CDs in those shops was not an easy thing to do, believe me.

Those East Village record stores were big business and had a very 'we are the coolest people on the planet' attitude, usually scoffing or laughing as they'd turn away local bands trying to distribute their own music. I smiled and told him that the artwork looked great as he happily handed me one.

He also invited me to come along to a four-show residency *The Strokes* were going to play at the nearby Mercury Lounge starting December 20th.

The residency shows were scheduled over four consecutive Wednesday nights. The first one wasn't crowded, but *The Strokes* gave an amazing performance. I didn't know if they had been rehearsing extra hard or if, somehow, the studio sessions had given them an energetic boost of confidence but, whatever it was, this show really impressed me and I was feeling proud of them.

Many more people came to see the second Wednesday night show. I arrived with Anne and by this time Julian would always greet me with a big hug and kiss. No one else really did that. I thought it was sweet and it made me feel special.

The third residency show was packed—completely SOLD OUT and the excitement growing in downtown New York City around the band was a marvel to behold.

The fourth and final show was to an overflow crowd, with folks who couldn't get in just standing around on the sidewalk in front of Mercury Lounge. This residency idea from new *Strokes* manager Ryan Gentles was really ingenious. I hadn't heard of an important downtown residency since Jeff Buckley's rise to superstardom at nearby Sin-é, in the mid-90s.

I'd met a beautiful young Hispanic woman around the Ludlow Street area and actually worked up the nerve to ask her to come along with me to that fourth *Strokes* show. We walked into the Mercury Lounge together but she was at the bar ordering a drink when I spotted Julian Casablancas entering the club.

I could tell that he was a bit tipsy. This time when he came up towards me, he gave me a giant hug and a kiss on the lips, but then didn't let go. He just kind of held me there about to say something and I could smell an overwhelming amount of booze on his breath.

"Hey Gordon, aren't you happy for us that things are going so well?" He slurred slightly as he spoke.

"Of course, Julian, I really am," I replied, hoping he might let me go.

He then came out with, "well don't you wish you'd made us sign something? 'Cuz you're not getting anything from those recordings now."

I knew he was drunk, but it felt like an odd, mean thing to say right then. I told him to fuck off, pulled his arm away and just walked away. I hadn't considered that at all; legal formalities and contracts for three demos?

The Strokes took the stage with a new level of confidence and played incredibly well on this night. It was electric and very magical, like a storm brewing at the beginning of something

HUGE. I had never once seen an audience in New York react that way for a local band, that's for sure.

After the show, I brought my lady-friend backstage to meet the band. Their dressing room was crammed full of people who were going crazy, drinking and partying. I chatted with Ryan, Fab Moretti and Nikolai and, when I looked around for that cute Hispanic girl twenty minutes later, I saw her sitting backwards on a chair, straddling Nick Valensi, full on kissing. The end of an intense night out, I left quietly and went back to my basement home in the studio.

18: Jumps Back and Forth Across the Atlantic

January 2001 was a major turning point, a cause for celebration. I was both sleeping and working at Transporterraum NYC recording studio, tucked away in the basement, producing a variety of bands and solo artists. Across the Atlantic Ocean, forces were at work that would influence and change my life "in such a permanent way," as one of Julian's lyrics would neatly phrase it.

Here's how it went down, according to rock historians:

Ryan Gentles, the young man who had become manager of *The Strokes*, asked his boss at Mercury Lounge where he might send the three-song demo, which the band had pressed into CDs and titled, *The Modern Age*. A copy of this disc wound up in London, in the capable hands of one James Endeacott, top A&R man at Rough Trade, a label that was world renowned for its innovative and forward-thinking artist roster. (They'd signed Robert Wyatt, *The Fall*, *Pere Ubu*, *The Raincoats*, *Stiff Little Fingers* as well as two of my personal favorites *Scritti Politti* and *The Smiths*.) James Endeacott played a few minutes of the first song, then ran urgently to find Geoff Travis, founder and head of the company. Together they listened to all three songs once through, agreeing that they NEEDED to sign *The Strokes* immediately and bring them over to the UK for a tour!!

I had no idea that this was happening until I bumped into Albert once again on St. Marks Place. He was beaming with that winning smile as he told me,

"Gordon, guess what? Rough Trade is gonna release the EP we made together and we're flying to England to play some shows next week!"

I was dizzy with excitement when he told me that, but also puzzled! I'd been a fan of British rock and British musicians my whole life, so the idea that something I WORKED ON was going to be heard in ENGLAND was blowing to my mind!

"But Albert, shouldn't we at least check the mix and fix it up a bit before it gets released? I mean they're only quick demos!" said I.

"No man, they said they like it just the way it is!" were Albert's comforting words. I did shake my head because I had never heard of a label releasing a demo as a record.

Days later I was browsing, as I often did, at the well-curated magazine shop on Avenue A, near my studio. I picked up the latest *NME* mag and was leafing through when I ran across a column showing that *The Strokes* had been picked for "Record of The Week," with a picture of *The Modern Age* EP cover and a short, glowing review.

Lord Jesus almighty Buddha God in Heaven, I was freaking out with excitement! I walked to the studio and sat with the magazine open on my desk, imagining what this could mean for the band and for me as their producer. I felt famous and successful in that moment, just from reading that *NME* column. What was I going to do with all that money and glorious attention? Why, I'd certainly NOT be working in the basement six days a week. No, I'd travel to cool places all over the world, recording bands instead. Also in this dream, my own music would have a chance to be heard as well, of course!

As *The Strokes* were overseas playing their first few shows, reports were coming back to New York that Kate Moss and members of *Radiohead* were in the audience. Well, the news was just getting better and better, filling my rock 'n' roll braincells with high hopes and big anticipation for what might come next.

Two weeks later, I was down in the lab at Transporterraum when my phone rang. It was Julian Casablancas asking if we could get together somewhere in the neighborhood for dinner and to talk.

I'd been hoping for a call like that, and the next night we met at 7A, across the street from my former living quarters at Philippo's place. Julian was a blend of cheerful, calm, tired and serious when we sat down. I couldn't wait to ask about their tour, he grinned and told me it was great and then we both looked at the menu. Our waitress was a tattooed East Village rocker girl, who took our order with a smile.

After she walked away Julian broke the news to me;

"Rough Trade really love the EP, but they want us to use a different producer that they've chosen when we record the album," Julian started, then continued with, "We all really liked working with you and we think you've really captured our sound."

I asked who the producer was that Rough Trade wanted for them and he told me it was Gil Norton. My heart sank and I felt suddenly hollow and afraid.

Gil Norton had been producing *The Foo Fighters* at Bear Creek Studios when I first started working with Anne. He had an amazing, incredibly successful career as a record producer going back to the early 80s with *Echo & the Bunnymen*, then *Throwing Muses* and, of course, he produced the gigantic *Pixies* album, *Doolittle*, for the legendary 4AD label. Gil Norton was a well-established British record producer!

Julian said, "Gordon, we need to make this decision based on what's best for the whole band. We have this one shot." Then followed with, "If you tell me right now that you're a better producer than him, then we'll work with you on the album."

"No fair...no way, this is impossible..." were some of the impressions churning through my mind in that moment. I relaxed a little bit and said clearly to Julian Casablancas,

"Look, we had a great time in the studio and we made that sound, together! I know that Gil Norton has sold six million copies of every record he's ever made and I have never even sold ONE record, so how can I tell you that I'm a BETTER producer than he is?"

Just then our food arrived and was placed in front of us on the table. Julian simply stood up and grabbed his coat.

He looked straight at me and said,

"Fuck you Gordon, now we have to use Gil Norton" and he just walked out the door into the Avenue A night, right along with my bright shiny dreams of fame and not having to work 12-hour shifts in the basement, six days a week.

19: New Digs & Developments

A persistent dull grey cloud of what-ifs and why-didn't-Is hung over me for a while, but I got busy producing more songs with other bands.

I would imagine *The Strokes* in some classic British studio making a great historic album with that other producer and then Julian's words would echo back to me about having asked for no royalty 'points' on *The Modern Age* EP. I was doing my best to concentrate on other things and get on with my life, telling myself that more good things would certainly happen at Transporterraum.

A couple of nice things did happen around that time; my dear short-term (she moved on) love interest, Carla, asked me if I wanted to take over the rent on her cool apartment at Rivington and Clinton on the Lower East Side. Simultaneously, my lifelong best friend, Ken Weller, told me that he'd packed a big truck full of his furniture, clothing and musical instruments and was setting off to drive from San Francisco to New York City. We were going to be housemates! That was very fitting because he was the one who handed me my first NY job by introducing me to Pamela Laws, thus saving me from imminent financial disaster. An extra cool benefit from having Kenneth move in was that he'd brought his gigantic Ampeg SVT bass amp and matching cabinet (that we used to call The Fridge) which held eight ten-inch speakers. This bass rig went directly into the Transporterraum basement, making the recording of bass guitars easier and better than ever. Extremely LOUD, but always the perfect rock bass tone.

In February, *The Strokes* invited me to see them play at the Bowery Ballroom opening for a band they'd always talked about, *Guided by Voices*. The Bowery was the biggest place they'd played in New York so far and it was another fast, noticeable step UP the ladder for them. The guys were very nice and friendly with me when I hung out with them after the show and they introduced me to the musicians in *Guided by Voices*. GBV's music was cool but I wasn't nearly as big a fan of that group as *The Strokes* were.

Two weeks later *The Strokes* were BACK at Bowery Ballroom opening up for British band, *Doves*. This was yet another level up, not only because the concert was packed and sold out, but there were long, shiny, black limousines parked around the block.

To me this meant only one thing: big fat major New York record labels were there to see what the buzz was all about regarding *The Strokes*! It was a heady, dazzling feeling to be so close to the intense aura which permeated that night at the Bowery Ballroom. Even though I had no part in their current activity, there was a bond and camaraderie between us, a knowing that together we made a three-song EP that certainly had gotten the ball rolling.

I was sitting backstage and happened to glance down at a pile of papers on the wooden chair right next to me. I absentmindedly reached down and looked at one and it was actually a real major label recording contract. I was shocked and looking closer realized it was actually a stack of such contracts from several different companies. No, I had never seen anything quite like that before and it only added to the electricity in the air.

On or around March 3, 2001, I was at home on Rivington Street in my new apartment chilling out, smoking some weed, when my phone rang. I was surprised to hear the voice of Julian Casablancas in my ear, so I asked him, "What's up?"

He asked me if I still had my studio.

"Yes," I replied.

He asked if they could come back there to record their album with me.

I said... "WHAT?? I thought you were recording with Gil Norton."

He explained that they tried working with him for a couple of days but didn't want anyone to hear that, as it wasn't the right sound. My heart was pounding and a fast wave of stoned joy was coursing up my spine, I felt like I was levitating.

He then said, "I have to tell you, we're also not sure if you'll be able to get that sound again. What do you think?"

I tried to reassure him that I could definitely get that sound back, and excitedly yelped, "Hey, let's just meet for coffee and talk about it!"

He told me that wouldn't be possible right then, 'cuz they were in Chicago still touring with *Doves*. He added that when they returned from the tour, we'd all have a meeting in the studio and that they wanted to play me some examples of their favorite music. I hung up the phone and literally jumped up and down.

My studio partner Jimmy had left a copy of *Rolling Stone* magazine that was spread open on our shiny wood table when I walked in to work. I saw there a small, glorious feature about *The Strokes* on tour and *The Modern Age* EP by veteran senior editor, David Fricke. He cited *The Fall*, *Lou Reed*, *Mission of Burma* and *The Jam* as references, to try and give the sprawling, mixed-up USA music audience something to grasp by way of a description of the band's music. It came with a bold full color action-photo portrait of the band, signaling MORE TO COME.

It was very rare to see *Rolling Stone* feature a band that was unsigned in the U.S. I think they stopped doing that in the 1960s!

20: So, We Meet Again!

When everyone was back in New York, we gathered in the studio to talk about how and when we were going to actually record *The Strokes'* first album. The musicians brought CDs of bands and songs they loved and respected, wishing to give me a wider picture of what they had in mind. This musical sharing included, *A Salty Salute* from *Guided by Voices*, intended to show me guitar sounds they liked, *Watching the Wheels* by the godhead himself, John Lennon, for drum ideas, and a few Bob Marley songs.

At this point they still weren't signed to a record company in the U.S., therefore we discussed how we could keep the budget as low as possible, in the hopes that we could do a great job and, hopefully, sell it on to a label for more money later.

There was a seven-week time window available, starting at the beginning of the second week of April, extending through the month of May. After that last day in May, the band was already hard-scheduled to be in the UK touring and then spend the entire summer playing festivals throughout Europe and Australia.

Their upcoming tours sounded like a dream to me and, when they told me about it, I instantly wished I could go with them and see it happening. They also informed me that there would be a handful of club shows between Boston and Philadelphia during our recording sessions, so periodically they would have to take their equipment from the studio. I disliked the idea of having those interruptions, as I thought that every day in that time window would be needed to do a great job, remembering how detail-oriented they had been with the demo, now known as *The Modern Age* EP.

It wasn't a long get-together that day, but there was a harmonious, unified group feeling. There was also a sense of fun in the air, along with a fair share of nervous excitement. To be honest, I was swimming in the giddy head-rush of having them BACK. We all felt confident and hopeful about really delivering a great album, running far with this rare opportunity which had been presented to us.

Our preliminary meeting gave me a couple of weeks to plan and prepare to do the best production possible. I called upon my secret weapon, former studio partner Scott Clark, and asked him if there was any great equipment he owned that he could recommend and lend to me for seven weeks.

He offered: a second 888/24 converter so that I could record up to sixteens microphones at once, six Neve 1073 preamps with EQ (truly the gold standard of recording equipment!) in a cool, heavy black metal rack and a strip of four API preamps, which he told me were the ones that *Pink Floyd* used to get their best guitar sounds. I ran to borrow Scott's equipment and wired it into our patch bay, thus increasing our firepower exponentially.

Since the beginning of Transporterraum NYC, we'd been using a pair of Alesis Monitor Two speakers which were cheap and not super-accurate, but they really filled the control room with a loud, powerful rock sound when I turned them WAY up. These speakers were on semi-permanent loan to me from Rick Robinson, our landlord.

Anne visited me one afternoon. She told me that she'd randomly met a guy at a restaurant the night before, who was a producer manager. He told her that he'd actually invented the field of producer management and was looking after the careers of some of the biggest music producers in the world. Anne said that she'd told him about me and that he wanted to come meet me, to potentially sign me. As always, I called Manny Hadlock back at Bear Creek, because I totally trusted her business understanding and instincts. I asked her if she thought that this was a good idea, which, after some research, she certainly did.

I was excited that my career was now suddenly of interest to such a top guy, imagining myself joining his roster of those really well-known record producers. My main interest in having a powerful, experienced manager was to make sure I got a good contract with *The Strokes*, unlike what had happened with the demos where I had NONE. Next, I wanted him to get me high-paying jobs with bands I liked so I could become financially well-off! Maybe I could get my own house somewhere, a bigger studio, more equipment and a cool car. I believed that a well-connected manager could help me get my own music signed and help me start my own record label, guaranteeing funds to develop the amazing new bands that I always seemed to be attracting or discovering.

Two days before *The Strokes* album project officially began, Mr. X (unnamed for legal reasons) came to my studio. He smoothly and slickly told me everything I wanted to hear. He assured me that he was capable of accomplishing all the things on my top priorities list. Within two weeks I signed a contract with him and have regretted it ever since.

It was a huge mistake, which I put down to a BAD combination of ego, drug daze and naiveté—all swirling together within my own shaky brain. These impulses allowed me to sign a terrible piece of paper. Of course, in that moment I was so cheerful, thinking I had just joined a high-ranking club of great producers, and wow, in two days we were going to start *The Strokes'* first album!

21: How It All Began

There was an energy and excitement in the studio even before we actually started, and I hoped it would last through the next seven weeks. Yes, there would be an incredible amount of hard work ahead in order to deliver an album that *The Strokes* would not only be proud of, but that could help them break through to bigger shows and a far wider audience.

I'd been in studios on my own for years making music and had also recorded many different bands, but NOW there was this feeling,

"Oh my God, the whole world is going to hear what we are doing and we can actually FEEL all those people waiting for this record to be born!"

It was a rare, electric and powerful BUZZ. I felt it as a great, wild new kind of trip—with adventure and fun ahead. I imagine that the band members probably felt, "We have this chance, we have to do it right, need to play our best and, oh, let's hope it's going to go well."

The day marked on our calendar had arrived, *The Strokes* entered the studio right on time. They set up in the same places as before except for Nikolai, who went a little further back because the mighty Ampeg SVT bass amp was so much louder than the one we had used before. Nikolai, Nick, Fab and Albert would be playing their instruments at the same time to create the same sound blending that we achieved on *The Modern Age* EP. It was important that the sound in the room was as perfectly balanced as possible so that it could be captured like a sonic snapshot.

Many producers and engineers believe in separating the amps and drums so they don't bleed into each other during the recording. Often this means putting a bass speaker in a closet and moving the drummer into a separate room or isolation booth. I always hated that vibe, especially when a guitarist can't stand near their own amp to feel it fully or create harmonic feedback. Putting musicians in different rooms also breaks a natural flow, because the band members are only allowed to hear each other through headphones and prevented from seeing each other face to face.

One time Fabrizio Moretti said to me,

"We don't care about the individual sounds; we just want to hear them dancing together in the air!" Sage words, indeed.

The extra audio converter I borrowed from Scott Clark meant that we could record up to sixteen channels simultaneously, but we only ended up using eleven for these sessions, three more tracks than we used on the demos. Ten microphones and one DI (direct signal for the bass) was much less than what was standard in those days, that's for sure.

In the late 19th century, the earliest recordings were made using a single microphone which was actually a conical-shaped horn attached to a wall. Later it was a big advancement to record a group of musicians using two and then four microphones. At Chateau Relaxo, during my experimental learning phase, I recorded Alan Bezozi playing a deep *Massive Attack*-style drum groove, using a single Neumann mic and the Manley Compressor. The sound that came from that was HUGE and had incredible impact. This taught me the power of microphones and that you didn't need to use too many of them.

Albert, Nick and Nikolai (two guitars and bass) didn't wear headphones during the instrumental tracking. The room was very loud and full of sound, starting from the very first chord, and they could hear themselves perfectly well, just like at a rehearsal or a show. Fab was the exception because he had asked me in advance for headphones so he could listen to the band and a click track. He told me in a very serious tone, that in the six months since we'd recorded the demos he had progressed in his drumming to the point where he could now hear areas where he slightly pushed or pulled the tempo in those songs. He asked me to help him make sure we didn't have any unwanted speedups or slowdowns on this album.

I'm sure that certain members of the band must have been a little surprised to see me rolling joints on the wooden table and smoking them regularly during the sessions. I wasn't doing it the first time we worked together and they wouldn't have seen that if they had met me at any point during the previous ten years. A couple of the band members enjoyed smoking pot, but some did not. There were beers coming into the studio but no one was anywhere near being slumped over or slurring their speech, that's for sure! And no, I certainly never drank any alcohol during these sessions.

In our familiar positions, the band played in the live room while Julian and JP Bowersock sat with me in the control room, carefully listening, checking to see if any parts or sounds needed improvement. I learned that JP had given guitar lessons to Nick, Albert and Julian, so they had ultimate trust in his finely tuned ears. He also demonstrated an encyclopedic knowledge of guitar history, both for the equipment used and playing styles. *The Strokes* musicians would ask him about pedal settings, amp tones and even consult JP for his suggestions regarding modes and melodies while crafting their guitar solos. I already described his characteristic way of shouting mathematical frequencies,

"Boost some 5k on Albert's guitar!" across the room when suggesting EQ tone improvements.

Yes, I often joke about that but, honestly, he was always helpful to the band and very complimentary, kind and supportive to me.

I don't have the kind of memory that can describe which song happened first, second or third, nor who said what during each moment of Album #1. I do have the back-up files and I could sleuth it out, but I'm not that obsessive! I also have original screenshots of a few songs, both the arrange and mix windows from the Logic sessions and can clearly see from those exactly how we recorded each part.

During our sessions, the band got very involved with the idea that every instrument should sound as close as possible to the ideal, BEFORE anything was recorded. This worked perfectly for me too, as it's much harder to turn a bad sound into a good sound or the wrong sound into the right sound after it's been recorded. It can be done but that process requires unnecessary extra work and time.

On every song I was experimenting. Crazy discoveries were made by putting an important mic in a place that I'd never tried before. One was six inches from the ceiling and as far away from the drums as possible, while another was two feet in front of the kick drum. Both of these created great but completely different tones.

Julian was not a fan of highly polished clean recorded instruments. He would say things like, "This sound needs to have its tie loosened!".

He also had a fantastic sense of listening to the recorded drum tones and noticing if one small detail was off. In one such case he turned to me and said, "The whole drum set sounds like a yuppie, but the hi-hat is out begging for spare change."

Some songs were very slow to capture, the band would do many takes before getting a version that everyone liked. There was NOT much editing done on the instrumental parts for this album. Sometimes a few notes would be played again (punched in) as a correction but looking at these sessions it's incredible how few audio tracks we used and how few edits there are. It's also mind-blowing to see that almost no plug-ins (software-based equalizers and compressors) were used at all, even in the final mix, to improve the sounds. Also, thanks to the challenge from Moses Schneider, there is no echo or reverb whatsoever.

Some songs were finished quickly, after two or three tries. We worked on one song for almost an entire day, but when the band came into the studio on the following day, they asked to record it again at a slightly different tempo. I didn't take that too well, as revisiting the same song a day later put me in a mild emotional slump! Their goal was reached by the end of that second day with the musicians being much happier with their revised, improved tempo.

During the first week, *The Strokes* would enter the studio and tell me about different horrible experiences they were having with big record companies taking them out to dinner. Words like jerks, idiots, douchebags, fake and boring were used often in their descriptions. One morning they came in and told me they had actually signed a deal with RCA. They were excited about that and told me that the people they'd met from the company were fairly cool, seemed like they really loved the band and were committed to doing great things to help them launch their career. They agreed to stay with Rough Trade for the UK, letting RCA take control for the rest of the world.

The day after the big signing, Nick came up to me at the beginning of the recording day, 1 o'clock in the afternoon at this point, and placed a huge bag of fine-looking marijuana on the big table. He said,

"Check this out, Gortron (they'd found out about my two old nicknames, Gordotronic and Gortron), this is for all of us to share."

He then looked me in the eye to see if I understood what "sharing" meant.

Truth is, I was neither gracious nor considerate with sharing marijuana, which I'm sure he'd already noticed by now! The new bag was soon opened and, while Nick rolled a joint, I dipped in and rolled one for myself.

Later on, Julian spoke with me while a couple of the other band members gathered around. He told me that their new A&R guy at RCA Records wanted to come visit the studio to hear what the beginning of the album was sounding like and to meet me. But then Julian's face looked a little concerned and serious as he told me that, for him, the studio space was so special, almost sacred like a musician's sanctuary, and he didn't really want this record company executive to come in. What could we do?

Well, I was honestly excited to meet a real record company guy from RCA, I mean, Elvis was on RCA, and my favorite star, David Bowie, as well! We all discussed this and came up with a plan.

There was a little construction area in the basement, right outside the front door of our studio. It was lit by horrible white neon tubes and there were piles of sawdust and chunks of plasterboard strewn on the floor. We would put a chair out there and bring him the three songs that were the furthest along, on a shitty plastic cassette player. How does that sound?

The next day, the A&R person from RCA came down the basement stairs and we all greeted him out in the little area, as described. He gave me a big (yet, fake feeling) hug and told me he had heard so many great things about me (with a tense smile). Then he said,

"So whattaya got for me? I can't wait to hear it."

Julian presented him with the cassette player and pushed play. The A&R guy moved his body, giving the impression that he was really grooving to the new sounds. He was practically snapping his fingers and saying, "YEAH!" but wasn't really. He said,

"That's great!" at the end of one song and, "Really great," after another.

Twenty minutes later he was leaving to go back to the office and said,

"Wow, you guys are doing a really great job," and then looked at me and added, "Nice work, Gordon!"

I distinctly thought that he was only pretending to like what we'd done so far and wondered if he was actually hating it.

The instrumental tracking parts for a few pieces were 'in the can', finished and ready, when Julian had a private chat with me. He told me that he wished we could use a drum machine on several upcoming songs. I was happy and surprised to hear that, because I would have never, in the relatively small amount of time we'd worked together, have suspected that Julian liked drum machines. He told me that he loved the sound and feel of his drum machine but, at the same time, didn't want Fabrizio to feel left out of any songs on their first album. His dilemma instantly triggered many possibilities in my mind. I told Julian that it would

129

be fairly easy to make Fab's drums sound like a drum machine and we could take that idea as far as he wanted to. I asked him to show me what kind of electronic drum sounds he liked, so we walked over to his (and Albert's) apartment on 2nd Avenue.

When we got there, I saw his small recording set up which centered around a Korg digital 8-Track recorder. He turned it on, pressed some buttons and hit PLAY. I wore headphones and heard a very cool demo for a song called *Hard to Explain*. I clocked the drum machine parts and also couldn't help but notice what a great song it was.

"Did you record the band playing this over the drum machine?" I asked.

"No," he answered, "I played everything myself."

It was at that moment that I learned that Julian had written all the songs right there on his 8-Track. He originated the hi-hat patterns, bass lines, guitar chords and countermelodies that would be played by the band on the album. Later, I saw firsthand how some of the guitar solos were developed by Julian working together with JP, and then Nick or Albert would finesse out the best way to perform them.

Back at the studio it was time to put my ideas into action, to create the sound of drum machines coming from Fab's drum kit. My background in industrial music was now going to come in handy.

In 1981, I'd borrowed a friend's Roland CR-78 drum machine and made twenty songs with it, including one of my best, *I Said*. One year later, my band partner, Tor Midtskog, bought a TR-808. Everyone laughed at those thin, artificial drum sounds, but lo and behold, it took over the world and is still revered in techno, pop, soul and hip-hop music to this day. Then in 1984, I was invited to the Greek island of Corfu by my friends Alan and Lisa. There we had a music studio in a mansion with marble floors in the middle of an olive orchard; plus, we imported an Oberheim DMX, one of the first affordable drum machines which featured 8-bit digital samples of real drums. Finally, in *Sky Cries Mary* we had TR-808, TR-909 and DMX in our basement, where I was lucky to spend all day, every day, making songs and insanely processed sounds with that arsenal of synthetic drums.

Drum machines do NOT have bleed. When you hit the snare button there is no trace of rhythm guitar noise and no ringing cymbals heard, unlike when you record real drums in a room with a band playing all around them. Furthermore, drum machines sound mechanical in their beat, as they are usually quantized to absolute, metronomic perfection. They play back pre-programmed patterns in mechanical repetitions, unlike the subtle variations that real, living, breathing drummers make. The individual machine drum sounds (snare, crash, rimshot, claps) are also 'unreal' sounding, a bit fake and plastic, which can be a very good thing when used as a creative choice. This was going to be FUN.

The first thing we did was to identify that the song *Hard to Explain* mainly used three pieces of the drum kit: kick drum, snare and hi-hat. We would record those three at the same time, without the band playing and then, afterwards, add a ride cymbal as an overdub in the chorus. I thought about Moses Schneider, the extreme, crazy ways he would invent unusual sounds. I applied that by working with Fab to see how far away I could move the hi-hat from the snare drum and still have him play his parts comfortably.

His left arm was stretched out much further than usual, it looked quite funny, but he could do it. In fact, he usually played the hi-hat with his right hand crossed over his left, with his left hand playing the snare, but I asked him to switch hands and he was also able to do that. Then I moved the kick drum to the right, much further away than any drummer would ever want it, but still within reach so that he could play it powerfully and accurately with his right foot. The way I placed the microphones for this setup really did keep the sound of each part separate from the others, like a........... drum machine!

To push those sounds further into the realm of abstraction, I reached into the toolbox of plug-ins and selected two Filterbank EQs for the kick drum (double boosting certain frequencies was referred to by my dear friend Griff Stevens as "radical EQ"); one EQ for the snare (modifying the single mic that was pointed at the snare) and an elaborate stack of: EQ, Noise Gate and three additional EQs for the hi-hat (truly unorthodox technique, haha!). There was also a single overhead mic placed three feet over the center of Fab's drums, which captured more depth from the snare and that channel had no plug-ins on it at all.

To make it sound robotic and mechanical, we recorded each different rhythm pattern in the song: Intro, Verse, Pre-Chorus, Chorus, Solo, Ending, separately—then joined them together by editing. Fab played each of these beats for a few minutes and we selected the absolute best performance for each section before placing it into the song. He was already using a click track, even for the live band songs, and Fab was able to play so TIGHT that way, very precise without ever losing his expressiveness. All of these extra processes we developed really did add up to a wonderful drum machine effect.

From the get-go, we all loved this new drum sound and I especially liked the way it contrasted with the other songs on the album. When we recorded the ride cymbal on its own, it really sounded like you'd just pushed a button and on came this cymbal noise. The ride cymbal was altered by using a Bomb Factory vintage compressor plug-in, that made it sound really grainy and swishy. After the real-life drum machine parts were finished, the two guitars and bass were laid on top. Two other songs on the album, Soma and Alone Together, were recorded using the same method as Hard to Explain.

Ryan Gentles approached me one morning and said that RCA had just called him because they were, as I had sensed, very unhappy with the way I was producing the record so far. He told me that they even went as far as offering to increase the album budget if The Strokes would promptly FIRE me and get someone else. Ryan then withdrew a small piece of paper from his pocket, telling me that it was the list of producers that RCA had recommended to take my place.

I was quickly getting upset about this, feeling strange clouds descending on my party in a very big way. He ended this discussion with the encouraging words that the band was on my side and that they really liked working with me. I did take heart in that and hoped that things would somehow turn out well.

One day later, Julian found me in the control room. He told me that the band really did want to keep me on as producer for this record but didn't want to risk alienating the label. To do so could mean that RCA wouldn't promote the album, ruining not only this opportunity for the band, but also the chance for the world to hear these songs. He spoke to me in a very supportive voice, suggesting that there might be a way for this to be resolved. I was asked to let the A&R guy come to the studio, into the control room and give me his ADVICE on how to make the record sound better! This didn't really feel OK to me, but I thought that if it could make a difference, allowing me to keep my job, then it was worth trying.

The next day, the A&R guy showed up and nervously smiled at me as I offered him the chair next to mine in front of the speakers and computer screen.

"So, where do you want to start?" I asked.

"*Last Nite*. Show me that song and go to the chorus," was his answer.

I did as instructed, and he told me that, "Everyone knows that the snare drum is supposed to get louder in the chorus."

So, I moved the slider for the snare up until he said, "Yeah, there, right there."

I looked behind me at Fabrizio who was sitting with Nick, Albert, and Nikolai on the couch.

"Is that ok, Fab? Do you like it there?" I asked.

He answered, "No man, sorry, it's too loud!"

I wanted to honor the fact that I had agreed to try, in order to remain the producer on this album, so I offered the A&R guy that I could turn it down just a little, but not all the way back where it was to begin with. I did this micro-adjusting a few times but each time Fab shook his head, no. The snare volume was returned to where it originally was and I asked,

"What else?"

A&R then said, "That distortion on Julian's voice is terrible. He's a great singer and he could have a great career, but not if you ruin his voice with that shitty distortion."

I asked Julian, who was sitting right next to me, "Jules, do you want to try singing with a clearer or clean mic sound?"

He replied seriously but softly, "No."

The A&R guy looked a little bit exasperated but wanted to remain in control.

We looked at a few more parts on two more songs and, in the end, ONE song on the album has a snare part that's a few tenths of a decibel louder than before he came. Nothing else was changed.

The Strokes, obviously, had already put their own ideas and preferences into the sounds and songs so far. I really wasn't making all the creative choices by myself or producing strictly from my own whims!

Everything we had recorded so far was sounding very cool to me. I identified something in the songwriting that was highly unusual when compared with most rock music. Instead of using big guitar chords, a bass line that just follows along with those chords and an occasional countermelody between the singing parts, which was common in many rock songs, Julian wrote in almost pure counterpoint, meaning every part was actually a melody! The two guitars each played a melody and so did the voice and bass.

It's no easy task to make that many different melodies fit together, let alone sound amazing. One of the best examples in music history for that kind of harmonization is the baroque composer, Johann Sebastian Bach. Certain *Strokes* songs completely knocked me out, striking me over the head as brilliant rock masterpieces even when all I heard were the instrumental parts being played together in the live room.

New York City Cops, I truly remember as being captured in one or two takes, with the sounds blending perfectly between the two guitars, bass and drums. The way Nick, Albert, Fab and Nikolai played together on that song resulted in a rare, exciting, synergistic spirit. It reeked of juvenile delinquency, skinny but muscular, with ripped-up leather jackets. It evoked the imagery of smashing a car headlight with a rusty old crowbar, just for fun. Their blasting loud sounds came bouncing off the walls, with that whole atmosphere pouring directly into the recording.

It was a real 'music listener's' thrill to be hearing *New York City Cops* while it was being performed for the album that day. It immediately felt like a true sonic breakthrough. I felt that same level of satisfaction with *Soma*, *Trying Your Luck*, *Take It or Leave It*, and the song *Is This It*. The band were locking together with dazzling musical results, no matter if the songs required only a few takes to get right or many wearying hours of incredible effort.

One of the most shocking sonic moments of the entire 'making of the first album' was Albert Hammond Jr.'s guitar solo in *Take It or Leave It*. They were all playing together and, when he HIT that solo, it just sounded like the whole room was trembling, with the red and purple glitter walls vibrating under the intensity of his wild and bent-up guitar notes. On many *Strokes* songs, I got the feeling that Julian was intentionally writing with a technique in which every section sounded GREAT, but the next part would sound even better!

One afternoon some very special visitors from London came to meet us in the studio—James Endeacott from Rough Trade and James Oldham, a very bright journalist working with *NME* magazine. Having them both in the studio was an honor for me and I couldn't wait to show them the songs we'd worked on so far.

135

The first song we played was *New York City Cops*, so I cranked up the speakers to a punishingly loud volume and let it rip. James Endeacott, with his headful of thick ginger hair, literally threw his hat high into the air and started shouting with joy. He truly and honestly LOVED it and seeing him react that way was all the reassurance I needed.

It was such a relief to know that the way I was feeling about this music was the same way he felt about it too. It was MAJOR vindication, 100% polar opposite to the RCA reaction and precisely the energy boost I needed at that moment. The two Londoners left after an hour and we were all invigorated, smiling and ready to carry on recording.

Working closely with Julian on his singing parts for this album was an intense and wonderful adventure for me. We used the Avalon preamp and Audio-Technica microphone, the same setup as *The Modern Age* EP sessions. I actually borrowed a beautiful vintage Neumann U87 from the studio next door, a much more impressive and expensive mic than the Audio-Technica. I said,

"Hey Julian, I borrowed a really great microphone. Here, try this Neumann U87!"

He looked at me doubtfully, tried to sing a few notes and then shouted, "I hate this mic, I don't even like the look of it—just get it away from me and bring the other one back!"

We quickly developed a process, like a ritual, for his singing. Julian would go out to the live room and we would record him singing the song once through. It was always perfect from the very first note till the end. He never sang out of tune and I never heard him fall off of the rhythm—no way, not even slightly! In fact, almost immediately into these vocal sessions I really noticed Julian's incredible sense of timing. He was so aware of exactly where the beat was, that he could lag behind like crazy or brutally push ahead, while always being in complete control. He'd often shift the feel of the rhythms profoundly which, I must say, is an extremely rare skill.

After he completed the first take, I would tell him through the talkback mic, "Wow. That was great!"

Then he would reply, "Yeah, well, I have a bunch of different ways I could sing this and I want to try them all."

So indeed, he would sing with different attitudes, different intensities and do experiments with the melodies or rhythms. These were all subtle variations, like different shades of a color.

Julian also did something throughout these vocal sessions that really puzzled and impressed me, furthering my understanding of how utterly sensational his musical skills are. If he became unhappy about how he was singing a certain section, he would just stop and ask me to "punch in" at that spot, but to start the recording ten seconds earlier so he could make sure his voice was warmed up for the lines to come. During those ten seconds of 'lead in', he would sing absolutely ANYTHING that entered his mind, often in a completely different range of his voice, with alien lyrics, in some new key, while using the weirdest rhythms imaginable.

Normally, even a great singer who would try messing around like that would fail miserably to get back on track when the all-important 'punch in' came. But Julian NEVER missed! I found those moments to be riveting, funny and next-level entertaining. Within an hour or two he would have completed recording ten to twelve different vocal performances of the song. But then the really HARD and painstaking work for both of us would begin.

My first job would be to color code each of the ten vocal tracks. Logic assigns numerical identifiers for each separate take, such as #voc12_04, but no one reads those boring things unless there's an emergency where a musical part gets digitally disorganized (moved out of place or lost). Instead, we had the red one, the orange one, the purple one, the royal blue one, the yellow one and so on.

Julian and I would both settle into our chairs in front of the speakers, ready to dig in. This was like us going into the trenches, ready to do battle and so the other band members would take this opportunity to go to lunch, go for walks or hang around chatting in the live room. Nikolai and Fab would often start a game of chess.

"Ok, play the first line of the blue one," Julian would say.

Then we'd go down the rows of colored vocal performances, listening to the first phrase of each (phrases were usually four or five words long) in order.

Sometimes he would say, "That one's good," and sometimes he'd say, "No way, throw it away right now. I never want to hear that one again."

At the end of round one, seven of the ten tracks of vocals might have survived, each represented by their team's color code. Fifteen minutes later there would be three contestants left, for example; the purple, the dark green and the lime green.

Julian would say, "Play me them in the order they are on the screen," and I would play them one after the other. If one still didn't stand out as the winner, he'd turn his chair around and face the bookshelf, asking me to play them for him in a random order and not tell him which one he was hearing.

Then he would shout out, "That one, that's the best, which one is it?"

I'd answer, "The lime green."

Mr. Lime Green, a phrase of four or five words would then go on a new track reserved for the champions of this careful, Olympic-style competition.

Because we both had to pay such close attention for long periods of time, this vocal compilation ritual was truly one of the most meticulous and mentally exhausting of all the studio processes. It was also one of the most important, as the voice is centerstage and the expression of words that tell the story is what drives a song deep into the heart of the listener. Selecting the best performances was mentally draining due to the sheer amount of concentration and super hard-focused, critical listening involved.

Julian's actual singing did not take long and each different performance was really fun to hear and watch, yet this compiling of the 'best parts Olympics' took two or three hours per song and really left us TIRED by the end. When we finally did have a completed vocal track, everyone in the room; the band, JP, Ryan Gentles and I, were all very satisfied and pleased with the results and so the time spent was extremely well worth it.

During these sessions, I observed something else about Julian. No matter how well we scrutinized everything or how creative our workflow was, there seemed to be one or two words that he thought he could have sung differently or a melody that he believed that, given more time, could have been stronger. I'd see certain looks on his face and hear him say these things more than once.

It did seem like he was carrying a heavy burden with incredibly high standards and expectations coming from himself, the band and probably ... the world! I believe this outlook is also how he developed his artistry to such a high degree. While we were recording, I personally thought the results on every song were solidly fabulous vocal tracks and that the WORLD was gonna LOVE THIS.

22: The Beat Goes On

Several days had passed since the A&R man from RCA had tried to assist me to make a better-sounding album. Even though his main suggestions did not gain approval from the band, Ryan Gentles never gave me any further bad news or threats from the label to have me fired. This was huge good news for me! I breathed much easier without those dark shadows hanging over our recording sessions and applied my energy towards interacting with the band and JP to get on with the rest of the songs.

Our days in the studio were now beginning at 2pm and we would leave the studio tired to the point of passing out, at around 3am. At this point we were making excellent progress with half of the album and I had an opportunity to spend a little time with Fab Moretti.

It started with a phone call one morning, well before that day's session was scheduled to begin. He asked me if I would meet him for pizza at Two Boots on Avenue A and then go early to the studio so we could both listen to the songs we had already recorded, paying special attention to his drum parts. I was happy to do this, thinking it would be great to hang out with Fab on his own, get to know him a little more and study the drum tracks in close detail.

Even though I had been working shoulder to shoulder with *The Strokes*, first on the EP and now the album, I wouldn't say that I had gotten much chance to know them as people, other than what I'd observed in the studio or what few items of information they had told me about themselves. Nick and Albert were always brimming with energy, very polite and friendly towards me. Nikolai was almost always smiling, very soft spoken and relaxed in the studio. There was an intensity in the interactions between Julian and I from the very beginning, because he needed to make sure that I would interpret his ideas correctly. He never wanted me to let him or the rest of the band down by not trying hard enough. As we went along and he could see that I wasn't attempting to pull any offensive ego trips by virtue of the fact that I was older than they were, or had been recording longer, Julian expressed genuine affection towards me and gave me more of his trust.

I was interested in Fabrizio from the moment I saw *The Strokes* onstage back at Luna Lounge. At first it was just the way he snapped his back and neck so hard when he attacked the snare drum but, as I watched him in the studio, it was apparent that he was such a sweet, lovable human being. He'd have his can of coke and wear his COKE T-shirt, as if that was his spiritual logo! He also wore a gigantic smile on his face most of the time, really bounced when he walked and his voice was mostly full of resounding joy. He was also hyped-as-hell to be a member of the band and recording in the studio, which he demonstrated when we walked through the East Village—he would gleefully press *The Strokes* stickers onto the crosswalks in the middle of the street.

Fab and I met up at Two Boots, each ordered two slices of pizza and ... yes, a Coke. It was the first time we'd sat with each other that wasn't in a club or the studio and the first time we had ever been.... alone together (joke, pun intended!)

Not much was said other than,

"How's it going?"

"Still tired from staying up late last night at the studio!"

And, "Isn't this the best weather for New York?"

"Yeah, springtime!"

I could tell that he was slightly nervous and anxious to get to Transporterraum to scrutinize his drum parts, making sure they were as perfect as possible, especially without anyone else being there who might start talking and interrupt us or want to inspect other parts.

We played the songs back in the order we recorded them and there were only a few parts that he had questions about. Upon further examination, some of those areas that he was concerned with turned out to be absolutely well played and fine, which made him very happy.

One song, *Soma*, had a drum fill between the snare and floor tom, which really bothered him (Fab's kit was super minimal, giving a signature sound for *The Strokes* beats—kick, snare, hi-hat, one tom and one cymbal). Under his direction, I edited the tom and snare hits in that section and moved each of them around 'in time' a very micro-amount.

We worked on that for twenty minutes until he said,

"No, Gordon, it was better before, let's undo those changes."

And, so we did.

That was how our friendly one-on-one interactions began and I was a little bit amused when he called me the next day and asked if we could meet at Two Boots and look one more time at that same drum fill, which he'd been thinking about in the back of his mind.

I answered, "Sure, of course."

And this became a thing for about a week: Meet Fab, have pizza and then readjust that one particular drum fill. Eventually he arrived at being satisfied with the changes we made between those three drum hits! We would check the final result several times and then he would smilingly accept it as DONE. In this way, we had forged a nice friendship and he was pleased that I took his concerns seriously enough to help resolve them.

Ryan had a message for me around the end of the first week in May. Rough Trade wanted a single to release in late June, directly before *The Strokes* summer tour would kick into high gear. The songs chosen were *Hard to Explain* and *New York City Cops*. He told me that we needed to prioritize those songs, work on getting them mixed well and then we'd all go to the mastering lab before sending the final versions to London for manufacturing and distribution. This pushed my excitement way up, but we also felt pressure to get these two songs in the best possible shape before our mastering appointment.

I really didn't know ANYTHING about mastering. I had never mastered anything nor had anything that I'd produced ever been mastered before. I had heard that the mastering lab would be the polar opposite of my basement studio. It was a clinical, scientific, million-dollar sound chamber with audiophile tube amplifiers and massive high-end speaker columns. (Their speakers were as expensive as my whole studio!) Furthermore, their rooms were built by top audio technicians and designed to be acoustically flawless. Here I was, working in a basement underneath a methadone clinic in the East Village, with cheap, inaccurate monitor speakers that only sounded cool when you cranked them way up, LOUD.

We pushed ahead with our work, mixing both songs until everyone was happy. *Hard To Explain* took every ounce of brain power that the seven of us (five band members, JP and I) could put in towards that final mix. *New York City Cops* was the opposite, it really sounded close to the way they played it together in the live room. Even so, we definitely spent a day of focused mixing, devoted to defining and balancing every detail.

New York City Cops shines as one of my favorite songs I have worked on and there are three wonderful things about it that ultra-please me:

1. The floor tom with tambourine in the very beginning sounds like a car door (taxi?) slamming. It's not a HUGE powerful, rock and roll tom sound as one might expect to start a song.

2. "Ow, ha ha, I meant Ahh... no, I didn't mean that at all, ooohh..." This crazy dialog from Julian was really just his way of fooling around, trying to take the pressure off during days and nights of long, intense vocal recordings. No one (except me) expected those funny phrases to remain in the song. They all thought I'd be erasing them sooner or later.

   When I said, "I like those, they should definitely stay" they all looked at me like I was crazy or joking—or both. Eventually they trusted my judgement and agreed... and now it's part of HISTORY! Ha ha.

3. Same with the 'sniff sounding' inhalation at the end. NO, Julian was not doing a line of cocaine off the Transporterraum floor! In those days I thought the solution for recording vocals

evenly and conveniently was to over-compress them with the Avalon. I just put so much compression on when we recorded Julian, that when he finished the loud singing parts at the end of the song, the volume of the mic suddenly swelled up to 'super loud' just as Julian caught his breath and inhaled. The result is just great, as a decadent, suggestive ending sound on a very perfect rock song.

We finished recording and mixing the first single just in time and took a taxi to the Chelsea Market for mastering. In my fear and eagerness to do my absolute best, I loaded our studio's G4 mainframe computer and my 888/24 audio converter into the trunk of the taxi. I wanted to be prepared, just in case we pressed play on those songs and suddenly, through that million-dollar sound setup at the mastering lab, we discover... there is really NO low-end bass or that the mix we made SUCKS. If that happened, my studio computer would be there so we could quickly adjust some levels to try and save the single.

The head person at this facility is one of the top mastering engineers in the United States, having worked with legends like John Lennon, Bruce Springsteen, David Bowie, Patti Smith, *Talking Heads* and *The Ramones*, to name a few. I was very happy to meet him and I wanted to favorably impress this guy who had worked with many of my musical heroes.

We walked into the lab and I quickly, nervously set up the G4 and my Pro Tools interface. I opened the first song's Logic session, plugged the outputs into the mastering console and we all got ready for the moment of SONIC truth.

I was at a small table, the band sat on a designer couch and, at that precise moment, who should enter the room but the A&R guy from RCA. Damn, as if I wasn't nervous enough!

The shadow cloud entered the room looking tense and stern as ever. The time had come, so I pressed play on *Hard to Explain*, bracing myself in case what came out of those expensive speakers just sounded awful, like ill-conceived garbage. I just dreaded the thought of Julian looking at me like, "What have you done, Gordon? This isn't the way it's supposed to sound."

The song started up and, after six seconds, when the guitars came in, I let out a huge sigh of relief—everything sounded fucking PERFECT, exactly like in my basement studio.

When the singing started, I actually yelled out loud, "YEAH!" and glanced over at Julian who was nodding his head and smiling too. It was the same sound as we expected, as we finely crafted, just clearer and louder than we'd ever heard it before.

When the song was over, I wanted to hear a round of applause, but what I got was a lecture from the A&R guy. With his arms crossed, it went exactly like this:

"Guys, this is the most amateur and unprofessional production I've ever heard. You will get nowhere with a sound like this."

And then, to my further dismay, the head mastering guy standing right next to A&R butted in with his TWO cents' worth:

"Yeah fellas, I mean, it's already hard enough to sell records, but ya gotta think of the listeners in Kansas. How are they gonna understand this song with distorted vocals?"

My mood plunged from elation, knowing that the sounds we made at Transporterraum NYC were really going to translate as we intended once they went out into the big world, to an anger mixed with fear that made my stomach hurt and a choking feeling appear in my throat. All I could come up with at that moment, my voice small, strained and shaky, was,

"I... disagree."

After that, the band members told the mastering engineer that this is how they wanted it to be and, for a few hours, I watched and somehow learned a bit about what mastering is. I saw that EQ and compression are applied to the overall mix to make it louder than it was before, while trying to preserve what was good about the song.[12]

---

[12] I am honestly still mystified by mastering. It just feels too technical for me to understand let alone do it—though I have tried. The mastering

We got through that day and the single was sent to Rough Trade in England. I was more than relieved to get out of there and we went back to the studio for the evening shift, to do more work.

Turning on the studio lights, I was plugging the G4 and audio interface back in when Nick let out a "HEYY!"

I looked around and he was staring at me saying,

"Gortron, what happened to our big bag of weed? Dude, that was supposed to be for everyone and now it's gone!"

"Guilty as charged, Nick.... I admit!"

This is what I should have said, but instead I just sat there, pink-faced and embarrassed. I had been presiding over that once full bag as if it were a gift to me, 'my personal lifeboat' shall we say, helping me focus and keep myself together during those hardcore twelve-to-fourteen-hour days and nights of work.

"I... I'll get us another one," I stammered, feeling silly and guilty.

Nick Valensi looked at me suspiciously, with some disappointment right then, but that didn't stop me from similar antics and more questionable behavior soon, after AND later. I never did replace that bag of green buds, I'm sorry to say.

---

process is supposed to make a song 'loud enough' to compete with all the other songs in the world so, when it comes on in a club after Kanye West (aka Ye), it doesn't sound small, weak or quiet. Often the mastering engineer believes he is improving the sound of a fully mixed song, but for me it's a matter of hoping they don't change and wreck it too much in the chasing of competitive loudness. I always wish the masters sounded exactly like my mixes, but they almost never do. Often the bass gets boomier and the effects and reverbs become too loud.

23: How to Cross the Finish Line

All eleven songs were racing towards completion as we moved closer and closer to our calendar deadline. We had no safety net of time in which to reconsider, add or subtract anything. After the first week of June, *The Strokes* would be overseas for a long, deep tour, starting in the UK then continuing with shows throughout continental Europe and Australia. Once they left town, there could be no adding or subtracting parts for this record.

The second mastering date had been reserved for our final day, long in advance. At the beginning of our fifth week, we moved into a marathon of musical energy and hyper-concentration. Our studio sessions were split between mixing the songs that were ready and adding Julian's singing to the rest.

There were several factors that added extra pressure during this critical time. The band had started a residency in Philadelphia, driving in their rental van once a week for an evening of live performance. On top of that, my studio partner Jimmy had booked the studio for a few afternoons, which meant that *The Strokes* would come in at night and we'd work until the ungodly hours of 6 or 7am.

The final hurdle was located in the notebook belonging to one Julian Casablancas, where there were a few blank lines in several songs, reserved for WORDS that had yet to satisfactorily appear in his imagination. I would often see Julian holding a pen, looking intently at sheets of paper, doing his best to conjure the perfect lyrics to make those blank spaces disappear.

Absinthee, the space age, dark, gothy music project that Anne and I had built up together during the past five years was, sadly... on the rocks. She had met a very cool girl named Eden and was often out partying with her or conducting artistic photo sessions. Anne had also met an L.A. rocker named Monte and she was frequently zooming off to California to see him or he would be

147

staying at her apartment. I even recorded Monte's comedic-hard-rock band, *The Bad Apples*, at one point. *Absinthee* had recently played a Tuesday night show at Don Hill's and, miserably, there was only the next band and their girlfriends in the audience. It was depressing for me to be in a band with someone I cared for and respected as much as Anne and still have no one turning up to our shows—five years into our project. I also didn't think it was good for her musical heart to face the impact of being ignored like that in the local music scene.

After much deliberation, I made the heavy decision that it was now time to call it off, to break up the band. When I discussed this with Anne, I sensed that she was in agreement with me, but also sad that this was now a tangible, hard reality.

One early afternoon during *The Strokes* recording, she called me up and was really upset about the ending of *Absinthee*. I told the guys I needed to take a lunch break, rushing off in a cab to her place to try and console her.

Anne was quite distraught and I could feel myself kind of splitting in half. Part of me was incredibly worried for her as she seemed so sad and upset, and the other half of my mind was highly stressed out about getting back to the studio quickly so we could make as much progress as possible. I was there to be as supportive as possible by being a listening friend, and luckily, she did calm down a bit after some talking. We were still very close and I never for an instant stopped believing in her as an artist or performer.

Back at the studio, JP Bowersock suggested that we find a better pair of speakers for the remainder of the mixing, (we'd already completed *Hard to Explain* and *New York City Cops* for the first Rough Trade single). Again, I called trustworthy Scott Clark and he lent us his Yamaha NS-10s which are strange, small, old-fashioned speakers. They were marketed in Japan in 1978 for home-stereos and, even then, received bad reviews! JP and I both knew that these unlikely speakers had become a recording industry standard, found in almost every studio in the world. The prevailing wisdom was that if you could make music sound good on these, it would truly sound great everywhere else.

I had heard NS-10s before and never liked them. They made music sound thin, harsh and weedy, so I didn't know exactly how to use them for reliable mixing. Gradually, I got used to them and now I really trust and love them—although I prefer to have a pair of super-booming, hi-definition speakers sitting right next to them for enhanced clarity and ear-deafening volume.

The final two weeks were like a pressure cooker. The band arrived at 3 o'clock in the afternoon and we left the studio after the morning sun was already up, baking the street and dirty sidewalks of Avenue A. The band would take taxis home to crash in their beds, while I walked in a thick, mentally exhausted daze to East Houston, crossing over to continue down Clinton Street to my apartment and urgently needed rest.

There was already a curious buzz around the East Village regarding the music we'd been recording at Transporterraum NYC and two great bands approached me to ask if I could somehow help them make quick demos during the mornings before *The Strokes* arrived for work or during the time that they were out of town playing gigs.

Steve Schiltz had been a sixteen-year-old super-guitarist with the band *Scout* when drummer/producer Alan Bezozi brought them into Chateau Relaxo to work with me. His new group, *Longwave*, reserved some morning shifts at Transporterraum and we recorded a small collection of demos. I really liked their music and it was great to have this reunion with Steve.

Immediately after that, a real live guitar rocker named Jody Porter asked me to do the same with his combo, *The AstroJet*. I was happy that both of these very talented bands had contacted me and knew that the magnetic power of being associated with *The Strokes* was largely responsible for that. It wasn't lost on me that *The AstroJet* and *Longwave* both featured master guitarists of the current New York City scene, whose ranks also included

Chad Swahnberg, Richard Fortus, Albert Hammond Jr. and Nick Valensi.

On May 19th (I know 'cuz the internet said), I hopped into a rental van with *The Strokes* and drove up the highway to T.T. the Bear's Place in Cambridge, Massachusetts, right across the Charles River from Fenway Park in the Boston area. I had a rapidly growing urge to go on the exotic sounding, summer long, European tour with them, thinking that maybe they would hire me to be their live sound engineer. I had this one show to demonstrate my unique abilities as front of house soundman.

There was really an odd atmosphere inside the club. *Black Rebel Motorcycle Club* was playing that night too and I remember that the crowd was very obviously made up of music tech students, musicians in bands that thought very much of themselves and Guitar Institute types.

How could I tell?

During *The Strokes'* set, the audience all had their arms crossed, scrutinizing the chord positions Albert and Nick were using on their fretboards, taking note of their pedals and wearing 'that's not so difficult to do' expressions on their faces.

I had done live sound before (back in Seattle I did live sound and 'dub treatment' for a young band called *Janus*, who were all stoned on acid and improvising off the top of their heads, to an audience of strippers hosting a nudist party at a sauna, for example) and usually preferred to take a confrontational approach, where the impact and attack of the sounds are aggressive and impolite.

After the T.T. the Bear's Place show, I annoyed Ryan Gentles, following him around asking him to give me his feedback.

"Well, Gortron (yes, he used the nickname too), actually there's someone else we are going to use for the tour, but we really respect what you're doing in the studio."

Once the equipment was loaded back into the van, we all went out for a late dinner near the club, and everyone was feeling fine. Our recording process had been difficult, mainly because the band had to sweat, concentrate and play their songs until everything was captured perfectly. My main job during the recording was to help get cool sounds and listen closely to everyone so that they could do their best work. The mixing was hardcore for me because, again, I had five or six very intelligent, observant musicians talking to me and making requests, all at the same time. My two eyes, two ears and both hands were the vehicles to channel all of their ideas and suggestions into reality.

What exactly is mixing? Well, Nikolai noticed that on my 1972 Fender Precision Bass, which he used on most of the songs, not all of the strings played at the same volume. Every time he heard a note that was too quiet, I needed to turn it up to match the other ones. Julian wanted the hi-hats to be prominent on one section but then more subtle on the next. Nick and Albert wanted each individual note from both guitars to be heard clearly, yet neither guitar should be overpowering, except during solos. For the singing, Julian wanted every word to be heard, but never too dominantly against the music. With the exception of the three songs which were meant to sound 'drum-machine-y' and more abstractly constructed, there were very few plug-ins used for EQ and no added effects whatsoever. The three songs: *Hard to Explain*, *Soma* and *Alone Together* had some extra EQ boosts on the guitars and that's about it—aside from those industrial drum treatments, detailed earlier.

On we went, poring over every note, combination of notes and every single word, till the magic balances began to emerge. Sometimes a vocal line would get a small re-edit, with other problem areas being attacked day and night by all seven brains in that control room.

As we neared the finish line, the sheer force of seven weeks at this intense pace was surely taking its toll. Patience levels were down, tempers easily triggered and sometimes it felt like we were gritting our teeth, wishing the goddamn clock would slow down. A day off or a few mornings of extra sleep would have been very welcome, but the deadline for our final mastering session was blowing towards us.

Ryan surprised me one night by saying that a photographer named Colin Lane was gonna drop by the studio to take pictures for the upcoming album cover. Apparently, the guys in the band wished to have my photo in there as well. I found this to be strange. I mean GREAT for me, but why would these amazing-looking young rockers want the ol' producer Gordon Raphael on their actual record cover?

The next day, I arrived wearing a stylish baby-blue leather jacket and tried to fluff up my hair to try and look at least a little bit cool. When Colin Lane came in, he was doing tight close-up portraits of everyone—yes, it was thrilling, but when I saw the photo of me I laughed because the lack of sleep, mega-long hours in the studio and stoner haze was clearly visible all across my face.

Still, it was a great honor that I can never thank *The Strokes* enough for bestowing upon me and it later gave me a public recognition that very few music producers ever have.

The story of the last day: Arriving at 2pm, yeah, a bit early and harsh for us all, having left work at 7am that same morning. There was, seriously, about a week of work still left to do and yet there were only twenty hours until we were scheduled to show up at the mastering lab.

One song needed light mixing, two songs needed serious mixing and one of those still had a blank space in the vocal track that needed a few CRUCIAL words.

Ok, I smoked a few joints as usual, got pretty high (still feeling the pressure), but the first part of the day went by smoothly. Work was getting done and things were getting crossed off the checklist with a permanent marker. Time flew by at a ridiculously elevated tempo and, when the missing, important lyrics finally made it onto Julian's notebook paper, it was the beginning of the night. It didn't take him very long to sing those new words and the editing wasn't painful or long either.

Then, a storm of very weird and unexpected elements came into play.

Around 11pm, very cool, important journalists from London came down to the studio to say hello. They were being led in by the two heads of Rough Trade, James Endeacott and Geoff Travis, and they were all vibrating with excitement to hear the finished new album.

I was in two minds already by this point; there was the wasted me, just at my outer limits via too much work and copious amounts of weed mixed with tobacco, and there was the inner-rock-fan me just dazzled that the actual Rough Trade president and British journalists were REALLY there in my fucking studio!

The fan in me wanted to meet them and talk and hang out, to revel in the attention and glory. The wasted, tired producer in me wanted them out of the goddamn studio quickly, so we could finish the work NOW!

After hugging the band, laughing, chatting and smiling, the visiting UK team could tell we were stressed for time and left the building, heading over to 2A, our favorite East Village bar directly across from Transporterraum. The plan was for us to bring the final mixes over later and play them on the 2A sound system, for a massive celebration of what we all did together and great things to come.

Midnight. Ok, there's a couple hours of work left to do, this is DOABLE. Tiring, we are so tired but we can probably get to the party around 2am, feeling victorious with the completed album in our hands and have some fun.

Someone from the band hands me a joint and I start smoking it by myself, as usual. Halfway through it, still puffing away, I'm gonna sit back down at my table and get into some serious listening, adding some mixing adjustments for fine, fine detail. I pressed PLAY on the Logic session for one song, zooming in with the cursor to get a closer look at some waveforms that need help. As I looked towards the colored regions of audio, I thought the screen looked blurry.

I blinked my eyes four times, trying to clear up my vision but, when I looked again towards the screen, it SLOWLY started moving backwards.

I felt crazy dizzy, watching the screen grow smaller and smaller and quickly realized that I was actually moving backwards. It wasn't my body, per se, it was my mind and my attention (consciousness), just leaving me and going in reverse motion, fast. I could barely make words to talk and I suddenly had the panic feeling that I was about to fucking DIE now.

If I looked away from the screen, I felt a few minor percentage points better—like I had a chance. But the moment I turned my head back towards the screen (knowing I urgently needed to get this work done for the band, the album and the great people waiting across the street), then the flying backwards would resume, the screen getting smaller and smaller, with the feeling of 'about to die'.

My next urgent thought was to write "Moongate hard drive / The Strokes Album folder / latest mixes folder" with a thin, shaky pen, so that if I died right then, at least SOMEONE could find the proper sessions and finish *The Strokes* album without me (I still have the exact notebook from the studio that day, with those words in shaky pen as a reminder).

The band were looking at me incredulously, as I still hadn't told anyone what was going wrong inside of me. So far, this mental episode had all taken place in the space of about five minutes. I found enough voice to say, "Hey, I can't …work… right now."

And that's it.

I have NO idea what that voice of mine actually sounded like. I heard a "WHAT??" and possibly a "No fucking way" in the room. I felt very much that I had mostly left my body, entering a constant panic that I was about to really and truly die.

I said, "Let me sit on the couch."

I lifted myself, don't know how, out of my producer's chair and moved back to the couch where I slumped down. Again, I noticed that moving away from the computer lessened the severity of the panic, but I still felt I was floating near, but not IN my body. When I tried lifting my head to look towards the computer, the death panic returned full force.

Just then, my dear friend Fabrizio walked into the control room and saw my face. I think he'd been over the road at 2A, hanging with the London contingent and he'd just come back to join us. He put his jacket around my shoulders and said,

"Let's go upstairs and take a walk around the block. I think you need some air."

He did manage to get me up the stairs but I was fearing with each step that the small string that was keeping me around my body would break and I'd be gone. He so kindly put his arm around my waist and steadied me as we walked, ever so slowly, down Avenue A and in a circle down 3rd Street, over to Avenue B and then back again.

It seemed to take a long time and I know I was saying things like,

"I'm not sure I can do this. I think I'm gonna fall... I feel so weird."

I have no idea how much time, in real life, this was taking. I was still very much aware of what I was meant to be doing, but I just couldn't do it.

Then Fab's idea was to take me into 2A Bar, through the huge crowd of regulars partying downstairs, past the bartenders I knew so well from the many late nights we'd all go there after our sessions. He helped me upstairs, where the music was blaring and the special guests from London were drinking, preparing themselves for the listening party. James Oldham from *NME* saw me with Fab, approaching to say hello with a big smile, and I was introduced to Jamie from Coalition (the UK public relations team that worked to promote the album). I wanted nothing more than to be cool and talk with them but, instead, I looked like a victim, a ghost being escorted by Fab through the crowd.

Then the Rough Trade guys saw us and started to come over, but turned back when Fab motioned something to them, while sitting me down on a small couch in a dark area. I stayed there motionless, closed down, with rapidly fluctuating waves of feeling that death would come at any moment, to momentary surges of almost calm stillness (still not feeling present in my own body).

The other guys from *The Strokes* soon arrived to have a drink and see what the hell was going to come from this horror. At some point, I signaled to Fab to take me back to the studio.

We got downstairs with the rest of the band following and I had enough clarity to try a plan. My panic was down from 98% to 85%, shall we say, and I told Fab,

"You go to the computer and I'll tell you what to do."

He tried.

"Ok, see the track marked Bass Speaker? Click on that and press the little telescope on the top to blow the view up bigger."

After a few more attempts like that, Fab shrugged saying,

"I really can't do this, sorry!"

I pushed myself to go to the computer and finish the work. I squinted my eyes and could see the screen enough to do my job.

I don't know if I worked like that, with the band clustered around me, for an hour. Or two? At some point late in the night, we went to 2A with a mixed, unmastered album that the band had decided to call *Is This It*,[13] to play it for whoever was still there and awake at that time.

I was still floating, but my panic was down to about 50% now. As the songs played over the upstairs bar sound system, some people looked very happy, at least that was my impression. I then had to ask the band for one more favor. I knew we needed to be at the mastering lab in about four hours and wanted to take the computer and 888 converter again to make sure that if anything sounded wrong, it could be fixed. I was so frail, ghostly and weak in that moment, I knew I wouldn't be able to lift the G4 into the

---

[13] This was the last song we actually recorded.

trunk of a taxi nor unload it at Anne's apartment, where I happened to be housesitting.

Someone from the band did help me put it in the cab, drove with me to her place and accompanied me up the elevator. Eventually I just laid in bed, still hovering somewhere nearby. I was exhausted and somehow got calm enough to fall asleep.

The alarm rang three hours later and I actually managed to get that computer and myself over to the Chelsea Market exactly on time.

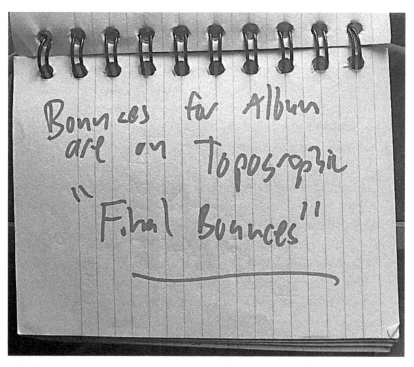

Exhibit 15A: The ACTUAL notebook entry during my extreme panic attack. Apparently, the hard drive was called Topographic and not Moongate as claimed in the story.

24: Unfinished Business

In the mastering lab I was feeling paper thin from not much sleep. I wasn't in panic state anymore, but not fully 'there' by any means. Again, by the grace of the music gods, the mixes sounded fabulous and the day was spent deciding which songs would be best mastered using the tape machine and which sounded better remaining in the digital kingdom. Some songs sounded better one way and some the other.

It was a long day this time, not just a couple hours. I took advantage of the mastering lab's well-stocked kitchen, in which we had full and unlimited access. I was basically snacking all afternoon in their modern dining area overlooking the Hudson River.

The highlight of the day, other than the fact that every song sounded amazing and well mixed, was when the mastering engineer transferred the song, *Is This It*, onto his tape machine for mastering and then rewound it for us to hear.

Julian's ear picked up the high pitched, backwards 'rewind' sound and he said, out of the blue,

"Can we put that sound on the intro of this song?"

Great idea from him, so we spliced that sound onto the mix quite spontaneously, which is the first thing you hear when the album starts.

After our mastering day was over, we were going to split up. The band were scheduled to play shows in Philadelphia and New Jersey before setting off to England. I already had a ticket out to Seattle for a sunny post-album recovery holiday, and my plan for after that was to see *The Strokes* play in London. Then I wanted to try and remain in Europe for the entire summer. As we were hugging, saying "goodbye" and "good job", I couldn't help but notice a serious, pensive look on Julian's face. I asked him what was on his mind and he just said,

"I don't know, I think if we'd had more time to work on it, there were a few spots that could have been better."

In that moment I felt a little bit sad that the album wasn't as great as Julian had hoped, but mostly I felt proud and happy that it sounded so unique and powerful. I also had no doubt in my mind that the world was going to love this.

The last thing I did before the summer break was go to Maxwells in Hoboken, New Jersey to see *The Strokes* play with *Longwave* on May 28th. That New Jersey venue was only a forty-minute train ride from my studio, and I arrived just in time to see *Longwave*'s very cool set, in their own inventive style. After the show, Steve Schiltz introduced me to a very striking-looking young woman named Terrah, who had rock-and-roll just sparking out of her eyes and a magnificent smile. She was dazzling in her hot pink pleather[14] mini skirt and tall silver glitter platform boots. Lucky for me, she was also a keyboard player, so we had an instant, fun conversation, bonding over analog synthesizers and British rock bands. I even got her phone number and told her I would call.

One bit of business regarding our studio that I failed to mention: By the end of our work on *Is This It*, Jimmy Goodman and I had been operating Transporterraum NYC for a grand total of eighteen months when we were officially EVICTED by our landlord Rick Robinson. From the first *Absinthee* rehearsal onwards, at least once a month he would tell me that the sounds coming from our studio were too loud and ask me to turn it down. I had warned him before we even signed the lease that I would be making the sound of rockets blasting off twenty-four hours a day in order to do my job the way I needed to, as an artist and producer. We did soundproof the studio as well as we possibly could during our construction phase, but we were limited by the funds we had at the time.

Rick had received complaints from Dangerous Music on the top floor of the building, five floors above us. They reported that some sounds from the snare drum went through our brick wall, into a metal pipe, then travelled up five stories, back out the brick

---

[14] Pleather is a somewhat shiny artificial leather.

wall, through their sound proofing and made some noise. When I went up to check this claim out, it was TRUE—if it was absolutely still and quiet in their studio, with no one doing anything at all, you could hear a sound about as loud as a pencil eraser being lightly tapped on a wooden desk. Rick had never approved of how loudly *Absinthee* rehearsed, so when Dangerous lodged their complaint, he sprang into action. There was one more (quite amusing) factor in Rick's decision to evict us.

One night, during the recording of *Is This It*, a couple of the band members were in an excited and cheerful mood. One could even say that they were a bit rambunctious after drinking several beers in the studio. As they went out through the dirty, junk-filled corridors in the basement, they grabbed two burnt-out, long white fluorescent lighting tubes and, as they stepped onto the East 2nd Street sidewalk, they gleefully smashed them on the curb.

Coincidentally, our landlord Rick was in his small studio upstairs on the second floor and just happened to be peering out the window as this spectacle unfolded before him. A few days later he stopped me in the hallway as I was on my way in to work (yes, precisely during the last week of sessions for *Is This It*), handing me an official EVICTION NOTICE.

His words to me as he gave me this legal document were, "We just can't have you and your friends rampaging through the building and smashing glass on the streets. I TOLD YOU many times to lower the volume."

I read that eviction notice in the control room twenty minutes before *The Strokes* were scheduled to come in. I was fucking upset about it, steaming with anger and disgust.

I put those feelings on hold as much as I could, but it was a small black vapor in the back of my mind that day, and for a long time afterwards. My studio partner Jimmy was very sad and angry about it too, and I'm sure he must have been irritated with me to some degree because the violations that had been used against us all took place during my use of the space. We had until the end of October to vacate the premises, so I pushed this stressful energy to the back of my mind while we finished *The Strokes* album. I wanted to fight this eviction and hire a lawyer, but first I needed a long summer holiday. Out to the beaches and sunshine of Mallorca!

My East Village in 2001

Top: L) Albert Hammond Jr. who swore he wouldn't shave his beard until the first album was done. R) The fresh, exuberant and ever buoyant Fab Moretti. Drummer extraordinaire. Bottom: L) Nick Valensi all strapped in. I just love this fun photo. R) Nikolai and Fab playing chess.

These four random polaroids, plus literally one more, were the entirety of visually documented evidence from the Is This It recording sessions. None of Julian! Fab made a lovely drawing of me while I was working, and I believe the photos inside the record cover were shot by Colin Lane at Transporterraum NYC, but that's it. There was no social media, and no one wanted to be distracted from the music by photographers or cameras. No one would do that these days!

The lovely musician Terrah and her electronic Korg KAOSS pad. Glam rock photo shoot by Anne Hadlock at her apartment on E 16th Street, Manhattan.

The special Audio-Technica 4033a microphone at Transporterraum NYC. This is the one that Julian sang into for both The Modern Age EP *and* Is This It. *Magical.*

Me reading a book while Anne sunbathes on the island of Mallorca. With Satellites for the "never ending summer" of 2001. Magical time.

(L-R) Camellia Clouse, Anna Mercedes and Kath Poulton, my dear roommates at Regent House in Islington, London.

Regina Spektor and I celebrating Rosh Hashanah at Giraffe on Essex Road, London. A few weeks later she would begin touring USA with The Strokes.

Scarborough Steve, Me, Carl Barât, Pete Doherty and Johnny Borrell. One of many nights at Su Goodacre's amazing loft in Covent Garden. What a way to start my London life.

Tim, bassist and singer for **Kill Kenada** *wearing black gaffer tape bra and beard in my Silver Transporterraum Studio in the Docklands, London. From a video I made of them playing live and LOUD. Drummer Stewart off to the right, epic guitarist Danny just out of frame.*

Outside Filthy MacNasty's pub on Amwell Street, London. (L-R) Ebe, Kat and India. It was an energy vortex that year and I had so many spectacular nights hanging out on these red thickly overpainted picnic tables.

ummer Overseas

After finishing the seven-week recording/mixing marathon that became *Is This It*, I was certainly looking forward to spending the summer running around in Europe. First, Anne and I flew to Seattle where I had the green bedroom waiting for me at the Bear Creek family farmhouse. The big bed there was fluffy and comfortable. I knew I'd be able to relax in that beautiful place and come down from my exhausted, stressed-out state.

I was safely out of the panic territory that I entered during the final session, three nights before, but I was still feeling beyond spaced out (spaced-out was 'normal' for me). My mind was still, truly, lagging two steps behind my body.

Anne always stayed in her childhood red room, across the hall from the green room I was in. It was the beginning of June, so walking around the farm early in the day meant radiant sunshine, lush meadows and those giant pines and cedars with their dark green branches waving in the gentle breeze.

Within a few days, thanks to Manny and Anne's wonderful cooking, lively conversations with the whole family (Joe and Ryan Hadlock were also there) and luxurious walks over the pasture to wander around in their ever-beautiful music studio, I was feeling much better. The air at Bear Creek is so fresh, with that stream flowing through their property and all those varieties of natural green surrounding, that I could feel it clearing out months of Manhattan's pollution, even from my aura. My inner electrical fields were rebalancing and soon I was only moderately more spaced out than usual. My inbuilt spacey mindset became greatly exaggerated when smoking my habitual weed mixed with tobacco.

One morning, Manny was kind enough to lend me her Jeep so I could drive into Seattle's U-District for breakfast and then accomplish some shopping—records at Second Time Around, old poetry and art books at the Magus Bookshop. I had a wonderful time in my old neighborhood and found all kinds of treasures. On the way back to the I-5 South freeway entrance at around 1 o'clock in the afternoon, I was stopped at a red light on 45th Street in front of The Blue Moon Tavern. The light turned green and at that moment an especially attractive young woman walked by on the sidewalk, dressed in that rainy day, thrift-shop, radical old-fashioned, weird Seattle style that I enjoy so much.

As I took my foot off the brake, I turned my head to get closer look and... SMASH! The driver in front of me had not yet moved when the light changed, so now my impaired aura and lapse of attention had caused a traffic accident.

The driver I had hit was an elderly woman and I had dented her car and Manny's Jeep. The police came and called an ambulance to check her out and make sure she was OK.

I felt more than AWFUL for what I had done, firstly to the woman and her car that I had stupidly hit and, as well, for the damage I had caused to Manny's Jeep. I tried to not dwell on that foolish, awful collision but certainly didn't drive any more on that trip. I did have a chance to see my family, telling everyone in my circle about the incredible events that had happened over the course of the last nine months.

While in Seattle, I solidified plans to fly over to London, to investigate and experience what it would be like when the first single, *Hard to Explain*, was released there later in the month. I also arranged to see a few *Strokes* shows at the beginning of their tour and then meet Anne afterwards in Mallorca for a long holiday on the island. By the end of my Northwest visit, I felt completely energized and ready for the summer.

A most shocking development: I got home to New York and had a few easy-going days to get ready to fly across the Atlantic. I was down in the studio when my phone rang. It was Ryan Gentles calling me from England with some really bad news: Fab had accidentally broken his hand and, on doctor's orders, couldn't play until it was properly healed. He asked me to make quick mixes of all eleven songs from the album and boost all the drum parts really loud. Then I needed to burn this new mix to a CD so Ryan's good friend and former bandmate, Matt Romano, could come and get it a couple hours later to... learn those drum parts on the plane, on his way to the UK to join the tour! I made those loud drum mixes, handed that disc to Matt Romano and off he went.

I landed in London on June 23rd, making my way from Heathrow to Battersea. There I had been graciously offered a couch in the basement belonging to Julien "Tiger Boy" Davis (Anne's friend who'd reported the bad news about London's closing rock venues and whose songs I'd recorded in New York) and his lovely bass-playing brother, Wood. They told me I could stay as long as I liked.

It was amazing to have a free pad in London while on my mission to scout around and see what I could discover. I had only been to London once before, during my penniless synthesizer-player days, trying to score a record deal for my self-produced *Colour Twigs* album. To give you an idea which year that was— *The Smiths' Heaven Knows I'm Miserable Now* video had just been shown on British TV; *Flesh for Lulu* had released *Subterraneans*; *Wham!* had a smash hit with *Wake Me Up Before You Go-Go* and *Frankie Goes to Hollywood* was about to rule the entire summer with *RELAX*.

My first day in Battersea was spent hanging out with Julien and Wood, cooking food, chatting and listening to songs by their band, *Hoodlum UK*. It was still two days before *Hard to Explain* would be released into the waiting ears and minds of the British public and then, three days after that, there was gonna be a huge *Strokes* show at a famous gay club in Charing Cross called HEAVEN.

Wood offered to drive me into Central London whenever I wanted but I was saving my energy for these two upcoming events, intuitively knowing that they would be mind-blowing experiences. Maybe even life-changing. Not at all intending to be overly dramatic but, since I began pounding the rock music trail at age thirteen playing shows in my earliest bands, this felt to me like the first time anything I was involved with was about to really go—wide!

When June 25th rolled around, I asked Wood and Julien to take me into town just to walk around and see if I noticed anything on the day the first single from *Is This It* came out. We piled into Wood's car and when we turned on the radio, we heard a DJ announce *Hard to Explain* and *New York City Cops*, and then proceed to play BOTH songs, two times in a row!!

We walked around for a while and there really did seem to be a buzz in the air. It was warm, grey weather and I felt a crackling electric energy in the city that day. We had some food and got back in Wood's car just in time to hear another DJ announce,

"Hello. We are in the tour van with *The Strokes* and we're speaking with Fabrizio Moretti!"

This was certainly a good beginning and that night we heard those two songs spinning in every bar they took me to.

Ryan had arranged a guest pass for me at HEAVEN and the place was packed, indeed the biggest headline show the band had played so far. It was a fantastic feeling, being completely incognito there, with not one person in that crowd knowing who I was yet, at the same time, being intimately connected with the band that all these people were going MENTAL for.

I loved the show even though it was weird seeing Matt Romano playing Fab's drum parts (yes, he played them perfectly well!) and sad seeing Fab off to the side of stage with his arm in a sling. Fab did go onstage near the end of show to hug the other band members, with the crowd erupting in cheers.

I made one horrible mistake that night. It was one that I'd made a number of times before and would again in the future; I didn't wear earplugs in the audience that night and, by the end of the show, my ears were absolutely aching. Near the end of the set, I was wondering if the sound system had broken or if the new soundman was having trouble, because I heard no high frequencies whatsoever, which made everything sound horribly muffled and bad.

Once the music stopped, I realized that it was, instead, my ears that were broken. Even the noise from the huge audience excitedly cheering and screaming sounded as if I was wearing those protective headphones used on heavy construction sites. I was in big trouble and I was panicking again, this time about permanent hearing loss. I was devastated and angry with myself as I was only hearing about one third of the actual sounds after the show. I must have looked tense and forlorn as I made my way along to the giant room designated for the afterparty, which I had been given the proper wristband to enter. I just went to the furthest table in the back, to sit down and try to recover.

The afterparty was quickly filling up and it looked like a quarter of the audience was in there. Even with my ear agony, I was super-hyped about being there, thinking that this was the exact crowd of people I needed to be hanging out with, getting to know. They were all at this party as fans of *The Strokes*.

Ten minutes later, a stylish woman sitting at the table next to mine smiled and leaned over towards me saying,

"Hi. You're Gordon Raphael, the producer, right?"

I don't know how she would have known that (as the album with my photo on it was still not out yet), but I smiled and nodded.

"Well, Gordon, I'm Banny and this is Peter," she said, sweetly pointing to an impeccably dressed young man sitting across from her.

"Peter's in a band called *The Libertines* and we'd love to speak with you about working with them."

A few minutes later Peter, wearing a very dapper suit complete with a trilby, grabbed my hand and led me across the room to a small clear space on the floor.

And then—I kid you not—he dropped to one knee, rolled his hat down his sleeve and serenaded me with a charming song that I can only describe as in 'an old English style'.

Not thinking about my broken ears for a moment, I was really touched by his performance, just for me. I smiled at him and said,

"That was very nice, thank you!"

When I went back to my seat, Banny asked me what I was doing in London. I told her that I was only there for a few days and that I was on my way to Mallorca for two months of summer holiday. We exchanged phone numbers and email addresses and then she handed me a demo CD saying,

"Listen to this while you are in Mallorca and write or call us when you can. We'd really love to have you produce *The Libertines*."

Just as I was looking for a place to put that CD, Nick Valensi came walking through the crowd with a very young dude who looked like a student, a high school student at that. Nick told the kid,

"Meet our producer" and walked away.

The youngster extended his hand with the biggest grin I'd seen in a while, saying,

"Hello, you're Gordon, right?"

"Yes. I certainly am," I said, while wondering what this was all about.

Then, trailing up behind this very self-confident kid was an older man also with huge jolly smile... um, his dad? The young one said,

"I'm Toby, I run a music website called Rockfeedback.com. Here is my card—and this is my dad."

Dad held out his hand and powerfully shook mine,

"I'm Roy, pleased to meet you, Gordon. Toby knows all about you." (I'm thinking, "Huh?")

Toby spoke up and said, "If you fancy, I'd love to have you write a column for Rockfeedback, you know. Could be about anything you feel like discussing."

I was instantly taken by this kid's clarity, confidence and forthrightness. I later learned that, so were *Radiohead*, *The White Stripes*, *The Libertines* and many other talents on both the musician and music industry side who volunteered to grant Toby amazing interviews, answering his deep, insightful questions as he worked his way up to his own illustrious career in music.

Of course, I agreed to write for him then and there.

The next morning, I flew to Amsterdam where I had also been once before. In September of 1999, I traveled with Anne to Gdansk, Poland to attend her brother Ryan's wedding. His bride, the very pretty and brilliant Maja, was a scholar who'd been working doing historical renovations of landmark buildings damaged in the war. Fittingly, their wedding took place in a gorgeous old stone church that was under reconstruction. This wonderful structure was still open to the sky; its roof having been blown off during WWII. After their wedding, I traveled to Amsterdam, lodging in an old schoolhouse.

The first time I visited the Netherlands I had been clean (off drugs), but this time my main intention was to get a hotel room (I'd rarely ever had a hotel room to myself before), score several types of high-grade marijuana and hashish from one of 'those' cafes and then retreat for a brain-vaporizing party. *The Strokes* were also going to be in Amsterdam for a radio broadcast at VPRO, driving to Rotterdam the next day to perform at Metropolis Festival. Showing up at VPRO in a very smokey state of mind, I was delighted to see the innovative duo of Adam Green and Kimya Dawson aka *The Moldy Peaches*. We hung out together and watched *The Strokes* play an energetic, tight 8-song set, again with Matt Romano on drums as Fab with his arm in a sling was still out of commission. The next day we all traveled together in a European rock 'n' roll tour bus to the festival in Rotterdam. It was great to see the crowd go crazy for both bands (*The Moldy Peaches* also performed) and that night I headed back to Amsterdam to get ready for my flight to the Balearic Islands.

A few days after I landed in Mallorca, *The Strokes* arrived there to play at Isladencanta Festival. To make matters even better, my dear crew, *Satellites*, as well as Sami Yaffa and Jimmy Goodman's band *Mad Juana* from NYC would also be performing there. Three of my favorite projects from Transporterraum NYC appearing at the same sunny summer festival! I was looking forward to seeing *The Strokes* in the blessed, beautiful setting of Mallorca, and this time I decided to buy some of that fragrant hashish and hand it to Nick as a way of saying,

"You know those one hundred times I've asked you for weed already? Well look, I finally got some for you!"

Hilariously, the interaction where I did exactly that was captured on a rare DVD issued exclusively to *Strokes* fan club members called, *In Transit*. Caught in the act.

All three bands were brilliant that day but, from that point on, it would be a long time till I'd see Fab, Nick, Nikolai, Albert, Julian and Ryan again and in circumstances that would be 'beyond freaky' to say the least.

Anne and I stayed in Mallorca for almost the entire summer. I went into Degrabación Studio there (the name translates to: "un-recording" or "erasing") which was an 'OK' studio and, just for fun, recorded five or six new *Satellites* songs.

One of these songs, *In Another World*, was based on a monumental rock guitar riff and is still one of my all-time favorites. Those sessions were a magical way to start off the summer; I was euphoric to be recording them in their native environment. The camaraderie between us all was growing and, to add even more fun, the *Mad Juana* band, Sami Yaffa, Karmen Guy, Wylie Wirth and Jimmy Goodman stayed for an entire month of swimming, smoking and hanging out in picturesque towns and on serene beaches all across the island.

Our time there was enjoyably peaceful and we were living at a stress-free tempo. I had the CD of *The Libertine*'s demos that Banny had given me in London, which kept brushing against my hand as I rummaged around in my suitcase. So, one fine day as we were getting ready for our daily trek to find a new amazing beach, I grabbed my portable CD Walkman, checking to make sure it had battery power left in it.

A few hours later, laying on a towel on some warm sand, I listened through, curious to see if *The Libertines* were a band that

I could see myself producing. The songs on that CD were what I can only describe as some form of well-presented, English folk music. It was similar to the short number that Peter sang to me down on one knee at the HEAVEN afterparty. *The Libertines* were using mostly acoustic instruments and I only imagined that their sound referenced late 19th century Britain.

I sent an email to Banny that night from an internet cafe. I told her that those demos sounded cool to me but it wasn't a style of music I knew anything about so I didn't really see how my musical ideas could be usefully applied as their producer.

By the middle of summer, I had the urge to go with Anne to visit our dear friend Moses in Berlin. I had been looking forward to playing *The Strokes* album for him, since we recorded it in our studio that was named after his.

It was very warm when we got to Berlin and there was a festive, expansive feeling in the Kreuzberg neighborhood where we mostly hung out. We enjoyed the Bauhaus Museum and joined in for The Love Parade; a wild outdoor techno party that snaked across the city, along the River Spree, through parks and wound up in the woods at Tiergarten.

When I played *Is This It* to Moses, he had a look on his face that said,

"Wow, you did great work here."

And, when it was over, he had a big smile and told me (out loud),

"Congratulations—and you didn't use any REVERB at all!"

I had to tell him the bad news about our eviction, but he assured me that, one way or another, he'd be back in NYC and we'd do more recording together.

Anne and I returned for more sun and swimming in Mallorca, which brought us towards the third week of August 2001. We were now ready to get back to the Big Apple and resume our downtown lifestyles. *Is This It* had already been released in Australia and was due to drop two weeks later in Japan and the UK, with the USA date coming up on September 25th.

I was not keeping track of where *The Strokes* were on their tours, but I knew they'd been gigging almost non-stop throughout that summer, all over the globe.

26: Good To Be Home

It was marvelous to be home after such a satisfying summer vacation. Now that I was back in New York, I called a lawyer to find out if we could fight our studio eviction. If it was not going to be possible to keep the studio, I would just wait until the next plan or possibility came to me. This was the first time in ten years that I wasn't actively playing in a band. I also hit up my manager to see if he could kick into gear, securing me high-paying production jobs and a record label to sign me as an artist.

There was one person who I had been thinking about during the summer, and I decided that this would be a good time to get back in touch. This was Terrah, whom I'd met at the *Longwave/Strokes* gig at Maxwells. I remembered finding her very attractive and we had a great shared interest as keyboard players, so I used that phone number she had given me. I called Terrah, and we had a few flirty emails back and forth. She dropped into the studio after her work one night and we just talked about music and smiled a lot. A few nights later, she invited me to a concert featuring new songwriters at The Cutting Room up around Times Square.

I wasn't so inspired by the performers that night, but I was super impressed with Terrah and her ever more magical smile. We went back to my apartment at 161 Rivington Street and just had the best sex ever. She was not only charming, but she reminded me of two girlfriends I had really loved, earlier in my life. Terrah told me she would spend the night but that she had to wake up early and get to work in Midtown.

The next morning, I was, needless to say, feeling amazing and woke up with her much earlier than I would normally, to walk her to the F train at Essex and Delancey. We kissed goodbye and I headed over, in very high spirits, to Clinton Street, entering one of my regular breakfast spots, Il Paradiso. I ordered coffee and a bagel, choosing a seat in the back corner, by the open side door and big window. It was a gloriously sunny, warm day outside.

Glancing at a small TV above the bar, I saw a curious live news report showing thin plumes of black smoke pouring upwards from one of the World Trade Center towers. The sound on the TV was off but the words at the bottom of the screen said something about a plane hitting the tower and that they were investigating.

I imagined that a seaplane had accidentally hit that tower on the way to a landing area on the waterfront. Just then, I stared at that TV and watched something very BIG flying into the towers again.

I simultaneously heard the giant BOOOM echoing in through the open cafe door, coming from 1.5 miles away. I wolfed down my breakfast, not really tasting it and ran outside to see what the hell was going on.

I couldn't believe my eyes to see people walking up from downtown covered from head to toe in whitish grey ash and dust. I quickly walked over to the Bowery where Anne was renting an artist's loft, as I knew she would be fast asleep at that time. I wanted to wake her up and alert her to the extraordinarily chaotic circumstances in Manhattan.

More and more people covered in ash dust were pouring up the sidewalks as I reached the Bowery and rang the buzzer. It took a few minutes for the sound to finally rouse her from sleep and she let me in.

I described what I had seen and she got dressed in a hurry, then we both stepped out to look around. At that moment, we didn't know if the whole city was going to be attacked. We instinctively headed for St. Marks Place and turned to walk down from 2nd Avenue towards Tomkins Square Park.

Ten seconds later, AGAIN, I couldn't believe my eyes—there was Roderick, the singer from *Sky Cries Mary*, walking straight towards me, dazed and in a worried panic. I asked him what the fuck he was doing in New York, and he told me that he and his wife Anisa (co-singer of *Sky Cries Mary*) had just moved from Seattle two weeks before and were now living in the

179

neighborhood. We were both shocked to run into each other under such ominous circumstances and it felt like an unbelievably weird dream. It was a time of fear and trepidation when NO ONE in New York knew what was going on, or what might happen next. Roderick had no idea where his wife had gone and was desperate to find her.

In a double flash of synchronicity, Anisa turned the exact same corner from 2nd Avenue and found us there. We were all amazed by this weird coincidence, a spontaneous partial band reunion as New York seemed to be disintegrating all around us. Roderick and Anisa were the ones who'd kindly offered me the entire basement of their home when I first joined their band in 1991. At the time, I was just making my way back from being penniless and homeless. Before I'd met them, I was sleeping on a stairway landing in the attic of my former bassist Mike Davidson's house, having just returned to Seattle from living in Los Angeles.

Around 1pm on the day that the World Trade Center was attacked, I was able to call my dad in Seattle to tell him I was alright and, moments later, the phone networks all went down.

Somehow, I found Terrah again, late in the day. She told me that her office was on a high floor, directly facing the World Trade Center, so there was no way she could avoid seeing the horror unfolding, until her boss decided to let everyone go home. 'Going home' itself had become an issue, because police barriers were set up all through lower Manhattan. You had to show your ID to be allowed back into your own neighborhoods. It was mind-numbingly oppressive to prove that I belonged on my own street and nerve-wracking to not automatically be able to enter my home when I wanted to without an ID card.

The next two weeks were bizarre and terrifying for all of us. A blackish grey smoke haze hung like a cloud over Manhattan, it had a death-flavored smell made from a combination of demolished buildings, burning jet fuel and the poor unfortunate victims trapped inside at "Ground Zero". We were told not to spend too much time outside in the city to avoid inhaling that toxic haze.

I was at home on Rivington Street or in the basement in my studio or at Terrah's apartment during the weeks after 9/11. I was already subject to increased paranoia and prone to mental panic thanks to my incessant pot smoking, but this was an awful time to be high on weed. Everyone was watching television, everywhere I went there was a screen showing the burning wreckage of buildings in Lower Manhattan. If one tried to change the channel, the same images were on the next station as well, from a different angle. I recall the waves of utter fear and sadness that would overtake me as I saw the stories about the people that lost their lives or lost loved ones in the devastation. In the second week of this nightmare, there came reports about letters containing ANTHRAX being sent in the United States and people dying from that.

For many days the streets were closed; it was macabre and eerie to see those completely empty streets in New York City. On every available wall and surface people were posting photos of missing friends or family members and there were candlelit shrines all over the sidewalks dedicated to those who had lost their lives.

For me, the events of 9/11 showed very clearly the results of the U.S. Government's foreign policies and military aggressions. Naturally I had been protesting (in my own way as a 10-year-old!) the Viet Nam war and I have been suspicious and distrustful of the U.S. political machine ever since then. Watching the Watergate scandal and resignation of President Richard Nixon cemented my satirical and distrustful views of the U.S. government. Reagan and Bush enflamed my anger and the events of 9/11 showed me just how vulnerable my country is to retaliation and attack. I wondered, for the first time, if remaining in the United States was a smart option. It made me reconsider spending my days working in a basement in New York City.

On top of all of this, the terms of our eviction notice were about to go into effect. With only two weeks remaining before we had to vacate the studio, I got a call from Ryan Gentles setting up an urgent meeting at Transporterraum.

The Strokes, their A&R guy from RCA, Ryan and I were there in the control room discussing the heavy topic of whether *New York City Cops* should be taken off the U.S. release, which was now being postponed. The band felt that, in the current social climate, NYC police and firemen were being hailed as heroes all across the country and so it could be counter-productive to release a song that had the lyrics,

"New York City Cops...ain't too smart."

This was not a decision forced upon the band in any way and, by the end of the meeting, it was decided that they would come in to record one new song and the album would be reprinted, repackaged and rushed for release in early October.

The Strokes brought in a song called, *When It Started*, which took us two days to record and mix. I agreed with the band's choice to take *NYC Cops* off the album for all the reasons that were aired during the meeting but I also felt it was a huge musical loss for the U.S. release, as it's a real signature *Strokes* song, bursting with energy, personality and band identity.

Boxes of vinyl LPs with the original track listing had already been pressed and were being stored in a warehouse. I was glad that someone snuck me a copy of one of those for it's surely a collector's item now.

The next single from the album was going to be *Last Nite*. The band had a strong resolve not to make a typically cheesy, lip-synch video for MTV, which I'm sure caused no small amount of friction and hair pulling over at RCA.

Ryan phoned me again,

"The guys filmed a video in which they play *Last Nite* live, there's a problem though—Julian says the word SHIT one time. Can you do something to hide that in the mix?"

"Yes, of course," and, in one of the last moments in the existence of Transporterraum NYC, I flipped that word backwards so that at two minutes and thirty seconds, you can hear the sound "Tish..." instead.

27: What I Did While Bush Went Hunting Evil-Doers

October: the month featuring Halloween, hauntedly rolled around. Our studio eviction was meant to take place right when kids wearing spooky costumes would be going out saying, "trick or treat" and filling their bags with candy.

Things were going well with Terrah and she suggested that, if I got a loft somewhere downtown, she would be happy to move in with me. Moving from the flat I shared with Ken Weller (which was not so expensive) to getting a loft in Manhattan was, sadly, far beyond my financial means.

Terrah shared some happy news: she and my former *Absinthee* bandmate Anne Hadlock had started an all-girl rock band called *Petal* (yes, named after Anne's beloved little Jack Russell Terrier), with a tremendous bassist named Hannah Moorhead and a fabulous guitar rocker named Tina Gorin, from *Bad Wizard* and *Helldorado*.

They'd been developing songs quietly at Anne's apartment, so I quickly offered that they could rehearse at the studio and that I'd be very up for recording them. They needed a drummer for that so I recruited my pal, Alan Bezozi. After a very few rehearsals they sounded great and we all had a few exciting, enjoyable nights recording six *Petal* songs. The band members looked spectacular together, their sound was raw and cool, with Anne's screaming voice perfectly suited for this group.

I finally did meet with a lawyer about trying to hold on to the studio but he informed me that there was no use fighting Rick's eviction notice—we wouldn't win. This felt like a punch in the stomach, but I already had a hunch that this would be the case. In my sadness and resentment about this I couldn't think about the incredible amount of effort that Joe, Anne and Manny Hadlock, Jimmy Goodman and Don Farwell had put in to help me make Transporterraum NYC come to life.

I didn't really go through the list of my five previous evictions: The band house I was kicked out of in my early 20s for my being rude, unhelpful and making too much disturbing noise. Apartment F that I was evicted from for having a strobe light in the window 24 hours a day and the landlady thought I was a devil worshipper. The church that burnt down with all my musical instruments and personal belongings which left me homeless for a while. Chateau Relaxo, because the landlord decided he could make more money from a retail business. And now this, being forced to leave our East Village dream studio under the methadone clinic.

I had two reasons bubbling in my brain that made me feel somewhat ok about this latest impending eviction. I had a nagging feeling that, after the trauma of 9/11, maybe I didn't need to be sat in a basement in New York City all day every day working. I also had a dream that maybe if *The Strokes* album became really successful, I could travel all over as a producer, and maybe even build a more amazing studio somewhere else.

In a solemn but friendly way, Jimmy and I split up the studio equipment (he bought most of it) and we parted ways as business associates. My personal collection of keyboards, guitars, books and decorations were loaded into a van and taken to Bedrock Storage where they could rest safely until I hatched a new plan. I was surely bummed out while riding out in a van to the West Side but dutifully placed my belongings into a big cage on the sixth floor and padlocked the door. The van driver, who'd helped me carry everything, left and I was about to go down the elevator and out on 11ᵗʰ Avenue to hail a taxi, when my cell phone rang.

A striking British voice was on the other end,

"Hello. Is this Gordon?"

"Yes, who is this?" I wondered.

"Richard Butler from *The Psychedelic Furs*. Richard Fortus gave me your number."

This was double WOW, insane and good! I'd been a *Psychedelic Furs* fan since their first album came out in 1980, listening to them constantly in my Seattle days. Now, here was Richard Butler, their amazing singer, calling to ask if I'd like to go on tour as their keyboard player! Richard Fortus would be playing guitar and cello in the band as well.

My next words to Richard Butler were, "But we've never met!"

To which he coolly responded, "Yes, there's always that!"

I mentally thanked Richard Fortus for suggesting me and for believing that I could handle the parts. I went straight home to learn nine songs.

The audition was five days later and—I passed the test! This new lineup of *The Psychedelic Furs* launched straight into rehearsals for a four-week tour of the U.S. and Canada, slated to begin in mid-November.

Two days before Halloween, *The Strokes* headlined Hammerstein Ballroom, a massive, classy venue, to celebrate the US release of *Is This It*, with its revised album artwork and track list. I was so happy to be there and continued my annoying tradition of going backstage to immediately ask Nick if he had any pot that I could smoke.

He would always smile at me and tell me where to find it and to help myself. After getting what I was after, I would then, of course, rifle through their dressing room for snacks, food and mineral water, also helping myself. The Hammerstein Ballroom show was a triumph on many levels. Because *The Strokes* had been touring all summer, playing so many concerts in a row, they were now MONSTER tight, more on the scale of *Led Zeppelin* and nowhere near the sonic texture of some kids making indie, garage rock. I was utterly shocked at how good and HUGE sounding they had become since I had last seen them play.

For me, it was the best and most riveting public performance I ever experienced from them, a true peak and a pinnacle. The party afterwards was also fabulous and, by the time I walked home, it was already light.

The Psychedelic Furs tour was a very well-paid job. We had a luxurious tour bus and stayed in fine hotels (yes, my own room) in every city. I bought my first laptop (a Powerbook G4) and iPod to provide extra fun on the road.

I said goodbye to Terrah and arranged to meet her a few days later when our bus would roll back into NYC to play at the plush Beacon Theatre.

Our tour began in Atlanta, Nashville and Washington D.C. These were our 'warm-up shows' to prepare for GREATNESS when we arrived back in New York.

I had made a serious deal with myself; I didn't smoke marijuana during the days of rehearsal, promising myself NOT to get stoned on the tour to make sure I wouldn't space out and make mistakes playing those revered classic songs onstage.

My keyboard parts were very specific, with many sound changes. I also played guitar and sang harmonies on several songs. *Echo & The Bunnymen* were out on this tour with us and we alternated the headlining slot.

The first shows went very well yet, even though we'd only been away from home for three days, I missed Terrah, as absence makes the heart grow...

We left Washington D.C. one morning and our bus drove directly to the Upper West Side, pulling over on Broadway, very close to Central Park (nice area!). We arrived just in time to check into our hotel which was right next the Beacon Theatre.

Terrah met me there, carrying a shopping bag full of cool black clothing I had asked her to buy for me to wear on the rest of the tour. I was happy to see her and she accompanied me to our soundcheck.

Soundcheck went super smoothly and, afterwards, there were three and a half hours till the gig so we went back to the hotel to 'rest and relax'. Well, the dear woman took out a perfectly rolled joint and my resolution to keep my shit together FLEW out the window. We smoked, and those two weeks of me "not being high" added some extra hallucinatory effects and way more potency than I expected.

Yeah, then we rolled around on the bed, earning ourselves two platinum stars up in rock-heaven. We both got dressed up for the show and walked over to the backstage area at the Beacon Theatre.

The Psychedelic Furs started each show with their smash hit, *Love My Way* (produced by Todd Rundgren, with the legendary Flo & Eddie on backing vocals), which required me to play a very steady riff using a marimba sound with my right hand and an analog synth melody with my left. We launched into that song as the red velvet curtain opened, which was a head rush in itself because this venue was immense, with a sea of faces and balconies up high in the air. I also knew that my dear friend Anne was out in the audience somewhere, for I had put her on my guest list.

The band was off to a perfect start and I was playing really well but then, in the middle of the first verse, I felt some BAD thoughts beginning.

The first bad thought was that we were sounding so perfect, it sounded just like the record... so was this a record playing? Or were we really playing this? My next thought, which was just as distracting and discombobulating, was:

"Oh my god, I shouldn't be thinking that right now. NO!"

My hands were nearly shaking, my confidence and concentration had dropped to 'frail'.

Was I powering through the song making the Butler brothers (Richard and Tim) pleased that I was a member of their band? Probably not! Then the third and worst thought entered into my drug addled mind:

"Oh, Anne is up in one of those balconies watching me and she is angry because I am onstage with *The Psychedelic Furs* and not with *Absinthee!*"

This was the clincher as I became certain that her being upset with me was somehow affecting my ability to play properly. Gradually these psycho-impressions drifted away and I was able to play my keyboards in an average/ok but not wonderful way for the rest of the show.

I was relieved to step off the stage that night and lucky no one in the band fired me or said anything devastatingly rude (which would have been justified). Did I learn from these negative brainwaves? Would this panicked nervousness help me maintain control over my urges to get high? No. I bought a bag of weed after the show, along with a pack of cigarettes and, for the rest of the tour, smoked piles of joints in the back of the bus.

That back lounge area was mostly empty, except for me 'cuz no one wanted to breathe all that smoke, except occasionally, legendary guitarist John Ashton would join me for a puff and a friendly conversation.

A few days later we were in Akron, Ohio and I'd just had breakfast on a cold, rainy morning. Some sad news crashed in via my cell phone, it was Terrah and she was crying. She told me that she had gotten into a verbal fight with Anne and whatever was said between them resulted in Terrah quitting *Petal* AND breaking up with me.

Unfortunately, I'd already had one long distance phone call breakup with a girlfriend, during a *Sky Cries Mary* tour, and I can tell you it's a purely miserable experience. You have nowhere to try and recover emotionally, except for your bunkbed in the bus or in the hotel room for a few hours per night before going back out to meet the band, the press and the public. I had been so happily looking forward to the end of tour, Christmas and the New Year, when this depressing call came through.

Our final shows were on the West Coast. Once we hit Portland, I was thrilled to be back in the region of the United States where I had grown up. Some dear friends of mine came out to the Portland show and we partied together late into the night.

The tour bus pulled out at 4am and we drove up the I-5 north towards my town, Seattle. Everyone in the bus went straight to sleep and we were told that when we arrived, around 7:30 am, those who wanted to stay asleep could remain in their bunks or we could check into our hotel rooms and catch up on more rest there.

I was zonked out, fast asleep when my body felt us pull over to the curb and stop. I lifted the little red curtain above the portal window in my bunk and saw, to my grinning soul, that the driver had parked the bus at 2nd and Lenora. We were directly in front of the DSHS office (Dept. of Health and Social Services) that I used to mandatorily report to every month in the early 80s, when I was receiving government-issued FOOD STAMPS. I had no job then, no money, and I would always walk into that place moderately stoned. In that miserable government office, I would sit alongside impoverished Vietnamese immigrant families, with multiple babies crying. Under those harsh white fluorescent lights, I would read my esoteric occult books (such as the one that channeled St. Germain, who, from a higher dimension was trying to teach me how to MATERIALIZE a crystal cross inside one of my shoes that was in a closet, back at Apartment F!) while waiting for hours to get my $60 per month of food stamps. The irony, that here I was touring with the majestic, well respected *Psychedelic Furs* in this exact location, was indeed magically enchanting. Maybe this is what I was materializing all those years ago?

The Moore Theatre, where we were performing that night, was located one block from that DSHS office. This concert hall had formed a major part of my musical history. I'd seen *Gentle Giant*, PJ Harvey, *Laibach*, *Nine Inch Nails* and many other intense, life-changing concerts there. Its grand old-fashioned interior, replete with ornate domed ceilings and crystal chandeliers, was acoustically gorgeous; perhaps the best-sounding venue for loud, crashing rock music in town. The first time I ever played there was with *Sky Cries Mary* and that was truly a golden moment, a peak in my musical career.

Now back in Seattle for one day, we checked into the Camlin Hotel, which is a wonderful building downtown, modeled on an Italian castle and famous for its Cloud Room bar on the top floor. I had a very swollen guest list that night as *The Psychedelic Furs* were being extra kind to me, knowing that this was my hometown.

My dad and sister Lisa were there, the Bear Creek family as well, along with my close circle of musician friends. The show went smashingly well and me 'n my peeps even had a special place in the venue reserved for us for a party afterwards. This night felt like a mythical kind of homecoming.

28: Gazing into the Future

After *The Furs* tour was over, New York got dressed up in Christmas lights once again.

I received an email from two brothers in a band from England asking what my rates would be to fly over and produce their album.

They lived on a farm in Abingdon, Oxfordshire, the same region where *Radiohead* originated. The brothers had an impressive plan: to record in Wales at the classic Rockfield Studios (*Queen's Bohemian Rhapsody* studio) and then go for mastering at Abbey Road. This was enticing to me, an ambitious, expensive project from the studio details alone. I quoted them a pretty high price, certainly more than I'd been getting in my own studio thus far.

To my surprise and delight, they accepted my terms and I was subsequently booked for my first-ever production in the UK! Because England was my personal fantasyland of rock 'n' roll, it was a dream fulfilled to finally have a chance to work there.

In early February 2002, I landed at Heathrow where I met the two brothers and we drove for an hour out to Abingdon. Since I'd landed in the morning we went straight to work, beginning a week of pre-production. This meant that I would check all the songs, musically and lyrically, offering suggestions anytime I thought something could be improved.

Their band sounded like a blend of early *Yes*, AC/DC and *Black Sabbath*; an unlikely combination of very complicated parts and basic, primitive hard rock. They managed to make these diverse elements sound cool and I was pleased to dig into our pre-production. I felt inclined to fine tune some of their lyrics, which they appreciated, and also helped them craft more compelling intros for several songs.

I gave them my philosophy that an intro(duction) should invite the listener in, making them excited to hear the story within the song. A boring or lackluster intro could easily make someone step away, yawn or turn it off instead. I also suggested changing many of the basslines away from just following along whatever the guitar was doing to, instead, creating independent melodies that progressed in contrasting motion.

Those days and nights in their remote farmhouse felt a bit monastic to me, just the three young men from the band and myself. No visitors, no trips out into the nearby town, no hashish, no parties and, worst of all—no women! I started to feel lonely and isolated.

I had imagined and hoped that my first experience working in England would have been more 'sexy, party, fun', to be honest. With that image firmly in mind, I asked the boys if they knew anyone they could call to deliver me some good hash. I also asked if there were any nightclubs around where we could possibly go meet some girls.

After our long work sessions, I connected to the internet and wrote emails to Terrah in New York, asking her if she fancied coming out to see me in England and stay for a while. She was amused, but...no.

Yes, I did finally score one small, dry, scratchy, weak gram of hashish and so we just got on with the band's preparations.

On the sixth day they spent the entire session looking for the exact metronome tempo they wanted to use for each song. My job was to nod my head if a certain tempo sounded particularly fitting but, in reality, they knew more than I did what felt right. After all, they had written the songs, had been developing them for a year and the musicians were the ones who had to play and sing them comfortably.

I did write down in my notebook, very officially, which tempo (in beats per minute) they preferred for each song. Incidentally, I think I have done pre-production like this a grand total of three times in my life and this was one of them. Usually, I just get off a plane, we go to the studio and start recording, having had crucial discussions in advance via phone or internet. In that way, I already know about the band's intended sound and we all have agreed on how we will achieve that.

The next day, day seven, there was to be one final rehearsal and then a huge shopping trip to buy groceries for our two weeks of recording at Rockfield Studios.

The band members liked to rise up early and so, by 10am, we were assembled in their frontroom for the last practice. The drummer announced that they wished to RE-CHECK the tempos to make sure that the ones they had selected the day before were correct. In response to that, I said a line that FOREVER changed my destiny:

"Oh, ok—here's the list from my notebook. Why don't you guys go do that while I write a few emails? Will that be alright?"

They double-checked their tempos again for a few hours. As I was writing emails in their office area, I could hear them rehearsing sections of their songs.

When that was done, we had lunch and went off in their car to a big Sainsbury's, filling bags and bags with food for the upcoming trip to Wales. When we returned to the farmhouse, they made cups of tea and then announced that they wanted to have a talk with me. The elder brother spoke:

"Gordon, we've decided that we don't want you to come with us to the studio."

Me: "WHAT?...Why not??"

Him: "We don't think you like our music and, actually, we don't think that you really know what you are doing, either! We don't trust you enough to be our producer."

Well, I was stunned. I felt hurt, like when I was thirteen years old and got kicked out of my first band. It just wasn't true. I DID like their music, it was cool, I just wasn't in the mood to sit through a second day of them checking their tempos, so I didn't.

I felt flustered, hot and jittery, needing to immediately figure out what to do (maybe a better person would have meditated?). I knew that I didn't want to be in that house with them and absolutely couldn't imagine spending another night there. What could I do?

I went outside for some fresh, cold air, with my mind racing for ten minutes. I did have their non-refundable first half-payment of £6,000 in my New York bank, so I could easily afford to change my return plane ticket. But I felt pressurized and didn't want to do anything right there in front of them. I had a grand total of two other people's phone numbers in England. I called Julien "Tiger Boy" but got a message machine. Then I called Banny and, thankfully, she answered.

I told her right away that I was in a serious bind, asking if there was any way that I could come to London, and if she would allow me to stay at her place overnight. I promised that if she did, I would sort out a plane ticket home to New York the next day.

She was totally relaxed and kind, answering,

"Of course—get the train to Paddington and, from there, get a taxi to (her address) in Islington."

I asked the brothers to drop me off with my suitcase at the Abingdon train station. The journey in their car was filled with what I would call an icy silence, quite the opposite from the hopeful friendly conversations we were having a week earlier when they picked me up from Heathrow. My head was swarming with confusion, disappointment and clouds of sadness.

I didn't really think I had done anything wrong, but being booted off the project made me feel 'less than', aka not good enough. But the moment I got my train ticket and stood on the platform under the London Paddington sign, I felt much calmer and more clear. I imagined that it would be fun spending a night in London and that I would find something interesting to get into once I landed back home in New York.

Three hours later I was ringing Banny's doorbell. She was cooking dinner when I arrived and offered me a cuppa tea. I put my suitcase in her guest room and sat down to tell my tale of woe.

Before I could really say anything, she spoke,

"Gordon, I'm managing *The Libertines* now and they have just signed with Rough Trade. They really want you to produce their first record and have just finished recording sixteen new demos that you really MUST hear. It's a totally different sound than what you heard before."

Those were her opening lines.

My head was still disoriented, spinning from being rudely fired that day and, on top of that, I didn't have high hopes of liking *The Libertines* on round two.

After we ate a delicious dinner, she persisted by putting on the sixteen song CD and pressing play.

Not only did I dislike the new sound, but I was offended— those demos sounded like they were attempting to copy the vibe and feeling of *The Strokes* album! Even worse, they only seemed to have picked up on the messy, distorted aspect, not paying attention to the clarity and definition that was essential to balance with the noise.

I told her directly that I was offended by this blatant copying, requesting that we just skip through the songs rather than hearing them from beginning to end.

Banny said, "Look Gordon, I understand why you don't like the demos but, please, they're having a rehearsal tomorrow and I want you to come along and see them."

I really don't know why, but I said ok.

The next morning, she made cups of tea and took me to a tiny cafe in Chapel Market. By 1pm we were at Rooz Studios in Old Street, entering a tiny practice room. The band were set up on the floor but had arranged themselves in a line, like a show, facing the two old wooden chairs on which Banny and I sat.

AGAIN, Peter, the gracious one, came up to me and smiled. He withdrew a small pouch from his pocket and handed it to me with the immortal words,

"Care to skin up?"

That pouch contained marijuana, tobacco and rolling papers.

"Care? Indeed, I'd love to..." And I rejoicingly did, as the band started into their first song.

Oh, it WAS good. No, *The Libertines* were amazing!

I was startled by each incredible song, the jolting vocal interplay between Carl and Pete, and Gary's insane fast beats. This was exactly the music for me. I felt like I had landed in my best possible future and was here meeting the next *Beatles* when they were 20 years old!

I asked, "Is there a notebook and a pen here?"

These I received.

"What was the name of that song?" I asked and started compiling a list, already filling my head with the ideas about how best to record and capture all of the GREATNESS I was hearing in that room.

I performed a rather cheeky move. Every time *The Libertines* stopped playing, I could hear, through the walls at Rooz, the sound of another band with a female vocalist. Even through those walls and for one-minute intervals, I could tell that I liked THAT BAND too! I made an excuse to leave the room, asking Banny where the toilets were, and wandered around the corner to find where the sound was coming from.

I knocked and a bass player opened the door. I told this new band that I thought they sounded really cool and that I'd be interested in recording them. They looked pleased but puzzled, as they had never seen me before and had no idea who I was. I just wrote my name and email address on a piece of paper, handed it to them, smiled and said goodbye.

A few days later their manager wrote me and very kindly asked me how much I would charge to record *Ripe* (the band's name), which subsequently led to several excellent sessions.

After the Rooz rehearsal, Pete and Carl returned to Banny's flat with me. They insisted that I walk with them to Filthy MacNasty's pub on Amwell Street.

Filthy MacNasty's had its entrance on the corner and was a heavily painted green-brick building with outrageously bright red wooden picnic tables with benches all along the outside. Inside were dark colored walls and an oval-shaped bar with thick brass fittings that served the front area as well as a tiny back room where bands sometimes performed. The stage in the back was barely big enough for a small drum set and a few musicians crammed up against it. That room was packed when 50 people were there and was a heaving sweaty event when 100 showed up. The whole thing had a divey bar feeling with beat-up rickety chairs and tables with old graffiti carved into them, clearly claimed from an auction. This pub was rustic, down to the collection of books along the walls that looked like they had been discovered in a charity shop along with some old board games such as Scrabble—but it was all very charming. Pete, Carl and I had a great chat and, as we smoked and they drank, more of their friends, 'the regulars', arrived.

So, from day one in London, I had *The Libertines* to hang out and work with and a small cast of lovely characters sitting all around us.

29: A Libertine in London

I was still staying at Banny's in Islington when she told me that The BRIT Awards were being held a few nights later. As a guy who grew up in Seattle, I had no idea what she was talking about so she explained that it was a high-profile show celebrating the British record industry. Then she mentioned that, in fact, my good friends *The Strokes* were going to perform there and had even been nominated to win a prize. This piqued my curiosity and I made a phone call to their manager Ryan, exclaiming breathlessly that I just happened to be in London and wondered where could I find the band? He informed me that they'd be staying at the Trafalgar St. James Hotel, giving me the exact time that they were expected to arrive.

The next evening, I took a black cab to their hotel, then just waited in the opulent lobby until they walked in.

Oh, they were so surprised to see me there, we greeted each other with smiles and hugs. I sat back down on a comfortable, chic couch in the lobby for a bit more waiting as they proceeded up the elevator to their rooms.

Soon Nick, Albert and Fab returned to chat with me but, after five minutes of catching up, I looked at Nick and asked,

"You don't happen to have any weed, do you?"

He smiled politely (as he'd already predicted that I would ask that) and handed me his room key, yelling after me as I ran off,

"It's in the small black bag on the table."

That night I was introduced to their official head of security, a big, powerful guy called Danny Yeates, who had a warm smile, bright eyes and was incredibly sweet. When I told the boys that I really wanted to tag along with them to the Brit Awards the next day, Danny stepped in and told me to come back to the hotel the following day and he would do his best to get me in somehow.

He really did! The next day I climbed into the van with the band and, when we piled out at Earl's Court, Danny just pushed me through the backstage door security. Yes, I was IN!

It was the 21st edition of The Brit Awards: *The Gorillaz*, Kylie Minogue and *The Strokes* played live and *The Strokes* won the prize for Best International Newcomer. I met Sting (who told me his real name was Gordon too) and Shakira that night, partied with *The Strokes* and discovered my new buddies, *The Libertines*, slinking around backstage as well. While the event was too corporately cheesy for my personal tastes, I admit that it also felt stimulating and amazingly fun to be there, hobnobbing with the cream of the British music industry that night.

The next morning, I went to see a lovely, musical friend that I'd met in New York the year before. Su Goodacre is her name and she invited me to her home in Covent Garden, right on Drury Lane.

That magical street was named in a song, *The Muffin Man*, that my mom sang to me when I was a little boy, but this would be my first real-life visit. Su was happy to see me in London and offered that I could stay at her spacious Drury Lane loft for a month or possibly longer. She also asked if I was planning to attend *The Libertines* show that night at Cherry Jam. Funnily, I hadn't heard about that yet and, of course, I wanted to go!

Su and I took a taxi together and all the way there I wondered what adventures this evening would hold.

Once inside, I immediately felt that Cherry Jam was definitely the most exciting place in the world to be. All of Rough Trade was there to celebrate their newest signing, the club was packed with top music industry chiefs and there were celebrated British rock royalty everywhere I looked. I felt very lucky to be part of this, positively giddy about the fact that I was close with Rough Trade thanks to *The Strokes* and already IN with *The Libertines* as their new producer.

Su whispered in my ear that the person I happened to be standing next to was Bernard Butler, from *Suede*, and that he had really wanted to be *The Libertines* producer. I looked over and saw him, then kind of stood up a bit straighter thinking (a bit too smugly, I admit),

"That job is mine now!"

The Libertines were incendiary onstage, lighting up that room with the perfect alchemy of chaos and beauty, sweaty aggression and poetry. This was the new London!

I'm sure that everyone in attendance at Cherry Jam that night would say that it was a high-water mark in their musical lives. The two singers, Pete and Carl, sharing one mic, were a hit and the accidental tripping over and pulling out of guitar cables from their amplifiers actually worked in their favor that night. From this concert alone, everyone would have anticipated that *The Libertines* were going to become the biggest, most well-loved British rock band of the new millennium.

I spied Toby L from Rockfeedback in the crowd. It was my third time encountering him because, bless him, Toby had had his dad drive him out to Abingdon during the fateful week I was working there, to interview me.

His questions had been, as I quickly learned to expect from him, astute and brilliant. When *The Libertines* gig was over, the club emptied EXCEPT for a marvelous bunch of *The Libertines'* friends, including my favorites from the Filthy MacNasty's crew, plus twenty more new faces that I instantly set about to meet.

There was a boisterous character named Alan Wass with his mates Ozandu and John Paul, they were in a band called *The Left Hand*. Then I was introduced to swashbuckling Scarborough Steve, photographer Vicki Churchill, French Carole, filmmaker Camilla Robinson and I said hello to the man himself, Geoff Travis, head of Rough Trade.

At some ungodly late/early hour, Su Goodacre and I arrived by cab at Teesdale Street in Bethnal Green, entering the Albion Rooms aka the flat belonging to Pete and Carl. By this point, the place was littered with most of the raucous guests from the afterparty in yet more heinous states of disrepair. One could only imagine the amount of alcohol, smoke, powder and pills contained in those bodies crammed into that small flat!

After a while, Carl offered to lend me his room so I could lay down and attempt to sleep. I followed him up the stairs whilst Alan from *The Left Hand* started pounding out chords on an acoustic guitar, loudly howling out a song,

"*Goodnight to the producer Gordon Raphael.*
YEAH goodnight, Gordon...."

It was both distressing and charming, as were many of my future run-ins with that fellow.

Up around noon yet feeling none too rested, I quietly climbed down the stairs, taking special care not to awaken the people strewn on floor, couch and chairs who seemed frozen in place from where they were six hours before.

I hailed a taxi and was driven through London town to Islington. There I prepared to move my suitcase over to Su's loft, thanking Banny for graciously rescuing me when I first called her and for all the great experiences with *The Libertines* thus far. Before I left her flat, Banny handed me an itinerary for an upcoming UK tour. *The Libertines* were hitting the road, opening for *The Vines* and performing two shows with *The Strokes*. I had volunteered to run *The Libertines* live sound, wondering what kind of mad adventure that might be. It was also another opportunity to smile at *The Strokes* a few more times while they were in England.

The next night, Peter, Carl, John, Gary, Banny and I drove up to Leeds University. It was the first night of the tour and *The Strokes* were headlining. I was guessing that *The Strokes* would find it amusing to see me mixing sound for *The Libertines* that night.

We had a rushed soundcheck before they hit the stage. It wasn't nearly as tight as the Cherry Jam show and there were several fizzles/malfunctions with the guitar amps. During the changeover before the second band, *Stereo Total*, took the stage, I was hanging out in *The Strokes*'s dressing room, yes, borrowing weed from Nick, eating snacks from their catering trays and generally taking up space.

When I went out to peek at *Stereo Total*, Pete Doherty approached me to ask if I would kindly introduce him to Julian and the rest of the band. In my stoned state, buzzing like a bee and still not deeply knowing the personalities of *The Strokes* or *The Libertines*, I did bring Peter back there and cheerfully introduced him.

I left quickly to see more of *Stereo Total* and no more than ten minutes had passed when I witnessed Peter leaving that dressing room in a hurry. Moments later I bumped into Julian, who told me in a very direct and serious voice,

"Don't ever bring him back again."

I had no idea what could have happened within such a short space of time to elicit that strong response![15]

The next night was a replay, only this time we were in Birmingham. I was doing ok running *The Libertines* sound and heard no complaints. *The Strokes* were incredible—on fire both nights and the UK love affair with them was palpably electric, a delightful spectacle to behold.

At the afterparty I was pleased to see young Toby L chatting earnestly with Carl Barât and let out a soft "Wow!" when I noticed Meg and Jack White of *The White Stripes*, joining our rock 'n' roll soiree.

The Strokes' UK love-fest reached new heights the next night when, once again, security chief Danny Yeates blagged me into The NME Awards. He somehow stole an extra chair from the banquet area, allowing me to squeeze in and sit right at the table with *The Strokes*.

This event was a super hipster, cheesy music industry affair, yet again, it felt stunning to be seated in a room full of great bands, rockers and heads of the UK music biz. *The Strokes* won Best New Act, Best Album, and Band of the Year. Hell yeah, I was PROUD to be at that table right then. EXCEPT, poor Fabrizio!

---

[15] Whatever happened in that brief space of time, I never asked and never knew, although there has been plenty of speculation.

He was sitting right next to me when they announced the third award and he just couldn't handle all of that intense adulation and admiration. The look on his face was one of extreme doubt, almost guilt, mixed with a profound sadness. He seemed distraught and said,

"No, no, I can't believe it. We're not that good. We don't really deserve another award. It's not right."

I guessed that this might have been the result of SO much happening SO fast, emotionally impacting their young lives (perhaps it also had something to do with the unlimited free champagne).

The Libertines' UK mini tour had a five-day break before we'd hit a few cities supporting *The Vines*. Our next show was in Brighton, a place I'd imagined many times as a dedicated fan of *The Who's* great opus, *Quadrophenia*. I'd studied the music, lyrics and the staggeringly evocative booklet of photos which accompanied that album, for years. This would be my first chance to be there, helping to contribute some searing, volatile rock in that seaside environment.

After the Brighton gig, I saw my ol' pal James Endeacott from Rough Trade, who said to me,

"... Hmmm, *The Libertines* are going to have to play much better than that to get where we want them to go!"

The next morning at our hotel, we were having breakfast together when Peter's girlfriend spoke up at the table. This was the lovely Francesca, from Italy, whom I really admired and who'd shown me the best place (Food for Thought) to get vegetarian food near Su's loft in Covent Garden. She was in tears and upset, telling everyone at the table that she was sick of Peter looking through her personal notebooks, stealing lines and phrases and then putting them into *Libertines* songs. This was alarming to hear, yet I had no reason to doubt her sincerity.

Only a few shows into their career in the current line-up (*The Libertines* previously had a very different sound and two different band members) and it was already emotionally difficult watching their manager, Banny, literally having nervous breakdowns, bawling and crying night after night in the van after the shows. Pete and Carl would take turns putting their arm around her, trying to calm her down. I wasn't privy to the inner workings of the band, certainly, but perhaps arriving late to the stage, drunkenness and missing press appointments were contributing to the pressure she was feeling.

On we went, playing a homecoming London show at the Camden Barfly, before ending that leg of the tour in Nottingham and Bristol. After the Nottingham show, Banny really had a particularly tearful breakdown about something, and again, Pete and Carl both tried to comfort and somehow soothe her.

At the beginning of this tour, I was given copies of The Libertines' most recent demo sessions. During the long van rides, I was working on my laptop, editing these and thinking of production ideas for their amazing songs. We decided that as soon as the tour ended, we would secure a studio and record their first single.

This plan and my dreams of climbing to further heights producing The Libertines did NOT come to fruition. On a cold, rainy London afternoon, I met the band for a quick meal before they headed off to a meeting at Rough Trade. They went to find out what our studio budget was going to be, pick up some money and ask when we could begin recording their album. We agreed to meet immediately afterwards to plan our next steps.

When we reconvened later at Su Goodacre's loft, Peter and Carl told me that Rough Trade was NOT on board with the idea of me producing them and they were all sorry—but nothing they could do. I was let go. My adventure with The Libertines was over. What had begun when I first met Pete Doherty and Banny Poostchi at The Strokes' HEAVEN London show roughly ten months earlier, was hereby cancelled.

It hurt, I admit, and I felt both shocked and sad. It took a few days (and several grams of hash) for that disappointment to subside but I kept going out to nightclubs and bars meeting new people.

One of the things that filled me with joy about staying in London, especially in Covent Garden, was the proximity to the National Gallery which has free admission every single day. I'm enamored with old European painters and that museum is truly a cathedral and church to me. It's full of dazzling medieval Christian art, Impressionist paintings, Italian Masters, even my entrancing Flemish heroes Breughel and Bosch are alive and standing there in spirit. It was like living my highest dream to gaze upon Renoirs, Picassos, Carlo Crivellis and The Wilton Diptych in the mornings before going off to lunch or recording sessions.

I confirmed my first studio date with *Ripe*, the band whose door I'd knocked on during that initial meeting with *The Libs* at Rooze. I also fell in with a couple of New Zealand ex-pats, filmmaker Marc Swadel and his friend Blair Jollands who hired me to produce his solo project, *El Hula*.

Blair is a very talented songwriter and a bold singer with a classic technique. It certainly helped my mood that Boy George was his label boss and George offered that I could do all the mixing in his gorgeous old mansion overlooking Hampstead Heath. Boy George wanted to know what kind of budget I required to do this work, so I requested £3,000, arranged in piles of 50 Pound banknotes, and one very large plastic bag filled with high-quality hashish.

The first day Blair and I visited George's beautiful mansion for the mixing, my desires had been fulfilled perfectly and lay gleaming in front of us on the mantel over his large stone fireplace.

Security man, big Danny Yeates, brought me a band that he was looking after called *D.U.N.E.*, and we recorded together at Premises Studios in Hackney.

Thanks to the fact that *The Strokes* generously included my photo in their album *Is This It*, I was beginning to be recognized in London, which often led to party invitations or being handed a CD from musicians who wanted to work with me. I felt socially and musically connected with the London scene in a way that I hadn't experienced since my time in *Sky Cries Mary* during the exhilarating grunge-Seattle days.

While living in Su's loft, I got together with Carole, who grew up in Biarritz. I was strongly attracted by her outgoing personality, vivid imagination, adorable French accent and ricocheting energy. She was very fond of using the word "beyond", and we constantly laughed during our long, beautiful walks together.

Carole invited me to stay with her for a few weeks in the flat she shared with a Filthy MacNasty's regular named Peter Wolfe, aka Wolfman, and his girlfriend. I smoked many hash joints with Wolfman, his raspy voice telling me of trials and tribulations from his own musical journeys in London.

Based on this new love I was feeling, combined with all of the swirling jobs, parties and possibilities, I decided to find my own place to live in London. I needed to retrieve my belongings from New York and...DO IT!

30: Regent House

Since all the action that season was taking place in the vicinity of Filthy MacNasty's, I popped over to Hotblack Desiato estate agency in Islington. I asked if they had a suitable property to show me, where I could throw parties, make noise and not receive visits from the police.

One very chatty agent drove me to 28 Florence Street, unlocking the door to a small, semi-detached house. Well, that house certainly had enough rooms and outdoor space for whatever might be needed, socially, for the rest of the year. I happily signed the lease for Regent House, then flew back to Manhattan a few days later to vacate my apartment on Rivington Street.

I did not have any regret or feel sentimental as I cleared out my very tiny room on the Lower East Side, readying for future escapades in London. I figured that I'd be coming back and forth quite frequently, and besides—Regent House was much larger and more elegant than my old flat! I literally had about two suitcases of clothing to pack, and then headed to my storage unit to get my guitars and keyboards. I had too much in there to take aboard an airplane, so I arranged for it to be shipped to Islington. I still had boxes of my artwork, vinyl albums and more music equipment in a deep basement at Manny and Joe's farmhouse in Woodinville, but I would deal with that slowly, over time.

As I wandered around the East Village, I walked into a music shop on 3rd Street and saw a gorgeous Memory Moog polyphonic synthesizer in excellent condition. For some reason it wasn't extravagantly expensive and so I traded my Roland Jupiter 6 keyboard, which I rarely used, plus about $1,500 and acquired something very special to add to my sound creating arsenal in London.

While I was back in my old neighborhood, I had a chance to record three bands that I really liked. The first was *HQ*, a very fashionable group led by a friend of mine, Charles Wallace, whom I had known for years through the East Village nightlife. *HQ* presented an authentic 60s-mod sound.

Next, my wonderful sweetheart pals, *Unisex Salon*, starring the glowing, irreverent Kenyon Phillips (a radiant, tattooed angel brimming with sex and philosophy) and his partner in crime, Gina Lee. I had already been close friends with Kenyon for four years so I did my utmost to help *Unisex Salon* push their music forward. Before, while I still had Transporterraum, we'd spent many days recording their first songs, *Sun Don't Shine* and *Kidprint*. Kenyon and Gina had an endearing habit of always calling me "Young G", which still carries on to this day!

The third band I worked with during this brief whirlwind trip back to New York was *5 O'Clock Heroes*, led by charismatic British guitarist Antony Ellis. Incidentally, since I no longer had my own studio in New York, I recorded all three of these bands in a funky, well-set-up studio called Melody Lanes.

It was located in the Lower East Side and belonged to Jay and Justin Braun from experimental noise-pop group, *The Negatones*. It was there, at Melody Lanes, that I had the smiley-faced pleasure to experience my first-ever interview as a producer! This was for the April 2002 issue of *Sound On Sound* magazine and it became a sprawling mass of words covering my ill-fated church/studio in Seattle, pawning vintage keyboards to buy drugs, the history of my Arp Odyssey synthesizers and *Strokes* stuff galore.

From New York I did a little cross-country dash to Seattle, home to Bear Creek for a brief Pacific Northwest holiday. I grabbed some musical instruments that I had stored there, clothing and, oh, one more thing—I asked my close friend and favorite singer, Anne Hadlock (who was about to modify her name to Anna Mercedes), if she wanted to come live in England with me. I already knew she'd fit right in with the mayhem and madness which was kicking off in London. She then asked one of her best friends, Seattle supermodel Camellia Clouse, to come with her. Camellia, in turn, brought one of her best friends, Birmingham's own supermodel, Katherine Poulton. Well, all three bedrooms in our Islington pad were now spoken for and it was time to get the ball rolling.

Anna and I landed at Heathrow in late April and began marching up and down the Caledonian Road looking for odd, artsy used furniture, preparing Regent House for our next level rock 'n' roll escapades. Unfortunately, during the short amount of time I had been away from London my sweetheart, dear Carole, had moved on to someone else. I suffered a twinge of sadness, as I was looking forward to being together with her in my new home. The universe did assist my heart in healing from this sorrow, however, by introducing me to two lovely girls that just happened to be hanging out at Filthy MacNasty's. Kat and India were both musicians playing in a glamorous band called *The Vincent Fiasco*. I was suddenly keen to produce their songs and went to see them play several times.

When our home was finally furnished and decorated, Anna, Kath, Camellia and I decided that we should let people know we were in London, ready to rock. We invited *The Libertines*, Ebe Oke and other faves from Filthy MacNasty's over for a housewarming party. It was a divine evening! Fun was had by all, with ashtrays overflowing, beer, weed and tremendous conversations. In the middle of our party (according to the memory of Toby L) one young man had the audacity to turn off the music, announcing that he was about to entertain/enlighten us with a reading of his poetry! He pulled out a notebook and began his poem until it was drowned out by BOOOOs and the music was cranked up loud again. That young poet's name? Johnny Borrell, who we started seeing quite often at the house. He would soon be singing in a band called *Razorlight*.

We were off to a good start when, by day, young journalists and fanzine writers (Twinstar Revolution!) would come around interviewing to find out what I was doing in London, who my nice roommates were and all things *Strokes* related. Toby L was one of those writers and he was now becoming a good friend. Very soon after we moved in, he suggested that we start a club night together, as he already had his eye on many up-and-coming new artists in town. Toby believed that we would make an unusual and good team.

He located and secured a venue—The Buffalo Bar (under The Famous Cock Tavern) at Highbury & Islington tube station. He even came up with a name, The Basement Club, and the boss there, Stacey Thomas, gave us the fourth Thursday of every month. Our first event, in October, sold out weeks in advance and featured live sets from *El Hula* and Ed Harcourt with the illustrious Boy George doing DJ honors.[16] Toby L reminded me recently that whilst Boy George was DJing that night, with a huge spliff in his hands, he played the same record four times in a row AND, upon leaving, said unto Toby, who was sitting with his dad behind the ticket counter, "You're a Poof!" This was the Basement Club's first night and we knew we had a hit on our hands!

Word was going around that I was now living in London. I started receiving calls from real major label heads of A&R, who wanted to meet me. I had been waiting all my rock 'n' roll life for record companies to talk with me and this is how it went: I would grab a black cab which would take ages snaking through London's horrible traffic. Then enter a flashy, hip corporate office with a HUGE silver or gold logo on the wall of the lobby. I'd be asked to write my name and the date at the front desk, be given a NAME tag and finally get buzzed in through a security gate. Once through, a young junior executive would lead me up the elevators to the office of the A&R president. That president, with beaming smile, would welcome me grandly, arm extended for handshake. NEXT, he would send the junior executive out to fetch cups of tea for both of us.

---

[16] *El Hula* was Blair Jolland's band that I had been working with thanks to Boy George.

While waiting for the tea to cool, the A&R president's words rang:

"So, Gordon what are you doing here in London? And, by the way, congratulations with *The Strokes*... fantastic album!"

I'd tell him that I was looking for great bands to record and that I had discovered some really incredible artists in NYC and London that I'd already produced!

This would elicit a puzzled semi-smile, indicating that they might NOT be so interested in my brilliant discoveries. I refused to be phased by their mediocre reactions and cheerfully asked if I could show them some of these fabulous artists to consider for their label. As I played one song from each my favorite new bands, the A&R president's eyes would glaze over, wandering sadly out the window. Then they would immediately glance at the clock on their desk.

"Wow, that's really great!" they would say, unconvincingly, and stand up announcing a 3:30 meeting they had to run to! It was lovely to meet me and, by the way, if I didn't mind, could I sign a copy of *Is This It* for their office, and one for their kids? These meetings were weird and not worth the time spent in traffic in the black taxis. I did get to meet one of my heroes, Steve Lillywhite,[17] who was Managing Director of Universal Music Group at the time. He was wearing a white tennis outfit and totally zoned out as I showed him the music I liked.

In May 2002 Blair Jollands (*El Hula*) and I jumped over to Berlin for a team remix featuring producer Moses Schneider and his great drum-chopper, Benson Lauber. My vision was to deconstruct one of Blair's songs, then reassemble it on several different planets. We chose *Arena of My Soul*, one of *El Hula*'s best tracks, and went wild remixing the living hell out of it.

My contribution was to add Mini Moog parts and harsh metallic chimpanzee sounds. Blair's label, Things to Come, loved it and head honcho Boy George was kind enough to release

---

[17] Steve Lillywhite did astounding work producing debut albums for *Siouxsie and the Banshees* and *The Psychedelic Furs*.

Gordon Raphael presents: Top Hits Vol. 1, a compilation starring *Soundtrak, Unisex Salon, Satellites, Absinthee, Van Der Meer, El Hula, D.U.N.E., The AstroJet* and *Colour Twigs.* These were the fine bands and songs that my lame manager, Mr. X in New York, and those major label A&R presidents in London couldn't quite grasp. I started dreaming of my own record label so I could finance and develop bands I loved.

It was now the perfect time to help Anna Mercedes start her own new group. I used the time-honored method of advertising in the back of *NME* magazine saying,

"*Strokes* producer Gordon Raphael looking for reliable, talented musicians to form a band with New York singer."

That ad worked fast and well. Soon we had Alex on bass, Vyvyan and Toni on guitars and a brand-new Gordon on drums. Anna took some of the songs she'd written with *Petal* in NYC, reworking them for the new line-up now called *Miss Machine.* Vyvyan Wyld, one of their outrageous guitarists, created a striking white-on-black image that became *Miss Machine*'s logo, symbol and T-shirt.

That June, David Bowie was chosen to curate Meltdown Festival. Anna Mercedes and I enjoyed seeing *Fischerspooner* at the Royal Festival Hall and, at the afterparty, I ran into Boy George, in whose charming mansion I'd recently been mixing *El Hula*'s album. George was sitting next to a young dance music producer named Andy Chatterley and, while I spoke with George, Anna got into a conversation with Andy. Those two hit it off very well and soon Andy was frequently coming around to Regent House.

In fact, there was a constant flow of nice friends and new faces coming and going. Our roommate Kath had a steady boyfriend in Greg Griffin, whose band, *Proud Mary,* were the first signing by Noel Gallagher's label, Sour Mash. I had met our rare and beautiful housemate, Camellia Clouse, in the queue for PJ Harvey and Tricky back in Seattle when she was seventeen. She was a quirky fireball, sporting tattoos, wearing hilarious clothing and accessories she had sewn herself. Back then she worked at Betsey

Johnson's where I often visited her, as she was a lifelong best-friend of Anna Mercedes before becoming a highly photogenic fashion model.

Camellia had a super-expressive, lovely face and we often smoked weed together at Regent House while she complained,

"What's wrong with these London rocker boys? They don't seem to like girls!"

Needless to say, she eventually flew back to the USA to pursue her modeling and acting career where boys from New York to Hollywood fell in love with her, left and right.

Hanging out at Alan McGee's Death Disco at Notting Hill Arts Club every Wednesday night was always worthwhile. The venue, sizable yet intimate, was completely rammed every week with gorgeous people. New bands and DJs were featured and the music was never lacking in ATTITUDE. Alan McGee was very kind to me when I showed up, sweetly offering me a DJ slot of my own. My personal DJ philosophy is one that makes people clear the floor and run back to their tables 'till my set is over. For this unusual style, I've received both nasty looks and nasty notes (even nasty notes in Portuguese when I DJ'd in Brazil).

What is that philosophy? Play my favorite cherished songs from 1969 -1984, the ones that make my heart sing. Typically, someone will come up to me and ask for something current and trendy (in recent years it's almost always *Arctic Monkeys*), then I sadly tell them that their choice just isn't in my collection, before proceeding to crash the mood of the party with electric-bebop from Johnny McLaughlin's first solo album, *Extrapolation*. To my DJing credit, I do have a few songs that people always come running up to ask me about, because they don't know them but think they're awesome (*Penthouse and Pavement* long version by *Heaven 17* and *Hey DJ* by *The World's Famous Supreme Team*, thanks for asking!)

Exciting up-and-coming rock bands would play during the Death Disco nights, hand-picked by main man Alan McGee. I met so many cool, interesting people there and it was a place where I was treated as a B-list musical celebrity for the first time. I had only just come up from the Z-list, so this was a lofty, heady experience.

On one such Wednesday night, I was hanging out by the bar (I only drank their delicious, healthy fruit-juice combos) entertaining a small circle of friends mixed with a few new G. Raphael admirers, when suddenly, in total synchrony, their heads turned away from me and gazed towards the door.

In a breathless voice, one indie rock fan near me said,

"It's DAVE GROHL!!"

Crestfallen...me? Yes. All eyes in the room were aimed at Dave and his entourage. I felt like yesterday's fourth page news at that moment.... until Mr. Grohl spotted me from across the room and, with everyone still staring at him, made his way through the crowd to come talk—with me!

I had never met Mr. Grohl and guessed that he was going to say something about *The Strokes'* album. Dave turned to his associates and directly in front of my friends said (precisely),

"Hey guys—do you know Gordon? He was the keyboard player in *Sky Cries Mary* and they were the BEST band in Seattle!"

Vindication. Proud smile. Evening MADE.

Another night out at Death Disco, I was queuing to hand my jacket in to the coat check when I noticed a phenomenally beautiful Asian woman working there. I tried to be cool, smile and small talk which, sadly, is not my best skill. This very cute woman responded cheerfully, small-talking back in a relaxed, natural fashion. From time to time during the night, when I happened to notice that she wasn't busy, I'd walk over and we talked more. She told me her name was Sarang, that she was from Korea and her name in English means LOVE. She also said that she wasn't really convinced that the indie rock lifestyle, as modeled at Death Disco, was of any interest to her whatsoever. I found that FASCINATING and, by the end of the night, she was leaving with me in a black cab.

214

It was an outstanding 'one night experience' of making love which, as anyone who really knows me will tell, didn't happen many times in my life. The next day I brought Sarang along to the video shoot for my own slippery punk-rock song, *2-Track Mind*. At first, she was reluctant to appear in this video but, at the end of the day, she gave us an incredible, wild dance performance against a silver wall, which is on film for the world to see. After that, to my dismay, I never saw her again.

Metro Club was located next to Tottenham Court Road tube station. The Blow Up club-night there presented important new bands including *Yeah Yeah Yeahs*, *The Killers*, *Interpol* and *The Kills*. That place was a social and musical hot spot for me and I went almost every week. One night, a young blond guy walked up to me and began asking many probing questions. My first impression was that he was overbearing and stood too close to me. I was high, as always, and tried not to pay attention to him. But he kept coming back and barraging me with more questions in an interview style, but with no tape recorder. His name was Paulo and he was soon to have a strange impact on my life.

A few days later he knocked on my door at Regent House, which was odd for I certainly had not given him my home address! My roommates and a few other guests were wandering around, so I let him in. He just sat down on the couch and began chatting with whoever was near him.

Paulo started showing up to our parties, often cornering me with more questions. I actually wondered if he was planning to write a book about me. He came all the way from Liverpool which was a long trek to London. Occasionally he'd need to crash on our couch, staying overnight until the trains ran again in the morning. Once, during his extensive 'information gathering', he asked me what I wanted most in life and one of the things I mentioned was "a record label of my own."

I almost had a label of my own in Seattle a long ago. My friend Tor Midtskog played guitar in *Colour Twigs* with me and also performed his own music under the name, *The Violet Caste*. He designed a very cool logo and we wanted to start our record company called, Ars Divina. By that time, I already had a briefcase full of cassettes, which included my own projects, Tor's music and several other bands I had recorded. We were in the process of calling investors, trying to get Ars Divina off the ground when, at that exact moment, *Sub Pop* formed and quickly became the center of attention in our town.

Two weeks later came another knock on the door and it was Paulo again. I wasn't so pleased to see him, but he asked if he could come in claiming that he had some big news for me. He told me that he'd walked into the offices of SONY at Great Marlborough Street in Soho and, using my name, had convinced them to give me my own record label!

What the-actual-fuck?

I had no idea how to accomplish that myself, nor that it could even have been possible—yet this twenty-year-old kid from Liverpool...walked in off the street and DID it. At first, I thought he was lying and full of shit, but he produced a business card with the name Mark Chung, under the company name, Sony S.I.N.E. I called that Mark Chung and discovered to my amazement that he had been the bassist for highly influential Noise/Industrial band, *Einstürzende Neubauten* (German for *Collapsing New Buildings*). Every punk and kid on the sidewalks of Seattle had worn the *Einstürzende Neubauten* logo and that crazy graphic of a urinating horse emblazoned on the back of their black leather jackets. Mark affirmed that he, indeed, thought it was a great idea for me to have my own label distributed and funded through SONY. He then asked when I'd like to come in for a meeting. I ran over to meet Mark Chung that week and left the Sony offices carrying contracts to sign PLUS the challenge of figuring out what I wanted to call my imprint.

While smoking joints I filled in my notebook with three pages, three columns each, of whacky, stupid, horrible or wonderful names that drifted across my mind. Each of these potential names had something to do with my personal 'VALUES'. I went to this supposedly healthy restaurant, Giraffe, on Essex Road almost every morning for breakfast and, one decisive day, Toby L, Paulo and Vyvyan from *Miss Machine* were there with me as I read them my top twenty favorite potential record company names, whittled down from two hundred. When I hit Shoplifter Records, Toby said,

"Stop there, that has a ring to it, go for that one."

What made me come up with Shoplifter?

This story goes back to my first attempt to make it big in New York, back in 1989. My then girlfriend, Debe, met and befriended a small group of Hungarians in the East Village. Every day, Bela, Shumair and Gundi would dress up in expensive, designer suits, rent a car and then drive all around New York and New Jersey stealing CDs from record shops. CDs were still a relatively new format then and quite expensive, $12 on average. Their *modus operandi* was that, while two of them would browse through the CD aisles, Bela would approach the cashier and start asking really impressive music-related questions.

"Do you have Brian Eno's *Before and After Science?*"

Or, "Can you recommend the best albums produced by Tony Visconti?"

While Bela baffled the people behind the counter with his brilliance, the other two would use razor knives which were tucked in their designer sleeves, to remove security tags. They had the skills to fill up the legs of their trousers AND stuff the inside of their shirts with stolen CDs. After they had taken as much as they could carry, they'd calmly walk out to their 'drive-away car' as they called it. By 5 pm they'd return with that car full of HOT CDs and take them to a few different record shops in Greenwich Village.

The managers of those specific record shops would pay them well, still saving money when compared with the normal wholesale price. With cash in hand, the Hungarian crew, anywhere between three and five of them, would take a taxi past Tompkins Park into Alphabet City to score a bundle (ten bags) of heroin and a bundle of cocaine. Then they would walk directly over to OUR apartment which was conveniently located nearby. Still wearing their expensive suits, they would roll up their sleeves (and ours), proceeding to inject.... well never mind, until 7am, when I had to get ready for my job as a 'hip' receptionist at an upscale ad agency. That receptionist job, along with my slender grasp on reality, did not last long. Hence the name—Shoplifter Records. That's it, really.

Flash forward to London 2002. Between my production work and going out almost every night (Metro, 12 Bar, Death Disco, Water Rats, Camden Barfly, 333 Mother Bar, The Hope & Anchor and *Lib*'s bassist John Hassall's favorite: The King's Head Theatre Bar), the year flew quickly.

My Christmas holiday plan was to visit New York and party in wild abandon for one week, then fly over to Seattle and relax at Bear Creek. Mere days before leaving London I got a call from my friend Alan Bezozi in Manhattan. He inquired when I might be visiting NYC again, so I told him,

"Funnily enough, this week!"

Alan then wanted to know if I'd be interested in producing an excellent pianist who sang her own songs, that he'd been working with lately. I told him,

"No, Alan, sorry, I've had enough of working! I've been going hard all year and produced so many great bands here. I just want to party and have fun when I get to New York."

Alan, not to be deterred (he's a REAL New Yorker), then asked,

"Well, will you at least come by and meet her? She's a twenty-two-year-old Russian girl and she is super talented."

Something about the idea of a twenty-two-year-old Russian girl who played the piano amazingly well did appeal to me and so I replied,

"Ok fine Alan, I'll meet her, but I'm not going to do any work, alright?"

31: Reginka (The Paperback Mummy)

Back in NYC, Alan Bezozi invited me to a spacious recording studio called TMF, on 13th Street near Union Square. He gave me a tour of the control room which was impressively equipped and featured a massive SSL mixing console as its centerpiece. A gorgeous 1927 Steinway B grand piano stood proudly in the huge live room, which radiated pure magic. Then Alan led me to a tiny room, just big enough for an upright piano and, while he was showing me that space, a young woman arrived. I was introduced to Regina Spektor.

She was dressed very 'bohemian artiste', had a head full of thick, amazing reddish hair and had a happy wide smile on her face. I shook her hand and asked,

"So, what do you do?"

She reached into her shoulder bag and pulled out a single drumstick. Then she took off her coat, positioned an old wooden chair on the right front side of the upright piano and then sat down on an old piano bench. After arranging all of that, she began banging the stick on the wooden chair using her right hand, creating the sound of galloping horses. With her left hand she played some mean piano, combining modern classical music with rock 'n' roll. Then, Regina opened her mouth to sing the MOST interesting, weird lyrics and all the while her head was up looking at me directly in the eyes.

Thirty seconds into that song (*Poor Little Rich Boy*) I thought, "THE WORLD IS GOING TO LOVE THIS!"

By the time it ended I was already burning up to record this person's music. I asked Alan if we could start recording immediately and he answered yes.

An unusual vision of exactly how I wanted this song to sound had already entered my mind, so I asked studio assistant, Josh Stoddard, to bring me seven microphones, observing that Alan looked amused that I would require so many for such a minimal song.

I placed two mics in the open lid of the upright piano and chose TMF Studios' amazing Neumann U67 condenser mic for Regina's voice, knowing that it would also pick up some of the rich, warm sound of the piano. Then I set up one microphone to focus on the stick hitting the chair and one placed up in the air to catch all the sounds in the room (with the singing too). My next trick was to add another mic up in the air capturing those same room sounds but, this time, the room mic would be wired into an old 1970s Fender Twin Reverb guitar amp located outside that room and down a hallway. Finally, the last mic went in front of that amp's speaker. Regina wished that we would record her song to tape and, since many of my London sessions were being recorded that way, I was more than happy to hear that.

It only took her a few tries to get a marvelous take of that song and, when she heard the play-back in the big control room, she was both satisfied and excited, and so was I!

She then wondered if we could try recording one more song, with both hands on the piano this time, called 8th *Floor*. For this composition she sang mostly in English but then branched out into her native Russian for part of it. I tried adding a few of my classic synthesizer sounds to that one but, in the end, Regina decided that she didn't need spaceships landing in the middle of her song, so they were erased. We all hugged when the session was over, the perfect ending to an abundantly musical year.

Twenty-four hours later, I was back in my spiritual home at Bear Creek during Christmastide, when the whole music industry goes into a quiet slumber. I made several phone calls to Regina, whom I was already calling "Reginka" for no reason other than it sounded silly and more Russian to me. I told her that I'd been listening to the two songs we'd recorded together, that I was completely thrilled with her music and that I'd really love to record MORE with her. She told me that she'd been listening to

The Strokes record and had become a total fan of their music, mentioning that she was particularly inspired and impressed with Julian's voice. Reginka also wished there was a way that we could work on an EP's worth of songs together, so I said I'd speak with TMF Studios and see if we could make this happen. After a chat with co-producer Alan Bezozi, I postponed my flight back to London and we reserved five more days at the studio.

Our first day back at TMF in the brand-new year 2003 was a smiley joyous reunion indeed. Alan and I agreed to complete an EP with Regina and we offered to pay all of the expenses up-front.

Later, we'd try and sell this potential masterpiece to a record label and recoup our 'investment'. We continued using two-inch tape on TMF's wonderful Otari MTR-90 MKII 24-track machine.

Right away, Reginka delighted us with her song *Carbon Monoxide*. For this we invited Oren Bloedow, from the atmospheric NY band *Elysian Fields*, to play guitar, and AB (Alan Bezozi) played powerful, crashing drums—all performed live with Regina's piano and voice as the song went down.

The next piece she chose to capture on tape was a bawdy, saloon style number called, appropriately enough, *Sailor's Song*. Her words painted scenes of a girl who would kiss you until your lips were bleeding, with a rousing chorus of "Mary Anne's a bitch!"

Bathtubs, blackjack, Kentucky, anchors and missiles are all mentioned in this crazy, moody song. Alan added some odd metallic percussion on that one and, in the middle, Regina and I set up a trash barrel on the studio floor, put a big brick inside on the bottom and, with two vintage German microphones overhead, smashed two empty beer bottles against the brick, perfectly on the beat! Recording the sound of glass exploding in a classic New York studio was a real treat.

Song #3 was *Düsseldorf* which describes hilarious, surreal adventures in many different European cities. I wondered if Regina had really been to all those places or if she was just doing some advanced creative writing? Though she tried a number of times, Regina never performed that song up to her own standards of excellence and so we didn't capture it!

Her goal was for every single piano note and expression, plus all the vocal nuances, to be perfect—otherwise the song would be immediately erased. She chose to sing and play piano simultaneously for every song as it was going to tape and was firmly against editing of any kind.

I had a challenging vision for Regina Spektor's music. Upon watching her play *Poor Little Rich Boy* for the first time, I tried to imagine what we could do that would make her songs really stand out and sound unlike any other piano-playing singer-songwriter. My instant mental answer was to approach it like a punk rock album. Since she was already going way out with her stories and piano abilities, I wanted to accentuate the aggressive nature of her creative world, rather than present it in a charming, relaxed fashion. I set the microphones and preamps in such a way that when she sang softly, intimately, the sound would be warm and inviting. But when she began to hit the piano hard, raising her voice to yell or get bigger—that change of intensity would slam the needles into the red. The results sounded like everything in the music, including the air in the room, was heating up, becoming emotionally charged.

I faced one big challenge in creating a good sound for Regina. Since she was such a mighty, powerful pianist and we had the lid of the old Steinway open to fill the room, I didn't want too much of that piano sound to go directly into the large diaphragm Neumann microphone I'd selected for her to sing into. I made a barrier by taking a few of the studio's couch cushions, cramming them on top of the piano between the lid and the keys. This funny sound fortress was rather unsightly, but it actually worked!

We had one day off so I wandered over to the Wiz Kid Management office on 7th Street, across from Tompkins Square Park. I dropped in unannounced, hoping I would catch some of the guys from *The Strokes* hanging out. Since it was now January

2003 and we'd recorded *Is This It* a year and a half before, I kept waiting to hear news about beginning a second album. It seemed to me that the band would want to keep up the momentum, based on the fabulous reception given to their first album.

I walked in, introducing myself to a new employee I hadn't met yet. She pointed me to the back office where Ryan Gentles and Juliet Joslin were working. They were both happy to see me but were super busy, offering that I could wait in the lounge area for some of the band members who would be coming over soon. I looked around the office glancing at the *NME* awards, a big TV and stereo, a world map on the wall with pins in each city *The Strokes* had visited on tour and a large green chalkboard. When I looked closer at that chalkboard, my eyes fell on a disturbing combination of words,

"Meeting with Nigel Godrich Thursday 1/9."

I had a sudden heart sinking, accompanied by a throat tightening feeling.

"God damn, I can't believe this is happening.... again," my brain moaned.[18]

Moments later, Fabrizio Moretti and Julian Casablancas entered the office and, when they saw me, walked right over and hugged me. They expressed surprise that I was there, wondering, "When did you get back into town?"

We chatted very briefly before I asked them what was going on with the second album, pointing to the chalkboard.

Julian told me that they wanted to try working with Nigel Godrich because they loved the drum sounds on the *Radiohead* albums. I came up with a sad sounding,

"Oh, I see."

Then he interjected, "Well, you know us, maybe we just feel better if we fire someone before we make an album, who knows?"

---

[18] Nigel Godrich is the ultra-famous producer of *Radiohead*. I didn't know *The Strokes* even liked *Radiohead*, and I was instantly flooded with the fear that if they started working with him they would consider him a much better producer than me.

I left a short time later, pacing around my familiar Avenue A territory, feeling a bit let down and nerve-wracked.

I had also scheduled an afternoon meeting uptown at MY manager's office. It was starting to wear on me that, in the first year and a half that I'd been signed with Mr. X, he'd gotten me zero jobs. On top of that, he'd made zero progress with any of the bands I produced on my own, the ones I'd asked him to help sign to record labels in the USA. In spite of his non-performance, that creepy guy was still taking twenty percent of my income at all times.

When I confronted him with my displeasure (I'd written and called him several times, but this was our first face-to-face meeting in a long time), he repeated his line,

"Well, *The Strokes* aren't really considered a mainstream success here in America and none of the labels I met with are interested in the bands you have produced so far."

I considered that particular meeting to be "Bummer #2".

Thankfully, that evening presented a very different world. Regina had invited Alan and I to see her perform at a magnificent venue called Tonic, on Norfolk Street near Delancey. She'd built up a loyal following by regularly playing at the Sidewalk Cafe, home to the Antifolk movement, spearheaded by Lach, which was also where *The Moldy Peaches* honed their stage show. Regina's concert that night was jaw-dropping and spectacular in every way. She looked radiant with her wild hair and self-styled fashions and the sound person there (my dear friend Kari Erickson, from Seattle) made every song shine brightly. The acoustics at Tonic were marvelous, adding to the sparkle in the air that night.

Announcing that she'd "Just finished writing this song today," Regina initiated one of the most haunting piano melodies I've ever heard, and then started singing about her KIDS! Well, I was so puzzled because again I didn't know if she truly had children? or if she was making it up with such conviction that we believed her? Suddenly that song became frightening, as it transformed into a doctor's office with a very serious conversation about cancer treatment—and Goddamn, this is a girl playing a piano so why am I feeling so uncomfortable and freaked out inside? The story finally morphed into a dream about riding in a limousine and "Crispy crispy Benjamin Franklin" kept popping in every few moments.

Everything about this song was melting my mind. It was exactly the kind of risk-taking adventure my inner MUSIC FAN craves, always. As this composition named *Chemo-Limo* progressed, it got so magical and GREAT that Alan and I were literally punching each other on the shoulder as if to say,

"Can you believe we are actually hearing this right now?? How phenomenal is this song?? Can we even comprehend how great Regina is??"

The next day we recorded that *Chemo-Limo* song and I felt inspired to push the sound even further. I invented a treatment where one of the special Neumann microphones, placed high above the piano, was fed through a rotating speaker in a wooden Leslie cabinet, which was sequestered in a small isolation booth nearby. The slightly distorted, crackling Leslie made the old Steinway piano sound like it was subconsciously swimming underwater, quavering into a mild hallucination. I thought that this special sound really complemented the 'dream within a dream' nature of the storyline.

On the last day, we recorded another song for her EP. *The Flowers* was another piano tour de force. Perhaps channeling the spirit of other historic Russian composers (Kabalevsky or Rachmaninoff?), Regina showed us how she could make floating melodic sounds with her voice, without using words, and also create percussion sounds with her mouth in a jolting off-rhythm against the piano parts. As in every song Regina had shown us, her lyrics were superb feats of writing. In *The Flowers* she sings,

> "The flowers you gave me are rotting
> And still I refuse to throw them away.
> Some of the bulbs never opened quite fully
> They might, so I'm waiting and staying awake."

And, in the second verse,

> "The papers around me are piling and twisting,
> Regina the paperback mummy.
> What then?
> I'm taking the knife to the books that I own
> And I'm chopping and chopping and boiling soup from stone."

This was CRAZY stuff that I was thrilled to hear for the first time and elated to be capturing on tape. I couldn't wait for the rest of the world to hear these songs.

During our final lunch break, I took Regina to meet a close friend of mine from the early Seattle music scene, David d'Heilly. He had moved to Tokyo in his early twenties, demonstrating his huge intellect by quickly learning Japanese. Then he worked his way up from being Madonna's translator to an expansive career in culture and international art dealing.

David had always been highly creative and was now in New York producing multimedia installations with Japanese designers. We met for a meal at Balthazar, in that intoxicating Bohemian atmosphere. Amid much laughter and telling stories, he told us that David Byrne was sharing his office space downtown and suggested that we all get together for a drink later in the evening. The first five *Talking Heads* records were massive inspirations for me and I was fortunate to see their very first Seattle concert at the Paramount Theatre. David Byrne and Brian Eno's album, *My Life in The Bush of Ghosts*, opened everyone's mind to what was possible with advanced technology, rhythm and human music. So... YES, I was excited for this chance to meet him.

After finishing our recording session at TMF, Regina and I walked to the Lower East Side to join the two Davids at a bar. Since this had been our last day in the studio, I now had five blazing new Regina Spektor songs in my laptop and was due to head back to London the next morning. Dave D'Heilly introduced us to David Byrne who was way more friendly and conversational than I would have expected, having studied old films of early *Talking Heads* performances at CBGB! Things were going so well that I dared to ask him if he'd give a listen to one of Regina's songs. He nodded and so I picked *The Flowers* (no pun intended). Once he'd plugged his own iPod earphones into my laptop, I pressed PLAY. When *The Flowers* finished, David Byrne smiled, saying it was an excellent song and that he really liked it. This bought great joy to Regina, Dave d'Heilly and I! Thus ended a Christmas vacation in the U.S., where I had promised myself not to do ANY work.

32: May I Borrow Your Bass?

Stepping back into Regent House, my roommates Camellia, Kath and Anna Mercedes were in high spirits as Anna's band, *Miss Machine*, was set to perform their very first show at The Basement Club! This would be the third event hosted by Toby and me at Buffalo Bar and I was glad to help my close friend and former band partner Anna have this showcase for her latest project.

Her guitarist, Vyvyan Wyld, always overflowing with energy, was now staying at our house, having come to London directly from her family home in Cumbria, three hundred miles away. Over the next few months, The Basement Club would feature live sets from *Electric Soft Parade*'s Tom White, *The Tenderfoot*, *The Libertines* (a boisterous acoustic set under the name *Libertones*), Blair Jollands from *El Hula*, *Ripe*, *Delays* and *Kill Kenada*. Not only did our club night establish itself as a hotly anticipated monthly social event, but it was already serving as the perfect setting to present the latest bands I'd been producing. *El Hula* and *Ripe* were among the very first bands I'd recorded in London and *Kill Kenada* was an explosive new discovery.

Alex Sexton was their manager and he'd originally contacted me to record a young, sophisticated band called *Machina*. We recorded two *Machina* songs at The Garden Studio and it went so well that Alex subsequently brought me *Kill Kenada*. The Garden was a brilliant recording studio founded by *Ultravox*'s John Foxx and then owned by *The The*'s Matt Johnson. It was located in the trendy-most area of Shoreditch, next to a wine superstore and a Roman-themed gay sauna. Other than that, the studio was also notable for its massive Neve console, 24-track tape recorder, classic microphones collection and secret weapon, Matt Hyde, a young, sharp-witted engineer who worked there.

I began bringing a steady stream of bands to The Garden early in 2003. I loved *Kill Kenada*. Our spontaneous, creative chemistry resulted in an ear-shattering EP and, later, a full album. They hailed from Bognor Regis, a seaside town on England's south coast. That name sounded humorous to me and the band made fun of their hometown constantly. Bassist Tim Smithen was also the singer, with a voice that could range from dusty poetry to a blood-curdling howl reminiscent of a locomotive screeching off its steel tracks. Danny Williams (they were all incredibly young) was one of the LOUDEST, most innovative guitarists I had ever met. In fact, one day while attending a *Kill Kenada* gig at The Barfly in Camden, I got so distracted by a group of drunken-overly-friendly rocker girls, that I forgot to stuff toilet paper in my ears (protection!) I was punished for this mistake by an annoying high-pitched ringing sound in my ears that lasted three years!

Their resident drum maniac, Stewart (Stoo) Fairhurst, was a complete show unto himself, flailing arms and flying hair, with more power and energy than should be advisable or legal. At the risk of losing fans (for Stoo, and for me), he reminded me of one of my favorite drummers ever, Carl Palmer from *ELP*, except reincarnated as a wiry, insane speed-punk.

Everything I ever produced with *Kill Kenada* was effortless and came out finished-sounding after one or two takes. You may find my favorite K.K. songs out there in the world somewhere: *Choke/Eastern Sun, Massachusetts Murder Medallions* (which has a sick video with them performing inside of a locked, fast-moving truck, falling all over and bashing themselves against the walls), *Hit the Floor, Kill Konversation, Sado Maso, We Got Down, Write Notes* and *Tear It Up.* Hmm, that's most of them!

By January of 2003, Anna Mercedes had decided to move out of our party-centric Regent House and was now living close by on Devonia Road, right off Essex Road with Andy Chatterley. Camellia and Kath had also moved out by then, so it made no sense to keep that place by myself. Andy and Anna suggested I move into a spare room in their flat and I soon made that my new home. Regent House had served exceedingly well as a foundation for launching many great projects and friendships for Anna and me.

That February there was the massive protest rally against the imminent war in Iraq, this was a direct reaction against Tony Blair's speech warning of "bloody consequences." I'd met a statuesque, dark-haired beauty named Emily Mann at Death Disco and we marched together along with 750,000 others through Piccadilly Circus and around Bloomsbury. My new friend Emily studied at the Bartlett School of Architecture, later becoming a successful fashion model and bass player for electronic band, *CLIENT*.

Following *Machina* and *Kill Kenada*, the next artist I bought to The Garden was none other than that highly accomplished powerhouse of musical innovation, Regina Spektor. We had never stopped communicating via phone and email in the three months since those miraculous recording days in New York at TMF Studios. Our new plan was to record more songs towards rounding out a full album. Two of these new songs required hiring a string quartet and, on another, she wanted to go completely crazy, with an entirely different sound. She envisioned a discordant, full-tilt punk band playing in shocking contrast with sections of delicate piano and sweet singing. That composition was called *Your Honor*, which was recorded live as always. Who do you think were the guest stars, providing that tumultuous punk sound? Yes, *Kill Kenada*, of course!

Regina tried to record her song *Düsseldorf* ten more times, but there would always be one word or one piano note that wasn't exactly the way she wanted.

"In Düsseldorf I met a clown, his nose—it was red."

These were the first words and the entire song was so amusing and cool on the piano, with such a funny storyline in the lyrics, that I grew desperate to capture it for her album. Though she tried as hard as she could to perform *Düsseldorf*, we were both disappointed when she just couldn't nail it in accordance with her own expectations.

I took a deep breath, suggesting we could use the best version we had so far and edit the part she didn't like. After all, there was only one error and this kind of edit is a normal, widely used technique. She looked at me like I was a deranged criminal for even suggesting such a bastardization (I usually call it a Frankenstein technique for it's obviously creating life from spare parts!), but I was confident that I could do it flawlessly.

I had so much experience editing, dating back to when Alan Bezozi first taught me how to rhythmically slice-up drums at Chateau Relaxo. I suggested that she go take a break while I worked meticulously on this edit to show her how, with magic and patience, it could be done. Matt Hyde transferred the two best versions from tape to Pro Tools and I made two cuts. Those audio regions needed to be moved around a bit, massaged into the PERFECT place and then crossfaded so that no bad clicking sounds could possibly be heard.

Wearing good headphones, I checked this edit several times before calling Regina back to listen. I asked her to look away from the screen so she wouldn't know where I placed the edit and handed her the headphones. She looked concerned from the get-go, but I pressed play and waited for her to LIKE it and smile.

When the edit came, she looked like someone had just slapped her in the face. Regina threw off the headphones shouting,

"What was that?? What happened?... I heard the air change!"

And that was that. She didn't try to play *Düsseldorf* again on those sessions and I certainly never attempted another edit on her songs.

The last two compositions she presented were *Us* and *Somedays*. The live takes of voice and piano went really smoothly and quickly, yielding excellent versions of both. The production method for most of her album was a process of setting up microphones and then dialing in a very warm, full sound using all the great vintage equipment that both TMF and The Garden studios provided.

Then my main job was to make sure Regina was comfortable with the headphone balance and that she liked the piano and vocal sounds. From that point on it was almost Zen-like. I simply needed to sit quietly while she played her music and sang, until she let me know she was absolutely satisfied. I would always, always say, "Wow!" or "Oh My God, that was AMAZING!" when she finished each song. This was not to hurry the process along or flatter her in any way. It's just that every time she performed one of her songs it was an artistic revelation of the highest human order.

It didn't matter what I might say, no, not one bit, for she knew exactly what she was looking for and knew immediately if she had achieved it or not. Sitting still was a very good test for my mind, producer skills and patience, which I'm famous for having very little of. I needed to wait for Regina to perform her music the way she wanted, and not rush in with suggestions or attempts to 'fix it'.

Since I was still relatively new to London and also since none of the so-called indie-rock bands I'd recorded required string quartets, I had to rely on suggestions from other people when it came time to hire classically trained musicians. We found out about a group of string players that were highly recommended and had even performed with Prince. I figured, if they were good enough for His Purple Majesty then they would fit with *Us* (and *Somedays*).

Three young women (two violins and one viola) and a guy named Merlin who played cello, came to work with us at The Garden. After pleasant greetings, I busied myself setting six old German microphones to soak up classic string tones along with a warm room sound. Since the songs already had the piano and voice recorded, Matt Hyde opened up six new tracks on the tape machine. As we dialed in the sounds of the string quartet, Regina sat at the piano showing these guest musicians the chord progressions for her song. She sang melodies for each of the string players to write down, as their parts. I was sitting in the control room with Matt, casually overhearing this process and I couldn't help but notice that while the string players were learning their parts, for some reason, they were really out of tune!

For strings, it's incredibly difficult, yet essential, to play precisely in tune. It IS like rocket science! String musicians learn how to use their ears to hear micro-details of pitch. Professional string players are required to stay in tune to the best of their ability, whether in an orchestra, jazz band or anything else. I gave them the benefit of the doubt, telling myself that they'd pay EXTRA attention to tuning up once they'd seriously learned their parts.

We started with *Somedays*. Once Regina was happy with the parts she'd spontaneously written for them, she came to join Matt and I in the control room showing a doubtful expression on her face. The string quartet then spent some time tuning up and we tried one take of the song.

Unfortunately, my ears were still rattled and miserable from being vibrated the wrong way by their out of tune instruments! I went out and asked them to please double check their intonation and pitch, and that we'd try again. I was fairly patient and kind, just doing my best professional job. They played once more, but still sounded abrasive and shrill from poorly tuned instruments. I became exasperated, as this string quartet was taking £1,000 of our budget and renting time in that studio was certainly not cheap either. I gave them ONE more chance. Still maintaining a professional smile, I asked them to tune up again and give it another try. Still sounded shit. With my patience gone, temper rising, I called them into the control room and asked them to take a seat.

Matt Hyde played the tape from the beginning, I walked over to the stunning Neve console, pushing 'mute' buttons which would let us hear one string player at a time over Regina's performance. My words:

"Violin 1, sorry, out of tune, I can't use it."

"Violin 2, listen, not in tune—can't use it!"

"Viola? Check it out, that's all played out of tune."

"Cello? Wow, Merlin, that's awesome, really nice playing and perfectly in tune, thank you!"

I told the quartet that I needed to send them home and that I wasn't happy about our time together. One of the girls cheekily asked,

"You're still going to pay us, right?"

I answered yes (but never did send them a check). As they were putting on their coats to leave, Merlin came up and confided to me that he also worked with another quartet that was really ON and they could come in the next day. I totally trusted him because of his exemplary cello playing. Merlin did return as promised with the 4 x 4 String Quartet and they nailed those string parts, bringing Regina's album *Soviet Kitsch* to a beautiful, higher level.

Regina was staying at our house on Devonia Road, sleeping on the couch during this trip. Toby L helped to secure her two first gigs in the UK, at 12 Bar Club and then at Kashmir Klub. She took the stage at both places with a rented Korg electronic grand piano and a wooden bar stool to smack while playing *Poor Little Rich Boy*.

When the London audience saw a cute young woman climb on stage to sit at a piano, they naturally just started talking louder, ordering drinks and clinking their glasses. The distracting crowd noise was growing, shall we say. Regina, smiling ear to ear, shyly introduced herself and then started playing some quiet yet demanding piano melodies. A touch of Beethoven mixed with *The Moldy Peaches* kind of vibe. Two minutes into her singing, the crowd fell under her spell, sitting still in rapt attention. She had them in the palm of her hand for the rest of the night, to rapturous applause.

This happened exactly the same way at both shows. The 12 Bar Club was a cramped wooden beer hall on Denmark Street,[19]

---

[19] When I was living in London, Denmark Street was a huge concentration of musical instrument shops, especially vintage guitars. In the past, it was a bustling center for musicians and songwriters: *Sex Pistols* lived there, David Bowie, *The Rolling Stones* and Elton John worked

while the Kashmir Klub, large and stylish, was packed with people eager for hot entertainment. She sold self-made CDs of her two previous albums, *Songs* and *11:11*, also signing autographs for her brand-new converts.

Toby L, his dad Roy and Emily Mann were with me for both concerts and we just loved every minute of watching Regina win over these audiences. When Kashmir Klub was finished, we all headed over to Roy's car for a lift back to Islington. While we were walking, a car drove by and slowed down. Someone opened a window and shouted adoringly,

"Oh, Regina you were so amazing tonight. Do you have any CDs for sale?"

She opened her shoulder bag, took out two CDs and got their money, with everyone smiling so much.

My own record label was starting to take off. Mark Chung at SONY gave me the green light to take *Miss Machine* to Miloco Studios.[20] We chose four songs to be released on vinyl and decided to use Miloco's 2-inch tape machine for that classic rock 'n' roll tone. The first single ever to blast off from Shoplifter Records would be *All American Girl* b/w *Runaway*,[21] both originally written for Anna's former NYC band, *Petal*, but given new life by *Miss Machine*. The second release would be *Not Another Pop Queen* b/w *Worthy*. The A-side was written by Vyvyan Wyld and Anna back at Regent House, while the B-side was a cosmic

---

there. Now almost all traces of that are gone.

[20] The Miloco company looked after and booked several really excellent studios in London. They were always extremely friendly and efficient to deal with, and both the equipment and engineers that came with the studios were brilliant/top notch! I worked at all three of the studios they ran at the time, including my favorite, The Garden Studios. Now they operate ultra-high-end studios around the world.

[21] b/w stands for "backed with", which was common in rock journalism back when singles were mainly on vinyl, ran at 45 RPM and featured two different songs, one on each side.

Seattle grunge hit, written and recorded by one of our favorite bands, *Lucky Me*.

The singer of that band was Nylene, who was a total inspiration to Anna and me when we first started working together. *Lucky Me*'s first album is called *GLUE* and if you ever find and hear it you shall be severely ROCKED.

All four *Miss Machine* songs came out sounding pleasingly abrasive and glam electric, in an exciting 'slap-you-in-the-face' way. *All American Girl* was pressed on hot pink leopard print vinyl and we shot a trashy, provocative video as well. In those days there was still an MTV and MTV2 that sometimes smiled on underground, alternative rock, so we were hoping for good fortune in promoting *Miss Machine* and Shoplifter Records.

I would frequently bump into Paulo hanging around at the clubs and he always came over to talk with me. He told me he had his own band in Liverpool and they wound up hiring me to take the train up from London to produce six songs. Naturally, my inner Beatles fan was thrilled to be musically employed in their famous hometown. His band was very young, but I enjoyed working with them and their songs rocked with a modern, serious outlook.

Since Paulo had shown fortitude and gumption in procuring my label deal with Sony, I decided to offer him a job running the day-to-day business of the label. He would attend meetings and liaise with Sony while I happily searched for new bands to produce and sign. Paulo was pleased about this arrangement and requested a new laptop and cellphone for use on the job.

I thought it would be hilarious in a true 'Gordon Raphael way' to send a twenty-year-old kid from Liverpool to deal with the more established old timers in the UK music biz. On the other hand, I certainly didn't enjoy him talking about *Oasis* so frequently, always trying to play me their songs in the hope that I might like one of them.

Toby L told me he'd never been on a plane before so, to thank him for being an amazing friend, I brought him to Mallorca to see *Satellites* play at a swanky, high-class theatre in Artà on the north-east coast. We enjoyed a few days off at singer Jordi's family home in the remote village of Maria de la Salut, basically going to the beach and smoking porros day and night. In fact, I was driving Jordi's car to the beach one day when I became alarmed seeing, in the side mirror, plumes of smoke coming from our vehicle! I was afraid something had gone wrong with the engine when in reality it was our own wafting clouds of marijuana smoke trailing out the rear window. It was great being with Toby in Mallorca but I was disappointed with the *Satellites* show. In my mind, sitting down on plush seats in a classy modern theatre was not a good setting for the brooding intensity of their music.

When I got home to Islington, I received an unsettling phone call from *The Strokes'* manager, Ryan Gentles. He told me that Nikolai had requested to borrow my bass, the 1972 Fender Precision bass he'd used on *Is This It* in my old studio. I felt a wave of jealousy, knowing that this meant they were really about to start recording album #2 with Nigel Godrich. My inner child wanted to pout and shout, "Fuck no!", but the deeper love and respect I have for Nikolai and *The Strokes* saw me saying,
"Sure, I'll pack it up and send it to your office."

One afternoon, Anna took me to see Andy Chatterley's studio in the Docklands, at Limehouse. I had always found Andy to be a very charming, mentally SHARP individual and was impressed to see that his collection of synthesizers rivaled my own. I mentioned that I wanted to start my own band in London and to build a recording studio/rehearsal room. Andy found a vacant unit in the same complex of rundown brick buildings on Cable Street that he was in.
Three of my top dreams were blooming simultaneously; Shoplifter Records, a new studio-to-be and forming my own band.

For the second time, I placed a cheesy ad in the *NME* classified section using my name 'n' credentials to recruit the best musicians I possibly could for my new rock band.

After I signed the lease for the Cable Street studio, Anna's parents, Joe and Manny, came to the rescue once again. They flew from Woodinville out to London to help me turn a nasty looking empty room into "The Silver Transporterraum of London", as I was keen to call it. This time I pulled an old-fashioned Gordon Raphael prima-donna routine (perfected and despised from town to town all through my late teens and twenties). I said,

"I don't care how much it costs, just hire some workers because this time I'm not going to hold a saw, hammer a nail, or put down one lick of paint."

Ok Gordon!

And so, it was. I auditioned my future drummer (and future studio owner, producer, legend) Matt Ingram in an empty space down the hall from Andy's studio, for my room wasn't ready yet. That empty room had piles of old school chairs in it and rows of giant glass windows which any acoustic scientist will tell you makes loud sounds reflect in an uncontrollably brash manner. Matt brought a 70s drum kit with monster-sized toms and, when he jammed with me, I instantly fell in love with my own personal John Bonham! That derelict and dusty room filled up with the biggest fattest groovin' rock-beats. Yeah! Instant win, so Matt was the first musician chosen.

The Silver Transporterraum of London was finished with a spray-painted silver brick wall (Warhol Factory, anyone?) and those same sweet purple velvet draperies and couches that had made our studio in NYC look cool, three years earlier. *Miss Machine* moved in straight away and used it as their rehearsal center. After those construction costs, I had no money left for recording gear, but planned to acquire some as soon as my next big jobs came though.

I did have enough cash to go to the town of Milton Keynes to meet Graham Sutton, who went around the UK collecting broken or unloved Hammond organs and Leslie speakers. He lived in a house with a big shed in the back where he had eight different Hammonds which he lovingly restored to their original perfection. Graham was so cool, he showed me this little radio system he devised so that he could play vinyl LPs of his favorite jazz organ recordings (Jimmy Smith, Larry Young, Jimmy McGriff) and beam them through his own small radio transmitter into an old-fashioned wooden radio.

This private radio station, that reached no further than his own shed, recreated the exact sound he'd grown up listening to. Graham sold me a breathtakingly beautiful 1967 Hammond A-100 with a matching Leslie cabinet for the new studio, something I'd always dreamed of.

Miss Machine's first single *All American Girl* was released at the beginning of April. Anna's band celebrated by going on tour in the UK with *The Buzzcocks!* I went along to several of the shows as *The Buzzcocks* records and their guitarist Pete Shelley's solo singles were majorly influential among my circle of friends back in Seattle.

Right near the end of that month I was at home when I received another Bang-Boom of twisting fate—in the form of a phone call. Ryan Gentles,

"Hi, Gordon...how would you like to come to New York next month to produce *The Strokes* second album?"

I probably should have told him I'd check my schedule and maybe if I'm not too busy...! Of course, I said an exuberant YES right away. He asked me where I thought we should record since I no longer had my studio there, so I asked him to send the guys over to TMF to check it out. Then I gave him a kiss over the phone and hung up, launching into a little celebratory dance with no music playing.

Auditions for my future band took place in the shiny new Silver Transporterraum, where I asked Jason Hart from Nottingham (who later became Jake Bugg's manager) to be my dedicated Jimi Hendrix style guitarist and ace harmony singer.

Pete Chenery from Sheffield came down by train to be my keyboard wizard and Matt Ingram brought in his old partner, Tim Smyth, to be our Mister Bass Guitar of 2003.

I called our band, *Crystal Radio*, after my father's and grandfather's passionate electronic hobby. A few rehearsals, a few dozen spliffs and multiple cans of lager later, *Crystal Radio* was swaggeringly ready for our first show.

The Basement Club was the natural choice for this first sonic assault. The musical mastermind that is Ed Harcourt kindly opened the show and there was a funny moment during the soundcheck.

I was delighted to have been contacted by CNN Europe, who asked if they could bring a camera crew and interview me at The Basement Club. I thought it would be great promotion for my label and *Crystal Radio* band. I imagined that they'd take me into a corner of the club or outside around Highbury & Islington station to ask me a few questions, but no, they arrived in the early stages of Ed Harcourt's soundcheck.

CNN Europe marched in, set up some blinding white lights and yelled,

"Everyone please clear the area!!!"

Scowls from Ed's musicians and the Basement Club's tech crew but they all cooperated as a gesture of goodwill towards me. The TV crew placed two chairs in the middle of the club floor, where a lovely news-gal with a great Swedish accent proceeded to ask me *Strokes*-related questions for twenty minutes. This was still the early days of me being interviewed and I very obviously relished the attention.

Later, when The Basement Club was in full swing, it was our turn to rock. We climbed onto that small stage and plugged in. I looked up, holding my sunburst Les Paul, and heard thunderous applause even before we played a single note. This, and the fact that we had a sold-out show, were true, glorious firsts in my entire career of performing my songs in public.

One of our *Crystal Radio* guys had been a bit nervous before the show and enjoyed one too many pints upstairs at The Famous Cock. Therefore, the first few songs of our set were slightly disharmonious and rough. We played *Seven Stars*, *View from Blue*, *Ring of Gold*, *2-Track Mind* and six more songs from my archives. The earliest was written on the Greek island of Corfu in 1984; some came from my Chateau Relaxo era in NYC and there was one new song I wrote in a few minutes during a Crystal Radio rehearsal. People from the audience told me afterwards that usually when a producer plays his own music it's quite laughable, they expected the same from me but were happily surprised.

Live room at Silver Transporterraum of London. A tangle of cables, my trusted SG guitar and various important rock 'n' roll pedals. Oh, ha ha, look, there's a UK platinum album award for Is This It!

Downstairs living room at Regent House. Scene of many meetings with Toby L, and parties galore. I get a great feeling from seeing this image. (L-R) Waldorf synth, Memory Moog, 1960s Clavinet and THAT 1972 Fender Precision Bass that Nikolai loved using on Is This It.

Aww! Julian and I sharing a together moment right before The Strokes *went onstage during their residency at Mercury Lounge. Downtown NYC, December 2000. This was after we recorded* The Modern Age EP *but before it was released by Rough Trade in the UK.*

The Strokes, me, JP Bowersock (L), with engineer Toshikazu Yoshioka (R) at TMF Studio NYC near the completion of Room On Fire. Summer 2003. The studio was very close to Union Square.

Hard at work, or hardly working? Building a recording studio for The Strokes in The Music Building, near Times Square. I'm obviously overexcited, and there's a Teletronix LA-2A compressor, two Distressors and an SPL Gain Station. Oooh and ahhh!

The day I met Dr. Robert Moog at Two Lines Music on W 48th Street, we kind of look related :) He invented the synthesizers that blew my mind as a teenager. Thanks Bob!

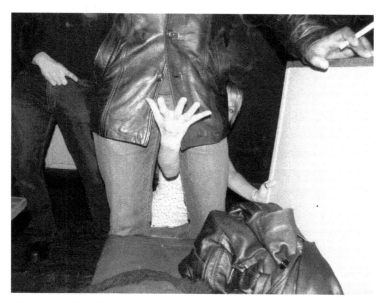

The vivacious Sarah Maguire on the very first night I met her, after our Black Light *show at* The Camden Barfly. *Here she is flippantly harassing some off duty policemen at* Trafik *bar in Old Street, London.*

My exotic EMS Synthi-A being rare and beautiful in the back of a white limo from JFK Airport, on the way to begin recording The Strokes' *third album.*

33: Room on Fire (June-July)

The Strokes agreed to record at TMF but with the provision that I do some decorating beforehand to make it look and feel more like our old Transporterraum studio vibe. To accomplish that I requested an extra 'studio-styling budget', hiring none other than Manny Hadlock to organize the creation and installation of long, thick purple velvet draperies. This was another precision rock 'n' roll seamstress job that had to be finished before the first session began—and Manny was right on time. The draperies and a few strings of tiny colored Christmas lights were enough to transform the big TMF live room into a place where these artists could cut loose and shine.

I flew out of London the day after our debut *Crystal Radio* gig, hyped out of my mind with anticipation and excitement. I took a white limo from JFK, carrying a crazy old peg-patch synthesizer called EMS Synthi A which Brian Eno used with *Devo*, *Genesis*, Bowie and *Talking Heads*. That synth looks like a black plastic businessman's briefcase from the outside, but on the inside lives the dashboard of a small spaceship. All the way into town I took sexy pictures of the Synthi A posing against rows of champagne glasses in the back of the limo, while out the window Manhattan skylines appeared...instant classic photos!

I was dropped off at Jane Street in the West Village, having rented a room in the apartment belonging to Charles Wallace from HQ and his lovely Swiss wife Tanja. I had a supreme case of jet lag and found myself falling asleep around 6pm then waking up at 2am, ready for breakfast. I did anticipate this and scheduled two days off specifically to get rid of the jet lag before re-entering the psychic kung-fu stance required to produce Julian, Albert, Fab, Nick and Nikolai.

On the second morning, I woke up at 4am feeling completely energized, ready to go party or run around. So, I laid in bed with mind buzzing when I had the odd, once in a lifetime idea to check the internet and see how early Jivamukti gave their first yoga class!

246

I had known the Jivamukti founder, Sharon Gannon, back in the earliest Seattle days when her art/poetry band, *Audio Letter*, played shows with my band, *Mental Mannequin*. Sharon was also close friends with Roderick and Anisa from *Sky Cries Mary*, so I was delighted when, in the middle of her 7am yoga class (is that even legal?) she played one of our songs, *Back to The Sea*, for the fifty other spiritual maniacs gathered there at that unholy hour.

After yoga, I had my favorite breakfast at nearby Cafe Orlin. From there I walked the easy distance to TMF Studios to meet Manny Hadlock who was making the final adjustments on her purple velvet decor. I considered that strange line which first connected me with Regina and now circled back to the same place where *The Strokes* album #2 was about to kick off. It was even more circular when I realized that Manny had been the first one to introduce me to Alan Bezozi, who then linked me to Regina.

One day later, I met *The Strokes* at TMF and they set up their instruments. Drums, amps, and oh!—there was my dear old bass guitar, safe and sound, saying hello to me again with a slight shine.

It was early afternoon when Julian asked if there was a small PA that could be set up. Fab told me that they wanted to play all the new album songs in a row, so that I could get a strong impression for what we were about to record. I placed a single chair in the middle of the grand TMF live room and got ready to enjoy the show! Before we started the first album, I hadn't heard any songs except the three we'd done for the EP, but that didn't bother me at all. Much of the real magic in a studio (or on canvas or a page in a notebook) happens spontaneously when one action initiates another, when one idea inspires the next. A studio is truly an organic laboratory in which songs grow, where new melodies, tones and words can be discovered.

I thoroughly enjoyed my private concert! It was a tight, powerful performance wherein *The Strokes* exhibited their mad musical skills, playing intricate yet slamming rock songs that would soon become their new album. They played SO amazingly

247

well, it was jaw dropping—nothing less. At the end I didn't know what to say that wasn't stupidly gushing, so I came up with,

"My God, Nick!!! When did you learn to play guitar like THAT??"

Next, we had a short conversation about how similar or how different our approach to recording these songs should be from the first album. I pointed out that there was a lot more high-quality equipment at this studio than we had at Transporterraum.

Julian raised an eyebrow, in his inimitable style, indicating, "Well, we all know that more is not always better,"

Bless him!

The budget was bigger, the studio was huge and TMF provided a top engineer, Toshi Yoshioka, plus assistants Josh Stoddard and Will Kelly. These three engineers had worked with Alan and I while we were recording Regina Spektor.

When the microphones were all set up and patched into the great SSL 6056 desk, we were ready for the next steps. *The Strokes* were huge fans of getting each sound as close to perfect as possible before they played a song for the recording. Starting with Fab's kick drum, proceeding around his drum set, Nick and Albert's guitars, Nikolai's bass; each musician's sound had to be carefully crafted and sculpted. This set of floating criteria would, naturally, change from song to song. Thanks to the combined efforts of Toshi, Will, Josh and I, we had all settled on the correct microphones, placement and instrument sounds. The band were now ready to play their incredible new songs.

Just before the band left the control room to start playing, I had one secret weapon I wanted to unleash.

My words: "Hey, I've been using TAPE for the last year in London and TMF has a great sounding tape machine, so let's try it!"

I had already checked that there were brand new reels of Quantegy tape ready to go.

Julian immediately rang in with, "I don't know, we've never had a good experience with tape!"

I replied, telling him they had never used tape with ME running it and at least we could give it ONE try.

He looked in my eyes, psychically saying, "Why are you wasting our time?"

After the tape was on the deck and levels set, the band ran out into the big room, tuned up and, with a count of "1-2-3-4," rocked out the first song.

I was at my station between the speakers listening closely, with J. Casablancas next to me. It sounded really great; I liked it very much. The band drifted back in and everyone paid close attention. After rewinding, Toshi hit play on the remote and the song played back from tape, sounding excellent. When it was over, I confidently asked Julian in a "see it's cool!" voice,

"Well, whaddya think?"

He just glared at me and rattled off,

"We just spent four hours setting up and getting every sound exactly the way we wanted and that fucking machine changed every single one of them."

Done, bad idea—and I certainly never suggested tape for *The Strokes* again! (insert cosmic smiley face here).

Moving right along, we spent days, weeks and eventually three months working on that second album which became known as *Room on Fire*. Despite the fresh new songs, brilliant sounding studio, increased budget and more time spent, the process and sound results were quite similar, by design, to *Is This It*.

Some songs were captured very quickly, while others were 'days long, sweating blood' to get the VIBE right. One thing I absolutely adored about producing this album was the fact that Julian sat in a chair right next to me when he sang, with both of us wearing headphones. This was so special and cozy to me and has never happened before or since. It was just the two of us in the room for those vocals, which was incredibly fun. Of course, we still did our three-hour marathons of selecting which phrases from which takes would make it to the gold medal circle of the singing Olympics. Who would win best first chorus line on 12:51;

the blue team? red? orange? or yellow?! Many songs had fake, placeholder names through most of the summer, though I only remember *Butt Cheek* and *Ze Newie*.

There were a few terribly rough waves on this voyage as well. The first one manifested quite early. I arrived to work and the band members came in and stood around me in the control room. Julian still gave me his special greeting of a big hug and kiss and then Fab smiled at me saying,

"Before we start today's song, we'd like you to get the exact sound of the drums from Michael Jackson's Billie Jean!"

I froze and probably turned a slight shade of pale grey.

They played the CD version of *Billie Jean* on the huge party speakers built into the wall at TMF and then Fab ran out to hit his kick drum, snare and hi-hat while I did my best to recreate Quincy Jones producing Michael Jackson.

I had no fucking idea how they did it. I wasn't a Michael Jackson fan (yet!) and I could only guess how, with millions of dollars at their disposal, in one of Hollywood's best studios, Quincy and his team of engineers might have gotten that sound. Sweating, I turned knobs and replaced microphones until I got 'close'. Two hours later the band agreed that I had indeed replicated the exact drum sounds from *Billie Jean* and we were able to proceed.

I recently learned that Michael Jackson's ace engineer, Bruce Swedien, had actually built a god-damned wooden BOX around the kick drum and THEN recorded those parts. Wow!

The Strokes went out and played the song ONE time before Julian told me,

"That Billie Jean drum sound actually isn't going to work at all for this song. Let's go on and try something different."

Within two weeks a few songs had been tracked, with our sessions running smoothly and harmoniously. Julian came in after a lunch break to tell me that on one of the songs we'd already recorded, the sound of the hi-hat was really bothering him. He asked if I could please fix it.

Pulling up the Logic session, I started opening plug-in equalizers, turning knobs carefully to correct that hi-hat sound to Julian's preference. This is usually not a big deal, something I can change easily... except when the first twenty solutions I attempted did not make him smile. There's an infinite number of creative avenues in the arts at any time, I just wondered how far towards infinity we would need to go.

The second hour saw me frantically patching in different analog outboard EQs and vintage hardware compressors. After turning more knobs and arriving at a sonic possibility, I heard a frowning line from Julian which I remembered well from the first album,

"Gordon, why would you even stop on that sound?"

During the third hour of searching for our golden hi-hat sound, Julian was sitting on the couch behind me watching over my shoulder. I sat in front of him, frustrated, aggravated and frankly, running out of ideas. I was silently fuming over the difficulty of my situation when Julian announced,

"I can feel your fists reaching back here and punching me in the face."

Another amazing line from empath Julian to passive aggressive sound engineer Gordon.

How this stressful, pressurizing search ended was almost too farfetched to be true. Failing with every creative or logical try and at the very end of my rope, I had an idea 'out of nowhere'.

I yelled, "Fab, go in there and when I signal you, hit your crash cymbal really hard, one time."

He smashed his crash cymbal perfectly well and, after that was recorded, I used a plug-in called Sound Replacer. I set it so that every single tap on the hi-hat would trigger a truncated, very quiet, crash cymbal sound.

"Yeah, that's the sound I was looking for," observed Julian and thus one particular trial by fire was over.

I had been a hardcore vegetarian for a long time. It started with my roommate, Dahny Reed, who lived with Pony Maurice and I, at the magical Apt. F, on Seattle's Capitol Hill. He had a beloved dog named Kizzy and one awful day a big dog bit and killed poor Kizzy. After being in a very dark, grieving mood, Dahny dealt with his pain by going to the neighborhood branch of our public library, reading everything he possibly could about ANIMALS. He would share his most interesting findings with all of our wonderful friends that would drop by Apt. F.

One day, he arrived home and announced that he was now a vegetarian, because it was the spiritually correct way to love and respect animals. This seemed exciting and cool until a few days later when he began to deliver sermons and lectures as I made my meager burgers or chopped up some chicken for dinner. After asking him to "get lost" several times, I converted to his philosophical way of eating. Originally, I did it to get him off my back, but then wound up really liking vegetarianism. I discovered great new foods and combinations such as chocolate spirulina shakes, black bean burritos and Thai food with tofu.

I had some notable lapses in my vegetarian times, most notably during my shitty year on heroin, during which I would eat anything I could get my hands on. My junkie diet consisted of Hershey's chocolate bars with almonds (almonds for the nutrition), Hot Tamales (candy) and gyro kebabs three times a week. That, plus slices of pizza with Coca Cola and occasionally Spiru-Tein milkshakes when we could lie or trick someone out of a little extra money. Oh yes, during my stint in the drug treatment center they were feeding me red meat to try and put weight back on my frame. However, all through my year in Hollywood and the grunge victory days with *Sky Cries Mary*, I stayed loyal to vegetarianism.

While recording *Room on Fire*, on one of my stoned-out, meandering lunch breaks, I found Quintessence. This was a RAW VEGAN restaurant in the East Village and, when I inspected the menu, it really tripped me out, piquing my curiosity. They created things that looked like spaghetti and meatballs, but the ingredients were raw zucchini cut in a spiralizer and different kinds of nut blends. This was topped with a sauce made from fresh tomatoes, sage and lemon juice. Their food was delicious and expensive and I started going there every other day.

Quintessence was a tiny place with five or six small tables and the manager would sit at a little desk in the back near the kitchen. After three weeks of eating there and loving it, I walked in for lunch one day and there were no other customers, just the manager smiling at me from her desk. I ordered a raw vegan lasagna and tiramisu for dessert, then waited whilst staring at the sunny East Village scenery out the window. The manager said that she'd noticed me coming there quite frequently. We got into a great conversation, I went on and on about my vegetarian history and how Quintessence was a new peak of discovery for me. I commented,

"I mean, don't you think that this is the most delicious and healthy food in the world??"

She paused for a moment and replied,

"Well, I used to think that, but now I'm not so sure it's very healthy."

I was dumbfounded. Why would the manager of this pioneering vegan restaurant have answered me like that? I needed to find out.

She proceeded to tell me that she had visited a PSYCHIC NUTRITIONIST in Midtown and that person had told her that raw food and a vegetable-only diet goes against the functions of the human body, becoming quite dangerous in the long run. In my marijuana addled mind this made me concerned and afraid.

Was I only inviting disease and ill health later in life by choosing vegetarianism, now shifting towards raw vegan? (Funny how I never asked myself that about the heroin, cocaine or my daily cannabis smoking habit.) I asked for the phone number of that psychic nutritionist and booked my own appointment for the next day.

Yellow cab to Midtown, then I was lying on an exam table (fully clothed mind you, except shoes off) while the psychic woman was moving her hands slowly up and down, twelve inches above my body, from head to toe. She said nothing and I just lay still in a relaxed state, occasionally she'd quietly intone a "hmmm?" or "ah-hah!" sound.

After about twenty-five minutes she said, "OK, you can sit up."

She told me that I was an unusual case because I rarely entered my own body and, when I did enter my body, I came in through my knees to visit for a brief moment or two. Then came the punchline,

"Your body told me that it's craving meat, chicken or fish."

I got a red flush of mild panic anger and pushed back,

"But I'm a vegetarian!"

She retorted with, "Don't get angry with me, I'm just telling you what your body told me."

She instructed me to at least eat potatoes, turnips, parsnips and other root vegetables which would have a warming, grounding effect. I paid her $100 fee, put on my shoes and left to walk, grumbling, back to TMF Studios in a 'fowl' (sorry, couldn't think of a better word, though it seems funny in this case) mood.

My fuzzy line of thought began shifting to analyze why I was so militantly defensive against what the psychic lady had told me. After all, I do believe in psychic stuff, so what was triggering me into panic at the suggestion of trying meat, chicken or fish? The walk to the studio was only twenty minutes, but two blocks before I hit TMF I saw a fine-looking SUSHI restaurant up ahead.

First thought, "I'm going in there."

Second thought, "I must check behind me and all around to make sure no one I know might see me doing this."

I went straight in and kept my head down, hiding behind the abundant menu before choosing crab sushi. It was so great, just delectable. I'd missed that taste more than I ever would have imagined. After lunch I tried to pull myself together, walked to the studio and plugged in to work.

Two hours later I took a short break and saw Fab sitting by himself in the little studio dining area, eating a bucket of General

254

Tso's chicken. I sat with him, chatting away and caught myself eyeing his bucket of chicken, repeatedly. I asked him if I could try a piece and he said,

"Fuck off, Gordon, we all know you're a vegetarian."

When I asked again, he gave me a chunk and as I bit in, Fabrizio RAN around the studio gathering everyone he could find to watch Gordon eating meat.

Halfway through the album project, Julian learned to hate the sound of the SSL preamps on the guitars. He started a crusade to "De-SSL-ify" the guitars that we had already recorded and we initiated a search for a holy grail piece of equipment to fix that. Luckily, it didn't take too long and by a joint suggestion from The Guru (JP Bowersock) and our engineer Toshi, they hooked up a Millenia preamp and ran the guitars through it for the rest of the summer. Problem was that thing overheated, broke down and blew fuses all the time.

Days later, Toshi had rigged up a solution by taking the metal top off that Millenia box and setting up a small fan to blow directly on it. That wasn't the only thing that blew up or melted down that summer—New York City (and the whole Northeast) experienced a big ol' BLACKOUT. We were beginning a session when the lights went out and, eventually, we all went home for the rest of that day and night.

I'd like to talk about Julian for a while, in relation to that summer of *Room On Fire*.

His songwriting, vocal ideas, vocal tones and lyrics were already on a supremely high level by the time we recorded *Is This It*. Julian's physical understanding of rhythm is just BEYOND (as Carole would say) and he hears pitch or tempo discrepancies of the slightest, most infinitesimal kind. *Room On Fire*, to me, displays some emotional darkness, perhaps anger and sadness inside some of the songs. *Is This It* was already pretty serious in vocal feeling as well, he's not exactly laughing or having abundant

255

fun on many of the songs from that album either, but people seem to be able to party more or get ready for a Friday night with the first album, while the second one is more lyrically contemplative.

The Strokes were a stunningly sharp, lean fighting unit on the second album. There's power, precision and creativity on display everywhere, throughout every song. The brain-numbing speed in which they went from playing a few shows on the Lower East Side, to spending months and years touring the world, had two definite effects. They became so musically tight and so solidly proficient on their instruments from those night-after-night concerts, but I'm also convinced, from observing and speaking with them in 2003, that being locked together on the road away from home for so long had a jolting, jarring effect on their minds and emotions.

This must have been profound, especially in combination with the partying and profuse mind-altering substances offered all along that trail. I mean, Fabrizio broke his hand and Julian was in a cast sitting down from a leg injury for part of the time between releasing the first album and recording the second. That must have been SO strange for both of them!

At 2am, after an extremely long day of work, there were just a few of us left in the TMF control room. The studio lights were dim and I was playing a song back for Albert while Julian was lying on the couch behind me. Jules had his eyes closed after twelve hours of work, with eight empty beer cans lined up on the floor below the couch. As the song played, Julian, with his eyes still closed yelled,

"Hey! The hi-hat just sped up."

Even close to exhaustion or unconsciousness he could still focus on these details with shocking accuracy. We located that ever-so-slightly fast hi-hat section, editing it forward by a few milliseconds.

One night in July after another long, mind-melting day with *The Strokes* fighting the good fight, Julian was peacefully lying on the couch in the darkened control room while I was consolidating and organizing the Logic sessions for several songs. When I finished, I looked over and said,

"Hey Julian, can I play you something I recorded here at TMF last Christmas?"

He opened one eye and glanced over at me, psychically saying, "Man, you must be feeling brave after what happened last time you tried to play me something!"

It was true, during the early days of recording *Is This It*, I wanted Julian to hear a few other things I'd recorded. I played him one band (not to be named here) which I had produced and loved. Forty-five seconds into it he asked me to please stop that song, using the words,

"I don't like that singer's voice. Don't ever play that for me again."

That stung a little bit, but immediately after that I thought that surely, since he likes me, he would like to hear one of my original songs! I picked a totally rockin' number that many people had complimented and, when it was over (I thought maybe he liked it, because he didn't tell me to turn it off) he said,

"Man, I'd hate to know what kind of dreams YOU have."

I did notice that before *The Strokes* took the stage at some of their concerts, they played songs from Eno's *Taking Tiger Mountain (By Strategy)* album, which I was often playing during short breaks at Transporterraum's *Is This It* sessions.

On this particular night at TMF, I patched my laptop into the console and pressed play on Regina Spektor's *Poor Little Rich Boy*. Julian listened till the end and was quiet for a few seconds.

"Play me another one," he said, and my heart was already happy.

I played *Carbon Monoxide* and, when it finished, he said,

"Will you please burn me a CD of that album? I want to listen to it when I go home."

Bingo! That's cool. I certainly didn't know much about his music tastes but, at that point, I wouldn't really have expected Jules to enjoy a young woman playing the piano and singing.

The next morning, I was already at TMF fussing around with something on the computer when Julian walked in. He walked up behind me and hugged me, then put his face very close to my ear ("This is weird," I thought...).

He sang to me in a quiet voice the words and melody from Regina's song, *The Flowers*. I was stunned and happy again—and couldn't wait to call Regina and tell her about this, I knew she would flip out!

Julian proceeded to pick up an acoustic guitar and strummed the chords of *The Flowers*, telling me,

"I wrote a song with the same chord progression once, but her chorus is way better than mine."

34: Room on Fire (August-September)

Time rolled forward to the end of July 2003. *The Strokes* were booked to play two shows in Japan in the middle of recording *Room on Fire*. After only a few moments of consideration, I asked Ryan Gentles if it would be ok if I went along. My main motivation was that *The Strokes* would headline Summer Sonic festival with *Radiohead* and *The Doors*! (The f**kin' DOORS! Minus dead Jim, of course). I had this vision of meeting Ray Manzarek and agreed to pay my own airfare and hotels just on the chance that this might possibly happen.

As a kid, *The Doors* were the second band I fell head over heels in love with, after *The Beatles*. I was inspired to become a keyboard player in rock bands because of Ray Manzarek first, then Rick Wakeman and Keith Emerson, thank you very much!

We landed in Tokyo and stayed at a stunning hotel. My room was one floor below *The Strokes* and I accompanied them to dinners (surprisingly, the most delicious Thai food I ever tasted was in Tokyo), a string of photoshoots and interviews. I was there as an observer, chatting with record company people and cute stylists. I love Tokyo with its human and visual overloads, having visited once before to play a concert with *Sky Cries Mary*.

On the third day we took the Shinkansen bullet train to Osaka where the first show of Summer Sonic would take place. I had plans to travel on my own to Kyoto, reconnecting with a friend from London, Noriko Okaku, a filmmaker and artist from the Filthy MacNasty's crew.

On the way, high-speeding from Tokyo to Osaka (I wasn't high at all, for in Japan I ran into NO ONE who used or even knew where to score weed. The penalty for being caught with it there is severe), I was taking pictures out my window while *The Strokes* and manager Ryan were conducting a meeting amongst themselves. I was sitting across the aisle from them and was able to overhear what they were discussing but didn't really pay attention until I heard the words REGINA SPEKTOR pop up.

Julian had clearly stated that,

"When this album is done, I want to tour with *Kings of Leon* and Regina Spektor."

Well, I just couldn't believe my ears! No way! Ryan Gentles jotted it down and the band discussed it for a few more minutes. I couldn't WAIT to tell Regina this BIG news, imagining the look on her face, the sound of her voice and what her reaction would be.

Noriko took me to see the Buddhist temples in Kyoto and afterwards we took a train together to Osaka where she stayed overnight in my hotel room (as friends, with her on the couch).

The next day we went to Summer Sonic, enjoying several good bands. Then on came *The Doors* who were exciting and impressive onstage that evening. Living rock hero, *The Cult*'s Ian Astbury, was tremendous singing with *The Doors*, putting in plenty of Jim Morrison but also showing plenty of his own power and style. Ray Manzarek and guitarist Robby Krieger were the only two original members from the 60s. *The Strokes* were in fighting form that night as well and the gigantic festival crowd got a chance to hear some of the new songs we were working on for their second album.

Ok, I have never been a fan of *Radiohead*, and not just because Nigel Godrich almost worked with *The Strokes*! I just never felt the kind of moods they seem to portray in their vocal tones and words. I think I would be very unhappy with my life if I did. This could be considered strange, because I listen to *The Smiths*, *The Cure*, *Skinny Puppy* and *Motörhead*, and feel perfectly fabulous! Yes, I have heard at least two *Radiohead* songs which I really did like, but generally no, no.

I enjoyed looking over their keyboard collection behind the stage while I was watching *The Strokes* play, but *Radiohead* pulled a weird move that stood out in my mind. After *The Strokes* set,

Radiohead's tour manager came to all the bands' dressing room trailers, announcing,

"When Radiohead walks towards the stage you all must stay inside and don't come out until they start playing."

Cut to the amazing hotel bar in Osaka with the 360° view of the city late at night and then sleep! The next morning Noriko needed to get back home so we went down to the lobby at the exact time for our entourage to check out and return by Shinkansen bullet train to Tokyo for Summer Sonic Part 2. I was milling around the lobby with my suitcase and THERE WERE THE DOORS! Ian Astbury, Ray Manzarek and Robby Krieger.

Normally, I would have been too shy but THIS is what I came here for! I walked right up to Ray Manzarek who was signing something for another fan (yeah, I was surely a fan too) and at the right moment—

"Hi Ray, I'm the producer of *The Strokes* and I have always been a huge fan of your work!"

He was relaxed, smiling, shook my hand and chatted with me for three minutes. He congratulated me on *The Strokes* album, and said that he really liked it, and I told him how influential he was for me getting involved with music and becoming a keyboard player.

We wrapped it up with, "See you in Tokyo."

The festival day in Tokyo was fun, *The Strokes* were projected onto a gargantuan video screen and I took my own videos on a 3CCD Panasonic camera that my pal Marc Swadel insisted I purchase while I was in Japan. They performed miraculously well and it was all quite similar to the day before. I did have a good chat with Ian Astbury, telling him that when *The Cult*'s *She Sells Sanctuary* video came out in Seattle, I watched as the girls in the club stepped away from their boyfriends, moving closer to the video screen for a better look! Ian let me know that he was writing his own new music and suggested that we meet back in London to work on it together.

Sayonara, Japan! We all left on a long airplane trip, followed by a couple days off in New York to recuperate.

Two historic bands blew into Manhattan that summer. The first one was Brit-pop favorites, *Blur*, who hadn't toured in a while as their singer, Damon Albarn, had started *Gorillaz* which became wildly successful. I chose to stay in the studio and do some editing while Fab, Albert, Nick, Nikolai and Julian went to Hammerstein Ballroom to enjoy *Blur*.

Around midnight, I heard some clamoring out in the hallway and when I looked up, there were *The Strokes* who'd brought Damon Albarn back to the studio. All of them were perhaps a little drunk? Some more than others. They all gathered in the control room with beers in hand and someone introduced me to Damon. The first thing he said to me was,

"David Bowie calls me every day."

"Hmm," I thought, "What an egotistical, bloated little quip out of the blue!"

I felt myself sigh and shook my head.

A few minutes later he sat next to me on the couch and out came, "I'm one of the few musicians in England who can sing ALL of the Beatles' harmonies."

My thought, "OK... strike two and even if you could, the way you are saying this isn't exactly making me like you."

This party was going nowhere fast when Julian said (while both he and Fabrizio were both looking slightly sad and nervous),

"Gordon, can you play some of our new songs for Damon?"

So, I dutifully pulled up a couple tunes and played them.

When these songs had finished, Damon confirmed the boys' worst fears.

"Oh yes, my, my, you'll have a very hard time selling this, now, won't you?"

That was the last thing I wanted to hear and it was pure bullshit to me. They talked for a while and a few minutes afterwards Julian said,

"Gordon, Damon thinks these songs need vocal harmonies, can you set up a microphone and let's record him."

My heart sunk even imagining one of these new songs with an extra vocal harmony. In my mind, that wasn't something that seemed to fit the vibe.

So out Damon went and he did try to sing on one song. I was grimacing, hearing what sounded more terrible to my ears with each new idea. Not only that, but this was already the end of a very long day at 3am and I wanted to go home.

But no, Damon had more harmonies he wanted to try and, in each case, none was getting better. With each spontaneous part he tried, I needed to mute the ones before it to give a clean slate. After what for me was 'too long' he shrugged and said,

"Well, I don't think any of those ideas are going to work, to be honest," and came back to join us in the control room. It was apparent that everyone but me was drunk and I was only high, ok?

Julian stood next to Damon and requested,

"Can you play back what Damon just did for us?"

I had an evil wave go through my diminished brain and quickly un-muted all ten ideas so they would all sound at the same time, then let it fly.

As you might imagine, this sounded like a tribe of wounded cats and everyone quickly agreed that Damon's vocals were not going to work. I asked immediately (perhaps a bit too joyously) if I could erase all of them, got the band's approval and pressed 'Backspace/Delete'.

On a much happier note, *Pearl Jam*, my ol' buddies from Seattle, were about to perform at Madison Square Gardens. Near the end of the *Is This It* recording sessions, *The Strokes* told me that they loved the music of *Pearl Jam* very much. When I told them that I knew P.J. from Seattle and that, in fact, I'd recorded Jeff Ament and Stone Gossard long ago when they played in the band *Green River*, they all got excited.

I wrote to Stone in 2001 immediately after that conversation, telling him about *The Strokes* and how he must hear them. Well, two years later the chance arose and I emailed Stoney again. This time I received passes for myself, *The Strokes*, plus Fabrizio's girlfriend at the time, Drew Barrymore, to see the show and get backstage to meet *Pearl Jam*. I relished the atmosphere in their dressing room at Madison Square when we all walked in, it was completely friendly with many hugs and wide smiles.

In the lounge area outside the TMF control room, I happened to notice a strange MTV News feature that made me feel very sad. There was a colorful, flashy graphic of Pete Doherty and Carl Barât from *The Libertines* and the reporter told the story of how Peter had developed such an intense drug habit that he was asked to leave his own band. As if that wasn't enough of a nightmare to hear about, the news continued with the fact that Peter had kicked down the door to Carl's flat while *The Libertines* were on tour without him and had proceeded to burglarize the place.

Pete seemed to be facing jail time and everything about this series of events made me feel very sad. Yes, I had been upset when I didn't get the job producing their first records but I always felt that there was SO much musical promise in *The Libertines*. I never in the world would have expected such a miserable twist in the plot.

I personally loved every song that we worked on for *Room on Fire*. *12:51* and *Reptilia* stood out all the way along, as towering musical accomplishments. For me, the *Reptilia* music video shot by Jake Scott is the perfect and ultimate portrait of *The Strokes*; how they looked and played all through the summer cooking up *Room on Fire*.

For *12:51*, I was able to incorporate a 'de-tuning' trick learned directly from my Arp Odyssey synthesizer which created a 'two oscillator' sound on Nick's thematic guitar part.[22] I had goosebumps and chills running up my spine when I heard *Under Control* being played in the studio, it sounded like the walls themselves were bending under the weight of those harmonic tones. That is SUCH a beautiful song, Julian's voice is heavenly while Fab's drumming opens an incredible sense of space.

The first song on the album, *What Ever Happened*, was the band's first choice for a single. Since it had been a while since the world had heard new songs from *The Strokes*, Julian thought it would be funny and ironic for the first words to be,

"I want to be forgotten."

That song was not the first single, however, because RCA suggested and the band agreed upon *12:51*, with its TRON-inspired video directed by Roman Coppola. The rhythmic interplay on that track is highly sophisticated and Nick's melodic guitar solo flows so gently. *You Talk Way Too Much* and *The Way It Is* are the most 'New York rocker' sounding of the batch and how cool is the sound of the drum fill that starts *The Way It Is*? It reminds me of imploding ping pong balls!

Years later in Berlin, I had an experience that will really make you wonder about my mental state. I hadn't listened to *Room on Fire* for around five years and I was out walking in Kreuzberg with my iPod set to shuffle. I was wearing really loud high-definition headphones and when *The Way It Is* started, I didn't recognize it at all. I kid you not, I got very jealous about how cool that intro drum fill sounded. 14 seconds later when Julian's voice came in, I felt rather foolish but certainly relieved that I was the one that had recorded and produced those unique drum sounds!

Mixing *Is This It* wasn't easy by any means but mixing *Room on Fire* was much more difficult. At least the producer didn't have a

---

[22] When using two strings or two synthesizer voices tuned to the same note, if you lower the pitch of one of them ever so slightly it can create a pulsating wide tone, sometimes bigger sounding than two notes that are precisely the same.

panic attack this time. Julian and I came up with a tricky two-channel method of mixing his voice. One channel used only the tube distortion from the Avalon preamp exactly as we'd recorded it, while the second was a duplicate of the same vocal performance but with added distortion from two Bomb Factory LA-2A compressor plug-ins.

For each lyrical phrase, both of these channels needed to be controlled separately so that the ratio between direct and processed sound would change, making each part of the singing as fabulous as possible. This automation alone, took ages.

Then Julian devised a new philosophy of mixing which, to me, was close to total audio chess. His theory was that, in a democratic mix, everything should be heard clearly but NOTHING SHOULD APPEAR LOUDER THAN ANYTHING ELSE.

Man, that is one tall order.

We struggled and we did exert ourselves, pushing our ears and minds for weeks mixing that album. Citizen hi-hat was not to be louder than citizen snare drum who was not to be louder than citizen Casablancas etc. Some critics said that the singing wasn't loud enough, but some critics also said that *Is This It* sounded like it was recorded by an amateur who had no idea what he was doing! Go figure.

As we were working on the mixes, Julian came up with,

"The kick and snare aren't friends yet."

And, on another song, he informed me that:

"The kick and snare are at the party having the time of their lives, while the hi-hat is outside in the rain and can't get in."

By now, I not only loved these symbolic observations, but I totally understood how to quickly fix these issues.

On we wrestled until we all agreed that album #2 was finished and we could finally rest.

There was one great story from the mastering lab, yes, the same place where I was originally confronted by the A&R from RCA and the head mastering guy. My sister Lisa and her husband Jose happened to be visiting New York on the day of our *Room on Fire* mastering session and I had permission from *The Strokes* to bring them along. They stayed for two hours, enjoying the sweeping West Side waterfront views and unlimited free use of their well-stocked kitchen. It was another long, slow day of mastering as all eleven songs got special, individualized treatment. The only thing that stuck out in my mind, other than the twice aforementioned Hudson River views and plentiful food, happened at the end of the day.

At 7pm, once the head mastering engineer had finished his best work and was preparing to leave the studio, Julian pulled one of the young assistant engineers aside and spoke quietly to him. It seems *The Strokes* were NOT convinced that *Room on Fire* had been mastered entirely to their liking. So, on we went into the night as the assistant engineer made significant improvements, thus completing the project.

I flew back to London with my bass and Synthi A, whereupon Julian called me to say that they'd discovered that I had accidentally left one channel on one of their songs 'out of phase'. This meant that when that song was played on a mono system, some parts DISAPPEARED completely. Luckily, our trusted engineer Toshi was able to print the mix again, this time properly. The band was none too pleased about this and so, maybe those critics had a point!

Some of the early reviews opined that *Room on Fire* wasn't as good as *Is This It*. Some complained that it was too similar, while others bemoaned the difference! But, in the years after the record was released, more and more people, especially musicians, have told me that *Room on Fire* is their favorite and that they can hear great development in the writing, playing and recording.

From my limited perspective, I think there were two factors that impacted the world's view of this album. First of all, it's difficult, if not impossible, to recreate the excitement of the first time you heard an innovative new sound or band. In my past, I experienced this with the band, *Portishead*. When the first song from their debut album, *Dummy*, came on the radio, I asked the driver of the car I was in to please go directly to Tower Records on University Avenue in Seattle, so that I could buy it immediately. I needed to study it, to try and find the secret of that completely new sound and I needed to absorb it over and over again for the sheer enjoyment of the music. When they released their second album, it was good but I already possessed a reference point for those sounds, so for me it wasn't WOW!

The second factor was, again as an outsider looking in, that *The Strokes* musicians were so young (twenty to twenty-three years old when they started touring crazily, promoting *Is This It*) that they probably got shellshocked from being locked in busses, planes and hotels together for two years. I imagine that they felt tremendous pressure doing that and possibly drove each other mad, as well. After those experiences they seem to have decided NOT to kill themselves with such long, extensive touring anymore.

35: Cogs In Cogs

Right before leaving New York and TMF Studios, I ordered and paid for enough recording equipment to fill up The Silver Transporterraum of London. That all arrived in the UK a few days after I did and it was a pleasure getting my new space in Limehouse ready and wired for action. I looked forward to working on my songs with *Crystal Radio* and finding new, exciting bands to sign to Shoplifter Records.

At the end of September, Regina Spektor returned to my flat on Devonia Road. Yes, she had been crazy-happy when I told her, back in early August, what I had overheard on the bullet train in Japan and now she had come over to discuss logistics for her real-life upcoming U.S. tour with *The Strokes* and *Kings of Leon*.

Toby and I invited Regina to play at our 11th Basement Club event along with my band and a new group called *Bloc Party*. Kele Okereke was one musician that Toby L had been keeping his eye on for years.

Regina's big U.S. tour was to begin in two weeks and, when she showed me that sweet-looking tour itinerary, I started imagining a side plan! I noticed that *The Strokes/Kings of Leon*/Regina Spektor tour would be hitting Seattle on October 25th with two days off afterwards. I jumped on the phone with Manny and asked her if there was any free time available at Bear Creek, in case I could entice *The Strokes* out to record on their days off. She said yes and *The Strokes* agreed to spend a day trying out a new song. My hope was that once they saw how beautiful it was at Bear Creek and heard how great the sounds would be, that maybe they'd want to record their next album there.

True to the plan, I flew from London into Seattle a little ahead of time, both for fun and jet lag removal. I brought my dad, sister Lisa and brother-in-law Jose as my guests to the big concert at the Exhibition Center. I especially thought they would all love Regina.

It was a powerfully touching moment for me seeing my two wonderful artists, *The Strokes* and Regina Spektor, play in my hometown in that same space where I had witnessed so many inspiring and influential shows.

The day after the concert I drove out to Bear Creek early to set up the studio equipment, feeling lucky to have the incredibly talented Ryan Hadlock engineering with me. By the time *The Strokes* arrived in the afternoon, all the tech stuff was ready and all they had to do was set up their instruments, soundcheck and play.

I was happy and surprised to see that they'd brought Regina with them, then became both overjoyed and mystified when Julian told me that the song we were about to record was a duet that he and Regina were going to sing together.

A Strokes DUET? Oh YES, here we go!

They all loved the studio and its outdoor 'farmhouse surrounded by forest' vibration. Joe Hadlock built a huge bonfire, one of his many specialties, and everyone was in high spirits. It was surreal being with *The Strokes* and Regina Spektor in those natural surroundings, so opposite to our usual meet ups in New York City. Bear Creek's rare magic was quickly apparent, because we didn't have to spend much time finding the right sounds.

It only took a few tries to get a great performance from Nick, Albert, Nicklai and Fab, even though the song must have been brand new. Once the instrumental tracks were done, Julian and Regina asked Joe if it would be ok to sing outside on the grass by the tall, wonderfully fragrant cedar and pine trees. Ryan Hadlock brought out two of his best large diaphragm condenser mics, placing them so that Julian and Regina would face each other.

They stood about ten feet apart with the studio dog, a big old German Shepard named Ella, laying restfully on the lush green grass between them. The two of them singing together was a sweet and powerful blend, and it didn't take many tries at all to capture an amazing performance. Perhaps due to the wonders of Bear

Creek, or the novelty of recording a duet, it was rather effortless to finish the recording.

The next day, we returned to mix that song and thus, *Modern Girls & Old Fashion Men* was born, becoming the B-side to *The Strokes* next single, *Reptilia*.

If you look on the back of that fabulous record cover (the front image is also wonderful!) you can see me with my blue 'Dealer of The Year' parka that Charles of London designed for me, and photos of these New York rock musicians happy together around a farmhouse bonfire.

Moses Schneider brought me over to Berlin to work doing 'vocal security' for a rock band with three guitarists called *Beatsteaks*. I was responsible for crafting the vocal tones, recording their singer, Arnim, and making sure that his English lyrics were grammatically right-on.

To be honest, Arnim knew very well what he was doing, his words and pronunciation were already great by the time I showed up on the scene. It was a fun, energetic job and also the most creatively involved I had ever been in one of Moses's productions. That record, *Smack Smash*, went gold and platinum in Germany and was a breakthrough for the band. *Beatsteaks* soon became one of the most successful bands in the country.

While working at the Berlin Transporterraum, I received a thrilling phone call completely out of the blue. It was Michael "Goldy" Goldstone from SIRE records in New York on the line. I knew exactly who he was even though we'd never met, as he'd signed my Seattle friends, *Mother Love Bone*, and later, *Pearl Jam*, to Epic Records. He'd also signed *Rage Against the Machine* and has a worldwide reputation for his music industry accomplishments and prowess. He'd heard the loud buzz about Regina Spektor touring with *The Strokes* and had a copy of her album, *Soviet Kitsch*. Goldy was calling to tell me that he absolutely loved the record and wanted to sign her to SIRE. (Seymour Stein's SIRE Records was Madonna's first label, having already launched *The Ramones*, *Talking Heads* and *The Dead Boys* among others.) I was exhilarated that this legendary A&R person was loving *Soviet Kitsch* and told him that I'd heard good things about him from both Seattle bands that he'd signed.

Mr. Goldstone asked me what I thought he could do to entice Regina to sign with S.I.R.E. and I simply replied,

"Take her out to dinner and tell her what you have in mind."

He did that and, a short while later, after the deal was done, I visited the SIRE Records offices at 75 Rockefeller Plaza (The Rock building!), meeting with Goldy and shaking hands with legendary founder Seymour Stein.

My label Shoplifter Records was the first to release *Soviet Kitsch*, originally having exclusive rights for the UK territories, but that story has a tragic final act on which the curtain fell much too soon.

Also tragically ending was my band's name, *Crystal Radio*. I got a message from Mr. Dave Davies of *The Kinks*, telling me that he currently had his own band with that name and I was strongly advised to change mine to avoid legal wrangling. I felt bitter about this, as I'd just hired Charles Wallace to design the cutest new *Crystal Radio* logo, borrowing heavily from the Day-Glo yellow and green lettering on Jimi Hendrix's *Rainbow Bridge* album. Plus, I had my own familial connections with the name *Crystal Radio*.

After filling another two pages with scratchy writing in my notebook, I picked a new name, *Black Light*. This moniker referred to the fact that my teenage bedroom with its signal-orange walls, was covered in psychedelic posters which tripped us all out when we turned on my black light (known as UV light in the UK). In my stoned-out mind, the name strongly symbolized how black music from Africa and the Southern States created rock 'n' roll to begin with. Please see: Little Richard, Buddy Guy, Muddy Waters, Chuck Berry, Willie Dixon, Howling Wolf, *The Beatles*, *The Rolling Stones*, *Cream* and *Led Zeppelin* for details.

Our year 2003 rolled on with *The Strokes* magically reappearing in England on December 4th to perform live on the Jonathan Ross TV show and play two sold-out nights at Alexandra Palace, or Ally Pally as the natives call it. *Room on Fire* had been released on October 28th, the day after our duet recording experience at Bear Creek. That album had been widely distributed within eight weeks of completion—super FAST!

The Strokes toured the U.S. and were now closing the year with a handful of European shows. Regina came to visit me in London at the exact same time and we went together see *The Strokes* play *Reptilia* on Jonathan Ross and also attended both Ally Pally shows.

Regina told me that she was on her way to visit some friends in Paris and would be staying at their apartment. When I told her I'd never been there before, she invited me along. I was very excited about seeing Paris for the first time and loved the idea that Regina would be my tour guide.

We boarded the Eurostar for a fast ride into France, staying in the 4th arrondissement close to Notre Dame. Regina's friends were delightful and the room I stayed in was full of ornate antique furniture. It was freezing cold outside but, as a first timer, I was enraptured with the visual feast that is Paris: the architecture, the Seine, the sky, the people. It was a heady, enchanting trip from the very first moments, but that high energy was further intensified when I was invited by *The Doors* to see their show at Le Zénith where, as the pantheon of gods would have it, *The Strokes* were also scheduled to play the following night.

The Doors thing should have been superb. I watched their soundcheck, then had a lovely formal dinner backstage with the band, featuring white tablecloth, wine and candles, with venison as the main meal (something I'd never tried before). Chatting with Ian Astbury and Ray Manzarek in that setting was truly a leap into the BEYOND!

When it finally came time for their concert, I stood at the side of stage rolling joint after joint, drifting in my own cloud of hashish smoke all night. Sadly, I did not enjoy the show. It was not a great performance like the ones I'd seen in Japan. Ian Astbury sang his parts perfectly, channeling plenty of Jim Morrison's spirit from the next world! I just couldn't stop hating the sound of the digital Korg organ Ray was using... You're the god-damned Doors! Bring some old electric organs and do it properly, gaaaah! Also, Ray was acting like a Las Vegas entertainer or clown almost the entire time, waving his arm like a circus showman while doing Korg organ solos with the other hand. Oh, and sorry to have to say, those organ solos were way too long, too frequent and too meandering for my intoxicated head.

Julian joined Regina and I the next day for some witty conversation and sightseeing. That night she and I watched *The Strokes* shred Le Zénith after a nice set from Regina's friend Ben Kweller. Christmas Eve was two weeks away and, as we returned to London, I was whirling with energy and satisfaction from the incredible year that was nearly over. I'm quite sure that Regina, sitting next to me in the Eurostar, was thinking the exact same thing.

36: Initiation of 2004

The beginning of an odd year with an even number. There was, disappointingly, not much reaction at all to the first two singles from *Miss Machine*. I was shocked because we had a good budget from Sony, were able to hire radio pluggers, press publicity agents, video pluggers and have a fittingly glamorous, sleazy video made for the song, *All American Girl*. *Drowned in Sound* printed a review for that song in which they wished we would just to go back to America, then further bashed us saying that we had to do more than "look cool" in order to sell records.

The whipping continued when they mentioned that they particularly disliked the production on the *Miss Machine* record, writing that perhaps I may have actually been sleeping on a couch while *The Strokes* records were being made. Nice warm reception, right?!

Meanwhile, Shoplifter Records was preparing to release Regina's *Soviet Kitsch* in the UK and I KNEW that this one was going to be a smash hit. I had spoken many times with Regina, asking her to please allow us to release her album. Because she trusted me, enjoyed our work together and had connected with *The Strokes* and *Kings of Leon* for that U.S. tour, she was willing to go for it. Albums by *Black Light* and *Satellites* were going to be the next two Shoplifter releases after *Soviet Kitsch*.

My noise-blast rock idols, *Kill Kenada*, came to The Silver Transporterraum studio to record a full album and it was superb! Dynamite! During one of their sessions, I pulled out my new video camera just to document the fun, whereupon bassist Tim Smithen proceeded to strip down to a leopard print thong, hung by his arms from some metal ceiling beams and performed aerial gymnastics. Then he sprinted into the live room and emerged wearing a black gaffer (duct) tape beard and matching black gaffer bra. This was not what I expected though I probably should have—it seemed hilariously fabulous at the time. In this profane get-up, Tim led the band through the next song. As they performed, I simultaneously recorded and filmed the proceedings, it was freakin' awesome too.

I was thoroughly impressed with *Kill Kenada* and loved every song I ever recorded with them. I tried negotiating to put *Kill Kenada*'s album out on Shoplifter Records, but their manager Alex refused my emotionally intensifying pleas over and over again. I was pissed off and sad about that and then even more so when he never sent me the second half payment for the producer fee and studio sessions. Bummer.

My other favorites, *Satellites*, recorded six songs in a cave in Mallorca before coming to The Silver Transporterraum to work with me on six additional songs. They called their new album, *Limehouse & The Cave*, which contains two of the most beautiful pieces of music I've ever heard. *Torna*, sung in the Mallorquin dialect, is trance-inducing, passionate and hypnotic with a relentless undertow pulling you down, down, down. The song features ultra-lush blending of their two live guitars. Joantoni's drums pulse eternally while Puter's bass cements it all together with dub reggae depth. Naturally, Jordi's singing soars into a vast dreamland.

The other master-piece on that album is called, *Where All the Promises Go*, which is pure, whisper-soft poetry. This one is sung in English and the first verse reads:

> *Where did all the promises go?*
> *The ones I've promised to myself,*
> *The ones I've done,*
> *Do they end up in a disaster box, becoming dust,*
> *Deep inside my own self?*

When it finally became time to record my music—the *Black Light* album—I played guitar with Matt Ingram drumming and Tim Smyth on bass, live for the main tracks. It took us one day to record nine songs, but I then spent two months adding keyboards, extra layers of spacey psychedelic guitar sounds, drum machines and singing. I wanted this album to be extra special, knowing it would be my first original collection of songs to be given a proper release, with a Sony-funded promotional budget, videos and tours.

I realize that I went obsessively overboard on the production and mixing. I would start at around 7pm, after my workday recording new bands including *La Momo, Todd, Zen, C33X, The Alpha Males*, Sara Hawley and *Yeti*, which was John Hassall from *The Libertines*' new group. Even the legend, Ian Astbury, made good on his promise to come over to collaborate with me.

I'd begin the night by going downstairs to the building's security guard, who was selling chunks of really low-grade industrial hashish, the kind with bits of wire and God knows what else in it. Then I'd slink up to my studio to fire up spliff after spliff, before 'tweaking-the-hell-out', turning knobs, pushing faders, screaming and breathing into microphones. Near the end of the tracking process, I was floating UFO sounds on top of space-kitten noises and adding a few door slams recorded with mics far down our concrete hallway, to make sure I didn't leave out any possible sonic texture. Then came mixing, mixing, mixing; neurotic dots of automation by the thousands, hyper controlling the volume of each letter and every word!

Well, one fine day in April the whole album was officially finished and I stumbled upon the title, "*Black Light—The White Album*". I simply thought the name sounded great, because after all, *The Beatles*' ninth studio album is actually called, *The Beatles*, not *The White Album* at all (ha-ha!). My completed album sounded great and one of my musician friends (Frank from the band *ray On)* described it as "an embarrassment of riches." I put so much micro-detail on that record that it can be truly said that I went 'over the top'.

Upon completion of *Black Light—The White Album*, a call came through from Wiz Kid Management requesting that I fly over to New York for a meeting.

"What??," I thought. "It's way, way too early for another *Strokes* album, I wonder what's up?"

A few weeks before my trip to New York, *Black Light* had a video shoot for my song, *2-Track Mind*, with ace director Tim Mattia. We filmed in The Silver Transporterraum and some trashed out, derelict areas around our Cable Street building. Tim Mattia and I also initiated a little side project.

We came up with the idea to produce our own creative video for *Modern Girls and Old-Fashioned Men* by Regina Spektor & *The Strokes*. I gave Tim my big box full of digital video (DV format) tapes that I'd shot on various tours, both with Regina and *The Strokes*, even footage from a rare New York concert where they performed this song together. Tim collaged my rock-on-tour videos together, intercut with abstract, absurd flashes of street scenes and shop windows in New York, Seattle and Paris. Our idea was to produce a video so mesmerizing that *The Strokes* would buy it from us and show it on MTV!

I was soon heading to New York, New York, excited to meet *The Strokes* and find what out what they wanted to discuss with me. I brought the *Modern Girls and Old-Fashioned Men* video with me hoping to dazzle them by showing it to them in person. We met in The Music Building on 8th Avenue, in the private rehearsal room that *The Strokes* had been renting for many years. To my delight and dismay, they told me their vision for how the third album should proceed. They wished for me to design and build a fully functional recording studio inside their practice room, then stay in New York helping them record demos first and a full album afterwards.

I was naturally delighted because—*The Strokes*! Album 3! Dismayed because I thought I had one more year to develop and promote *Black Light*, *Satellites* and Shoplifter Records before *The Strokes* would have been ready to call on my services. After that meeting, I stayed in the city for three days purely for fun and, on the last day, I invited the band to come over to my hotel and watch the *Modern Girls and Old-Fashioned Men* video that Tim and I made for them.

They band really liked it, with Julian saying,

"Whoa, you made us look so cool!"

I handed it to them so they could discuss it further, but.... further, it did not go.

I flew back to London with about four weeks to organize the plan for constructing a studio in The Music Building. *The Strokes* gave me a very good-sized budget from which to carve their future studio and, immediately upon re-entry to London, I got busy calling Vintage King audio shop in Chicago. I intended to give *The Strokes* a very special environment that they could use for many years, even producing other artists if they wanted to.

It was fun designing a dream studio, contacting acoustic technicians to make the room sound good, ordering by phone and email all the equipment we would need to make classic sounds. Chandler, Neve, Amek, API, Avalon, SPL, Telefunken and Distressor were a few names on the gear I selected.

May 14th was scheduled to be my first day unboxing everything, putting the plan into action and wiring it all together. Before I left London for this unknown quantity (of days!) that I had signed up for in NYC, I moved out of Devonia Road and put a few valuable things (like my precious framed poster of *Eno: Here Come the Warm Jets*) in storage at The Silver Transporterraum studio in Limehouse.

The last big hurrah was a concert featuring *Black Light* and *Satellites* at the Camden Barfly. We had a smooth soundcheck that evening and afterwards I went downstairs to the bar for thirty minutes before our set began. I went to get my classic party drink, bubbly mineral water with a slice of lemon, and was happy to see a woman that I really liked, sitting at the bar. It was Kirsten from the band *Ripe* who I'd met early in my London days. *Ripe* recorded with me twice and I'd also gone out to dinner with Kirsten one time. Truth be told, I had a crush on this talented, attractive singer. It flashed through my mind (as these things do!), that perhaps if she liked our show, it would improve my chances to go out with her again.

I said hi to Kirsten and she smiled before introducing me to her cute blonde friend, Sarah, who was standing with a huge glass of beer in one hand and two shot glasses of tequila somehow balanced in the other. Our *Black Light* set went very well and the Barfly was jam-packed. I stayed upstairs to smoke joints with Jordi and Puter before their *Satellites* set and then watched them rock from the side of the stage.

One month before, *Satellites* had played at The Dublin Castle, also in Camden, and I was running their sound. The house audio engineer had shown me a big LED level meter mounted on the front wall of the sound booth. He told me that if I made the volume in the club too loud and "hit the red" on that meter, then he was gonna shut me down. It sounded stupid to me, that they had to worry about loud sounds in such a well-established rock club, but I agreed. I wanted *Satellites* to make the best impression possible since they rarely performed in London. The show was going well, the crowd was indeed getting into *Satellites'* set. I just felt the sound was a bit too tame, so I figured out ways to increase the compression and boost certain frequencies to make it 'seem louder' and more aggressive. The house engineer came running back to the booth and said,

"Turn it down. It's too loud!"

I pointed to the level meter on the wall and it wasn't in the red yet.

This was my way of telling him, "Fuck off."

He just charged over to the sound board intending to turn it down, but I wasn't going to let him interfere with *Satellites* sound. I had not violated my part of the agreement we'd made at soundcheck. The Dublin Castle sound guy came rushing at me and tried to push me away from the mixing console and I just shoved him back. He went flying out of the sound booth, landing on his ass in the middle of the crowd.[23] That was only the second time in my adult life that I entered into a physical altercation with a fellow human being.

The first one was in Seattle at club WREX (decorated with wrecked car parts) with my band *Mental Mannequin*. That time, I was fighting with a soundman who told me it was impossible to put my echo signal in the monitors. I mean, I could do that at home, so why couldn't I do it live onstage?

After the Barfly show was over, I ran downstairs with stars in my eyes, hoping to find Kirsten again. Yes! She was at the bar, exactly where I last saw her—good! Excellent! I asked her if she enjoyed the show, and she responded,

"Oh yes!," with an even bigger smile than before.

I was trying to talk with her but that blonde girl Sarah was, annoyingly, making herself the center of attention with another large bottle of beer in her hand. They were both very drunk. Kirsten asked me if I wanted to leave with them to go party elsewhere and I emphatically answered YES. I grabbed my coat from the backstage area upstairs, beseeching my band members to "Please forgive me, here's the keys to the studio. Can you kindly unload the equipment without me? I have a hot date! I'll make it up to you."

The two women put their arms around me and we walked through the club, out the door onto Chalk Farm Road where we hailed a cab to Hoxton Square. They wanted to go to 333 Mother Bar but, after queuing for a while, the doorman stopped us saying that these girls were too drunk to be allowed in. We settled for Trafik next door and stepped inside.

Every time I wanted to stand close to Kirsten or talk, her friend would interfere and be distracting. They ordered drinks and we sat in a comfortable booth with me in the middle. I did notice that Sarah, even with her annoying behavior, was quite adorable. I had been taking photos with my camera all night at the show

---

[23] He did not try again, and after the set he came up to me and told me that I hurt him. I said I was sorry.

and now began snapping pictures of Kirsten and Sarah. I offered to get them their next drink and went to stand in line at the bar.

Up popped Sarah and she joined me. She was standing next to me looking at me with her beautiful blue eyes.

"So, you're the big *Strokes* producer," she said mischievously. "Oh, Mr. Producer, I'll bet you'd really like to go to bed with me."

I had my heart set on Kirsten but this new girl was bold and sassy, so suddenly I had a seed planted in my head that maybe this was going to happen instead? Then Sarah hit me with,

"So, you're the one responsible for those tiny drum sounds."

I felt slapped, so I asked her, "What's wrong with my drum sounds?"

She snapped back, "Well, they're a little bit "tinny," aren't they?"

She was disturbing me but something about having someone in London not putting me up on a pedestal actually felt refreshing.

We got back to our booth and I sat down with Kirsten while Sarah wandered off. This was good, and we were just starting a conversation when we looked over at the DJ booth and there was Sarah! She'd snuck into Trafik's DJ booth (uninvited), where she was wearing the DJ's headphones and dancing out of control. Again, completely distracting.

Five minutes later there were a group of big, tough looking, off duty policemen having drinks. They came and stood directly in front of Kirsten and I. Suddenly an arm was reaching forward between one of these guy's legs, it was Sarah's hand going into a peace sign.

The two girls wanted to hit yet another bar so we left. As we walked along Old Street's sidewalk a red double-decker bus was stopped at a red light. With no warning, Kirsten knocked on the closed front door of the bus. It opened, she stepped in and the bus drove off leaving me confused and alone with her disturbing friend Sarah.

Since leaving the Barfly everything had turned crazy, and now—this situation.

"So, Sarah...um, where do you feel like going?" I asked.

She told me she was hungry.

I knew at that time of night most places in the area were closed except the kebab shop. I flagged a black cab and asked the driver if he would take us somewhere open that served good food. We drove for ten minutes before he let us out, I have no idea where, in front of an open restaurant.

Down a stairway and across a black and white checkered floor, we found a big comfortable booth. I sat down to look at the menu and Sarah proceeded to take off her shoes and socks, then laid across the booth resting her head directly on my lap. Looking up at me provocatively, she began to talk. She told me that she'd moved to London to study vocal performance.

We ordered food as she told me sad tales about how she desired to sing for a heavy metal band but, in London, that scene was a boys' club and she wasn't being respected or taken seriously at the auditions. In an effort to help her, and to help her like me more, I offered assistance in finding musicians for Sarah to work with and also, of course, suggested that I would record her songs.

I particularly liked her speaking voice, the accent sounded somewhere between Scottish and Irish to my naïve American ears. The more we talked, the more beautiful she became.

Finally, around 3am, she was tired and wanted to go home. I suggested that we share a taxi, drop her off at her place and then I'd continue on to mine. We talked more on the short journey back to Shoreditch and, when the cab pulled up at her address, I cheekily asked if I could come in. I was pleased when she answered yes and we went up to a very tiny, half-size studio apartment just barely big enough for a bed and a few pieces of furniture.

We sat on her bed and, though my mind was wondering if we would have sex, it was instead lively conversation until she really

DID need to go to sleep and so I wished her a gentlemanly goodnight.

Some of the *Satellites* guys had stayed at my flat and, when I woke up at around noon, I took delight in showing them the wild photos from my night with Kirsten and Sarah. I had some especially cute pictures of Sarah and asked them,

"Isn't she amazing?"

Two weeks later I was at Heathrow, en route to New York for god-only-knows-how-long. It was totally weird to be heading off to a job with no set schedule and no return date. Perhaps I should have put more thought into it but, well, that's hard to do when you're smoking weed constantly.

I had been spending my time thinking about Sarah and I did have her number in my phone. I called her up from the airport and we chatted for a while. Again, I noticed her accent, which seemed different from any of my other English friends and made her voice sound extra sweet to me. I asked her if she was Scottish but she told me she was from Sheffield, in the North of England, and that her last name was Maguire. I asked her if she would like to come and visit me in New York while I was working there, and she said... yes.

37: First Impressions of New York

The Strokes provided me with an elegant room at Gramercy Park Hotel, which was to be my home for quite some time. On May 14th I entered The Music Building where the acoustic experts were fastening small wooden inverted V shapes to the ceiling of *The Strokes'* live room. I looked like a pirate in my maroon corduroy trousers, shirtless, with my razor knife slashing open cardboard boxes full of the best-sounding audio equipment in the world.

We had an entire month until the band got off tour and I intended to have the studio ready by the time they arrived. Even though it was only halfway through May, you could already feel the Manhattan scorch of summer. Since The Music Building was only a seven-minute walk from Times Square, I took my lunch breaks there, often returning at night to soak in that madness; the lights, flashing billboards, huge crowds of people spilling across the streets and sidewalks. Wiz Kid's management team, Ryan, Juliet, Esperanza and Matt were always in touch, helping me find everything I needed to get started with upcoming album #3.

By this time, many of my former pals had split from New York, for it was already a vastly different city from when Anne and I moved there in '98. The East Village was completely unrecognizable from when Debe and I had lived there ten years before that. I feel extremely lucky to have explored that neighborhood when it was truly the most vibrant, unpredictable and energetic mecca for young, creative people in the western world. Artists, musicians, filmmakers, poets, drag queens and queers of every variety flocked to this tiny, compressed area to cross-pollinate ideas, party and work. I have never seen anything as intoxicating as that cohesive yet mixed community with its collective display of creativity and sexual intent.

Alphabet City was where dope dealers once proliferated, empty crack vials literally crunched under your feet as you walked and junkies were seen nodding out, up and down both sides of the street, often unconscious while leaning their heads against metal traffic poles.

This same neighborhood was now filled with exclusive multimillion-dollar condos and organic vegan moms pushing designer prams while drinking their coconut lattes. The sleazy Chameleon Club on 9th Street, which I managed for two weeks, had been turned into a chic Beverley Hills-style restaurant with a long waiting list, a Maître D' and was decorated inside with imported trees. Insane penniless artists, gone. Poets living on cigarettes, baked beans and cans of Café Bustelo coffee— nowhere to be seen. Boys and girls partying nightly with nothing to trade on but their colorful personalities and drop-dead good looks, all disappeared. Instead, students from wealthy families, investors, lawyers and financial advisors had taken their place.

I felt a bit lonely during that first month, especially since the guys from *The Strokes* hadn't come back to town yet. I missed my action-packed life in London and new circle of friends there. There was also a strong pull within me to seriously focus on pushing my own freshly mixed *Black Light* album.

Regina's *Soviet Kitsch* was scheduled to be released on July 5th making it the first full length album on Shoplifter Records. In my mind, this was a brilliant way to start! I was sure that the excitement around those songs would put us firmly on the map. Paulo was coordinating a UK tour for Regina and I made it a priority to sign *Black Light* and *Satellites* as the next artists on the label.

One morning, as I was waking up at the Gramercy Park Hotel, I became shocked and irritated when Paulo showed up, unexpectedly and unannounced. I wondered what the hell he was doing in New York and who was paying for it? He told me he was on Shoplifter Records business, which irked me even more because it was supposed to be ME steering the label. His job was to help carry out my ideas. I had very little patience for him, especially when he told me he was going to the town of New Paltz to meet with Char Johnson. She was a brilliant singer and songwriter that I really wanted to sign and produce. I told Paulo that I really needed to jump in a taxi and race over to Cafe Orlin for breakfast, before heading to the studio. He asked if he could go with me as he had some important papers from Sony for me to sign regarding the release of Regina's album. I begrudgingly let him ride with me and signed my name in two places on those thick documents that had the Sony logo on top. Luckily, he got out of the taxi immediately after that and I was able to have breakfast in relative peace.

My phone rang two weeks later; it was Regina Spektor freaking out.

She was in Cardiff on her first Shoplifter Records tour, calling me very panicked and upset.

"I was just leaving the hotel this morning and was stopped by a manager who said I needed to pay! What the fuck, Gordon, I thought you and Shoplifter were supposed to pay for my hotels."

Of course, we were—this was a promotional tour for our very first album release. I had to find out what the hell was going on!

I called Paulo and he said that he did pay for the hotels, then I called Mark Chung at Sony who told me that they'd released money to Paulo for the tour. None of us could figure out what had gone wrong. Mark said he'd make sure this didn't happen again and I didn't hear any more bad reports, but this seemed awful and totally unnecessary.

The Strokes had finished their tour by the third week of June. They met me at their newly converted rehearsal space that sported a new, uplifting look; it was now a cutting-edge recording studio. We had mighty firepower in the control room and the live playing area had been acoustically improved. The band had rescued those thick purple velvet draperies from TMF Studios after our *Room on Fire* sessions and they were proudly hung along the back wall.

During our first gathering we outlined the initial phase of the upcoming work we would do together. They made it clear that some days I wouldn't be needed at all but, when they had ideas that were ready, I'd be called in to work recording their new demos. *The Strokes* told me that they had four shows booked over the summer headlining massive festivals in the UK, which would mean time away from developing these songs. I wasn't worried about that because we weren't on a tight time schedule. I did ask the band members the daring question,

"May I ask Ryan to contact those festival organizers to see if they'll add my band, *Black Light*, to the bill?"

Pretty brave for me, but I DID make that request and felt pleased with myself for trying. Word came back from Wiz Kid that, ok, *Black Light* was added to two V Festivals in England, T In the Park in Scotland and Oxegen in Ireland. RESULT!

The demos, which would eventually lead to *First Impressions of Earth*, took place in a subtly different spiritual atmosphere than the previous two albums and *The Modern Age* EP. It all felt a little bit strange although, admittedly I was in a wasted, pot-smoke atmosphere, not able to grasp the emotional and psychological nuances at play. It seemed like time had moved on and I felt that the excitement level and interpersonal chemistry between the band members had...mellowed.

Maybe it was because they'd just come off a tour and had already jumped right back into working. It was also the first time that we started a recording session with no songs already written. I was present enough to notice that each time our short demo sessions ended, the band members would say polite farewells before heading off in separate directions.

This was already a contrast as I reflected on the way they used to move as a gang of brotherly friends, together in groups of two or three most of the time. From the moment the band entered the studio, they would be open and relaxed with each other but the writing work seemed serious and a bit formal. They appeared to be doing their job (yes, a very creative and highly skilled musical job), working among friends that genuinely cared about each other. A vision of how they used to bounce into the studio laughing, pranking and joking boisterously was still hanging around in my mind.

I was calling Giorgio, a new dealer I met who sold potent strains of marijuana and different types of hash. My good per diem and handsome salary enabled me to spend $50 per day at his place and then I'd just walk around Times Square, Tompkins Park, Washington Square Park, Union Square; my eternal trails through Manhattan. I would ritually space out all day long.

Along the way, I'd be sure to visit Souen macrobiotic restaurant or Angelica's Kitchen for their amazing meals, which were some of the most delicious and nutritious in the world. There were many days off and sometimes, when I felt lonely, I'd drop by The Music Building and say hi to the guys for a few minutes, checking out their rehearsals and hearing sections of possible new songs in formation. I never stayed long, as they didn't seem to be in the mood to chat with me and I felt it was best to let them get on with their work. They were focusing hard, deep in concentration.

In those first few weeks I was rarely called in to work, but sometimes I'd hang out by myself in the control room playing keyboards or listening to some of my own music. I wanted to prepare for *Black Light*'s four upcoming UK festival shows, so I visited Ludlow Guitars and bought a sunburst 1979 Stratocaster and a few pedals. Then I hit Chelsea Guitars scoring a mint condition 1970s Fender Twin Reverb amp. Back in my room at Gramercy Park Hotel I set up a music station (I already had my ASR-10 sampling keyboard there) and began practicing by myself, thankfully receiving no noise complaints! Thick walls, old building.

Sitting on my bed at the hotel, enjoyable hours were spent reading *Hammer of the Gods*, a Led Zeppelin biography, before segueing into *Please Kill Me—The Uncensored Oral History of Punk*. Both of these books provided perfect visions to fill my mind and highlight my own rock and roll dreams.

During an introspective moment, I looked at my photos from that unhinged night with Kirsten and Sarah Maguire and heard Sarah's intriguing Northern accent in my mind. I decided to send her an email. I asked, for the second time, if she'd like to come visit me in New York. I told her I'd really like to see her, suggesting she could stay with me at this fine hotel. I clumsily borrowed a line from John Lennon's *Norwegian Wood*, joking that I'd sleep in the bathtub.

Well, the message she sent in reply wasn't nearly as fun as I expected. In very direct language she told me that she had a steady boyfriend and that, since she barely knew me, the invitation to come to stay in my hotel room really irked her. She ended with clear instructions for me to leave her alone and not write to her anymore. Ok, the curtain fell quickly on that idea.

Snippets of scenes in July. Wiz Kid found me a different hotel, closer to the studio. I far preferred the Gramercy Park area but could clearly see that developing the third album was gonna be a l-o-o-o-n-g process! The new hotel, though comfortable enough, was much more businessy/corporate, as one would expect in that 'north of Times Square' location.

Albert brought wonderful musician, Sean Lennon, to the studio and soon he was visiting quite frequently. I was majorly excited to meet him because... SEAN LENNON! He was very kind, cheerful, open and, although we didn't really have long discussions together, I always enjoyed seeing him. Albert had been spending time at Stratosphere Sound, hanging out with James Iha from *Smashing Pumpkins* while Sean was there recording his own album.

48th Street in Manhattan had been the home of great music stores since my dad bought his first saxophone there as a kid. It wasn't far from *The Strokes* studio so I went there often to look around and play new keyboards. Sam Ash and Manny's Music were the two biggest shops but a brand-new place had appeared called Two Lines Music, which specialized in vintage and brand-new analog SYNTHESIZERS. I found my fun there in the form of cool instruments, effects pedals and a very turned-on staff of young, knowledgeable, electronic music enthusiasts. They told me that the stellar being known as Dr. Robert "Bob" Moog himself, would be stopping by for the MOOG 50th Anniversary event and I was cordially invited.

Moog was the pioneering synthesizer company founded in 1953 but they had gone out of business by 1987. Gloriously, by popular demand, they came back IN business around 2002. Two Lines rearranged their shop on that special day to feature every new Moog product and it was a magical, sparkling moment when I got to have my photo taken with Robert Moog. He even signed a promotional picture of himself and asked me what I wanted him to write on it. I instantly thought of, "Keep on tweaking, Gordon" and, as he started writing, he paused to ask,

"How do you spell TWEAKING?"

This blew my mind and I found it perplexing. My entire life had been spent tweaking knobs on Moog and Arp synthesizers, I mean, where do you think SPACE NOISES actually come from? Yet, here the MAKER, the inventor himself wasn't really familiar with that term. God, send some tweaking angels right now to give me help!

I flashed back to 16-year-old me, the first time I ever walked into Bandstand East music shop in Bellevue, Washington— seeing before me a real live Mini Moog synthesizer for sale. I turned it on and started riffing around, improvising some incredible funky melodies, when that grumpy old guy behind the counter yelled,

"Hey, get your hands off that, KID! You don't have enough money to pay for that. Leave it alone."

That traumatizing moment of reaching for the dream, touching it, playing with 'that magical sound' and then being cast out. Maybe that's why I spent the next two decades with a circle of electronic keyboards all around me? AND, two decades later, when I did find my very own mint condition Mini Moog model

D at (where else?) Trading Musician in Seattle, I truly felt a missing chunk of my soul flying back to me.[24]

Amidst my morning emails, I received a message from Leigh Johnson in London. She manages the artist Skin, from *Skunk Anansie*. Leigh inquired if I might be available to record Skin's second solo album. I HAD heard of *Skunk Anansie*, as they were popular during the high-profile ROCK days of MTV, but I hadn't heard their music and didn't know anything about Skin.

I pressed play on the three-song demo that she had sent me and was utterly floored by this intense, soaring singer. Skin's voice was sharp and clear, cutting like a laser beam with tremendous light and focus; always warm, very human, she sounded incredibly real yet shockingly urgent. I was torn at that moment because I knew there was no way I could commit to a new project, not even one as exciting as this. There was still an unknown length of time that *The Strokes* needed to complete their new album and we were still very early in the process.

I wrote Leigh back and said, "WOW!!" regarding Skin and that "though I would love to be her new producer, I just don't know when that could possibly happen".

Small chunks of songs were forming. There were demos underway. *The Strokes* were busy working together, searching through the universe for new melodies, chords, beats and words.

One day, when I had some time to myself in their studio, I began working on a couple of my own songs. I fired up the computer and uploaded some instrumental tracks I'd written during the *Absinthee* days, eight years earlier. Using a wonderful mic, preamp and compressor, I made up some words and sang, finishing two songs (*107 Club* and *Superhit*) that I was very pleased

---

[24] The Mini Moog Model D was the world's first portable synthesizer and all my favorite bands suddenly appeared on their album covers and concert stages with one or two of them. I primarily use the Mini Moog for the deepest earth-trembling bass sounds.

with. I even plucked up the courage to play one for Julian, and he said,

"I wish we could get drum sounds like that."

I told him I had used a very early Big Fish Audio Drum Loop CD, which was ground-breaking new technology back in 1995! At least this is an actual story involving Julian, for you would not be wrong to notice that there was very little personal talking or interaction between me and any members of the band during this time. I was just called in to record them a few times each week. The musicians were always kind and friendly with me, but there wasn't much conversation or camaraderie going on between us.

The summer festivals approached and I flew to London for one big rehearsal with *Black Light* before we traveled to Ireland and Scotland for the first shows. I was personally (not Shoplifter Records, not Sony) footing the bill to fly my five musicians plus sound man Nick Abbott and tech helper Jordi (from *Satellites*) along with our instruments to these festivals. In addition, I agreed to feed the band and crew, pay them and provide hotel rooms. It was a significant chunk of cash, but this seemed like a golden moment for me to play my own songs, having never performed for big UK festival audiences before.

We landed in Dublin and drove for an hour to the Oxegen site, arriving early in the day. We were taken to a small building which was quite a distance from the Main Stage, like, way off to the side. We set up our equipment in a tiny tent where it was pretty much guaranteed that no one would see us. Whoa, anti-climactic for sure!

Thirty people wandered in during our set, having no idea what they were seeing, nor how they were supposed to feel about it. Later that day we watched *The Killers*, *Franz Ferdinand* and *The Cure*, in addition to *The Strokes* and *Kings of Leon*. In my Rockfeedback Column #18, I wrote (and I quote me here!):

"Kids are dressed in free plastic ponchos embossed with the logo of some insurance company (how very rock). Nondescript Heineken logos

293

replace what might once have been original art-work and creative backdrops during the original hippie rock festivals. Scorched hot dogs mingle with the chilly wind and black summer clouds. One boy looks grumpy and blank as he passes out on his rain-soaked girlfriend, his pills and vodka kicked in way too early (it's only noon) and he probably won't see any of the bands."

After that, we encountered some shitty luck at the Dublin airport as Ryanair had erroneously booked one plane to fly to two different destinations. We were bumped off our flight to Glasgow and had to sleep rough-style on a filthy airport floor in bitter cold, with bright fluorescent white lights on and noise galore.

Indeed, the next day was also fucked, we missed our ride to the hotel, just grabbing any old sleep we could on long bus rides and one more airport floor. Like jet-age bums we were. When I finally took my pointy silver shoes off, after three days of having them strapped on, my feet were shaped differently.

In an unwashed, slightly comatose state, we all arrived at Glasgow's T in the Park festival starring N.E.R.D., *Kings of Leon*, PJ Harvey and *The Strokes*. For the first two and a half hours we were marched unceremoniously around the fairgrounds in a harsh, comical way. *Black Light* were booked to play The T Break stage, and the security guards, parking lot attendants and guest-list staff each took turns provoking us, shoving their pent-up disrespect and bottled-up aggression in our faces. In my sleep deprived state, it all seemed a bit cruel.

Finally, Steve, one of the festival promoters, came to our rescue, just as my grumpiness level was escalating towards wild rage. He totally sorted us out with amazing meals and entrance to the rockstar encampment, where all the mega-musicians and top billed bands were hanging out, having FUN together. That was our Sunday turning point. Well-fed but still hallucinating from lack of sleep, *Black Light* stormed the T Break Stage. We performed an excellent set with our sound engineer Nick Abbott crafting the perfect mix all the way through.

Our successful show here redeemed an otherwise horrible weekend. In a very happy state, we watched *The Strokes* give one of the best shows I'd ever seen them play, in front of a sea of very happy fans. People were stretched out as far as the eye could see and even the dark foreboding clouds stepped back to reveal a bright, biblical, moody sky. I was a-movin' and a-groovin' on the side of their stage with Jordi Satellite, Drew Barrymore (the nicest woman in rock), Amanda de Cadenet (tied for first place in her sweetness), Wiz Kid Ryan Gentles, Booking Agent supreme Russell Warby and the Rough Trade family: James Endeacott with Kelly Kiley. In fact, Drew Barrymore was holding my hand partway through *The Strokes* first songs, staring at the drummer saying,

"Oh, my GOD. Fab is SO CUTE!"

The massive white clouds became ice cream castles and *The Strokes'* set blew everyone right out of this world.

I spied Mr. Pharrell Williams backstage. Paulo insisted and prodded me until I went up and introduced myself to him. We wanted to show him the music of Char Johnson, the fabulous new singer/artist that Shoplifter was about to sign. I got really nervous, thinking: "I can't just go up and say hello to Pharrell Williams. I mean, I'm sure he has no idea who I am and how can I even talk with him?"

I did work up the nerve though and, much to my delight, he congratulated me on the first two *Strokes* albums. Then he told me that he wanted to write some songs for *The Strokes*, and would I please ask Julian what he thought of that idea. I did pass Pharrell's message along, but I don't think any actions came of it.

By the beginning of August, I became so bored with my sterile New York hotel room in that I requested Wiz Kid Management to rent, instead, my old guest room on Jane Street in the home of Charles and Tanja Wallace. It was a psychic relief to be back in a vibrant, friendly environment with them, in the heart of the throbbing West Village. Charles quickly introduced me to the modern joys of marijuana delivery service. He dialed a phone number and thirty minutes later a young dude on rollerblades came zooming out of the elevator. We could select from different sized bags marked Purple Kush, Orange Crush or Maui Wowie. This became our big thing to do together, and the apartment was permeated with the reek of weed smoke.

The Strokes reconvened at The Music Building after that first round of festivals. More songs were coming into focus. I remember recording the first versions of *Razorblade* and *Heart in a Cage*. I was also there for the first run-throughs of *Fear of Sleep*, which I thought was an eerie piece with a strikingly depressive atmosphere painted by the lyrics, for sure.

Julian asked me two powerful questions in a row while we were hanging out at their studio one evening.

"Gordon, when I'm in a club and hear a Nirvana song it's SO huge sounding and then one of our songs comes on afterwards and it's, like, thin and small. Why is that? Is it a production thing?"

My inner producer-child felt a little twinge of hurt as I interpreted that he was unhappy with our previous records when they were played after *Nirvana*. For a full fifteen seconds I wanted to blame myself for just not being good enough. But, after some mental analyzing, I shared my thoughts. How did Kurt Cobain write *Nirvana* songs? He used BIG giant full chords on the guitar that hit all the strings at once and ran that through a chorus pedal. And what about the songs on our first two *Strokes* albums, *Is This It* and *Room on Fire?*? Lovely, amazingly well played single-note melodies on one guitar with sparse two-note, three-note or openly played chords on the other. *Nirvana* has a more typical ROCK compositional approach with unique genius twists, while *The Strokes* songs feature unusual counterpoint techniques of layering multiple melodies, again with ingenious ideas all the way through.

Julian did not smile after my explanation, seeming to be unsatisfied and unanswered in his soul. Then he wondered,

"Isn't it possible to make something cool that also sells?"

He (and others in the band) had rightly observed that several very popular recent groups admitted being heavily influenced by *The Strokes* sound and style. These new bands borrowed or copied elements directly yet were selling more records and making more money than they were. In this case, the followers appeared to be more successful than the originators. Julian definitely did not see the justice in that and this led to inner searches, quests for answers and new directions.

August zoomed by and I was again in a jet plane bound for London. There I would gather the team of *Black Light* and Paulo for two back-to-back V Festivals, first in Chelmsford and the following day in Stafford. This time we rented a van and drove to both locations. The first V Fest was OK but certainly not memorable. The stage given to *Black Light* was small and our early time slot ensured low attendance. Unfortunately, next day was even worse. The worst. Paulo, as day-to-day coordinator of Shoplifter Records, had been responsible for our itinerary and logistics for the summer festival dates. He had been working in the UK while I was in New York recording *The Strokes*. He thoroughly miscalculated the driving times, so we arrived to the parking area of that festival a mere thirty minutes before our set time. This was bad, but what was fucking devastating was the fact that it took us an entire hour to find a place to park because Paulo failed to secure parking permits ahead of time.

We truly FUCKING missed our set at a major British music festival!

I was inconsolable and god-damned angry about this. There followed a shouting match between Paulo and myself, and I gave him a piece of my mind. After that, I spent the rest of the day walking around the festival in a miserable funk and certainly not speaking with Paulo.

38: Second Thoughts

For the first days of September 2004, I was very shaken up. I landed back in New York, trying to cut through my own mental fog to understand, in whatever way I possibly could, that I had just missed and wasted an opportunity the size of a V Festival show in England. Anger and confusion were ricocheting around inside of me.

The studio sessions with *The Strokes* were moving ahead steadily. There was now a bunch of completed demos from which we could envision an album shaping up. The next step would be to re-record all of them in a final form. In my view, the demos sounded like they were already pretty close to being album worthy, after all—I had recorded them and the equipment in their studio produced excellent tones. I thought that we could just re-record some parts, do a great job mixing and we would have a very cool third album. *The Strokes* definitely did not agree with me about that at all.

I called Paulo who was back in London working with Mark Chung on Shoplifter Records' next phase. I told him that I wanted my *Black Light—The White Album* to be released in three months' time and to release our *2-Track Mind* video immediately. I also told him that *Satellites* needed to be signed right away and given money for their living expenses. Since I had promised them a deal with Shoplifter Records, *Satellites* had all moved from Mallorca to London. They had rented a house in Stoke Newington, preparing for many upcoming concerts. I also wanted Sony to pay me back for the two months spent in The Silver Transporterraum recording their album, *The Cave and the Limehouse*. I couldn't wait to release that album and send *Satellites* out on tour.

Abruptly Paulo shot back with the worst sentences I'd heard yet, "Gordon, we aren't ready to release your album or Satellites. We are going to wait a while."

I told him to FUCK OFF, that it was MY label, I was in charge and I would make the decisions!

He announced that, in fact, Shoplifter Records was now only fifty percent my label because those papers I signed in the back of that taxi in NYC were documents he had paid a lawyer to draw up (with Shoplifter's Sony funds), which made him an equal partner in my business!

At that moment, I was phoning him from a restaurant and there was so much rage in my body, yellow fire in my brain, that I bit my fork, chipping a tooth and really hurting my mouth.

I had thought that it was going to be so funny and cool to have this young Liverpool dude representing my fresh rock 'n' roll record label, the one I'd dreamt about having for much of my life. YES, it's true that I was uncomfortable with Paulo from the beginning, so why had I ever trusted him? I gave him a job to reward him for having helped me start Shoplifter when my supposedly high-powered New York manager and all my own efforts had previously failed. As I slammed my mobile phone down on the table after that call, my mind went into a hyper-feedbackloop of sweaty rage and violent revenge fantasies.

The shitty news from London became EVEN WORSE. Mark Chung called me and said that Shoplifter Records had not provided the necessary receipts for the budget that was being spent. Mark Chung was apologetic when he told me that, without receipts and proper accounting, he had no choice but to drop Shoplifter immediately from Sony S.I.N.E. He really did like me and believed in my musical vision, it's just that his company couldn't work with me under the present circumstances.

I called Coutts Bank at Charing Cross and they confirmed that the Shoplifter Records account had been cleared out completely.

Shoplifter Records: dead on arrival.

Subsequently, I had a miserable, heartbreaking talk with Regina Spektor. She called to tell me how shocked, disappointed and upset she was about the fiasco of the Shoplifter tour, but worse—we mishandled the release of her album.

Now I needed to enlist the help of Manny Hadlock to call Michael Goldstone and Seymour Stein at Sire Records to untangle the legal, financial mess made with the UK release of *Soviet Kitsch*. Regina was a lovely friend of mine and we'd done great artistic things together. From that point on, however, she wouldn't speak with me or return my calls or emails, and of course I certainly understood why.

Years later, I did hang out with Regina for a short visit backstage after her 2009 Berlin show. It wasn't until 2017 that I finally had a relaxed and open talk with her, also in Berlin. Losing her trust and friendship was tragic to me, on a par with losing my own record label.

Somewhere in my churning G. Raphael mind, a voice from my former drug-recovery program began to shout at me. It was my own voice saying loud and clear,

"YOU are the one to blame for all of this mess and fucking fiasco. Who was too busy getting high, unable to hear your own inner impressions telling you that you didn't want to be around Paulo from the very first moment? Who was the one, too stoned, too often, to perceive this whole thing going down? YOU are the one that wanted to party constantly, handing Paulo the power to make you miss your festival show and lose your label."

In a rage of truth and righteousness, I quit drugs AGAIN, doing it instantly with no pain except for the massive regret of losing Shoplifter, my festival slot and Regina's respect.

One might think, "But Marijuana isn't that harsh of a drug!" Well, in the hands of hyper-addictive personalities such as mine, with a history of chemical dependency, YES it really is! My emotions were conveniently spaced out and I excelled in anti-social behavior.

It actually wasn't that difficult, quitting drugs. I was so angry (at myself) that I really just snapped out of it. The first time I experienced this was after the rehab center in 1989. Back then, it took me a while to find my way back to wanting to do creative things once I got off drugs. So much of my identity and creative confidence came from being 'high'. I remember finally breaking through and writing music 'straight' and then going on stage straight for the first time at the age of 33. It was strange at first, but soon it felt normal to NOT use drugs.

I found an apartment to sublet down near Canal Street, knowing I couldn't stay at Charles' place anymore with the ghosts of marijuana delivery, or smelling pot smoke. Ryan Gentles agreed to transfer the rent once again, instantly providing me with a quiet sanctuary in which to recover from my four-year complete relapse. I entered reset mode, starting over once AGAIN.

By October, the demo sessions were very close to being finished. Soon there would be a blueprint for the third album, mapped out in fine detail. As election year fever swept USA and our microcosm in New York, we were all sick of seeing propaganda and campaign bullshit from George W. Bush, his wars and his talk of evil men; we desperately wanted him gone. The election was now a constant background noise in our lives and Times Square looked like a dual ad campaign for Bush and Kerry, blown up in LED billboards and neon lights.

The Strokes and I were listening to the demos, discussing how to take these songs further when the actual album recording began. Albert approached me in the studio one evening and told me about an engineer he'd met named David who was working with Sean Lennon over at Stratosphere Sound. Albert asked me what I thought about the idea of bringing David in as a second engineer to help out when the next phase began. I immediately thought that this could be a good idea. I had the pleasure of working with Matt Hyde in London and Toshi at TMF. Having an extra engineer meant less time staring at the computer screen and more time to be creative and involved with the band while producing. I also thought that if this young engineer worked with me, he would probably learn a lot, and that being affiliated with

The Strokes would be great for his career. So, I said, "Yeah, that sounds fine."

Yet another change of residence for me. Ryan Gentles told me that he'd secured a very impressive studio apartment for me on the Upper West Side, next to Riverside Drive and Hudson Parkway. This was a Donald Trump building full of actors, models and other generally wealthy people. This Trump apartment building had a concierge who smiled and told me when I had mail or packages, but there was a downside. The doormen expected a crisp $5 bill every time I came home in a taxi. These doormen would open my taxi door with their white velvet gloved hands waiting to receive a tip.

While I was living in this tiny, sophisticated, marble-floored apartment, I discovered eBay and online shopping for the first time in my life. Soon I had a Teac A-3340S 4-track tape machine shipped from San Francisco, three vintage guitars, four synthesizers, turntable and speakers. My big suitcase, clothing and all of these new online purchases formed a circle surrounding my brand-new ultra-comfort mattress (made in California and hands-down the best bed I ever had). I was fortified now for the long winding pathway up through the high, high mountains I foresaw producing this third *Strokes* album.

The day of beginning. We convened at 3pm in the studio, waiting to meet the new engineer, David Kahne. When he walked in, I was quite surprised, for this was not a twenty-something new engineer—he was at least my age, possibly older. Of course, this was fine, just a funny twist on Gordon's classic jumping-to-conclusions. David shook my hand and started looking over the equipment I had chosen to outfit *The Strokes* studio. Albert told me that David had recently produced Sir Paul McCartney in Russia, another surprise, indeed.

After briefly perusing our studio gear, David pointed to a few pieces he liked and many that he didn't care for. He told us that he'd be bringing a few racks of his own Wunder Audio recording equipment and this is what we would use.

The band were anxious to start the first song. I already had microphones set up around the drums and also for the guitars, but David didn't like the way it sounded, asking if he could rearrange a few things. We told him OK and soon the Gordon Raphael instrument sounds were being changed to those of David Kahne.

The next movement, like a ballet I will never forget, as I stood in front of the Amek mixer, David motioned his arm towards the studio couch which I clearly understood to mean that he wanted me to TAKE A SEAT. The next performance, in that psychically spinning and rotating control room, was the drum sound check.

Usually, I put a few mics in front of the drums and ask Fab to play his kick drum. After making a few minor adjustments, the kick drum sounds great and we move to the snare drum. Normally, it takes me twenty minutes at the most to get a great drum sound. It does take me a couple hours to set up all the mics for recording, but as I've mentioned, I like to do that the night before the band arrives, so as not to bore them or waste their energy. David (like most engineers I'd worked with on my own music before I trusted myself enough to do it) spent two or three hours dialing in sounds for the drums. I truly wouldn't even know what to do for that long and I'd be very impatient to start hearing songs being recorded! For me, sitting on a studio couch for three hours hearing drums being tested was NOT something I enjoyed.

The first time I experienced long drum soundchecks was with my band, *The Sorcerer's Apprentice*, at Kaye-Smith Studios when I was eighteen years old and I never warmed to this process.[25]

The third movement of this rather heart-sinking recital was when all the tones were finally dialed in and sounding much cleaner, bigger and more professional than I was used to. *The*

---

[25] This studio was started by famous Hollywood actor Danny Kaye and, for many years, was the premier studio in Seattle. It turned into Bad Animals which was owned by the band *Heart* during the grunge times.

Strokes ran through their first song with a click track for about an hour. At a certain point David asked if the band and I would please adjourn to the TV room and he'd call us back in a while.

On the television was some horrible news report about the election, which was quickly switched off and replaced by a video game that some of the guys were playing. Much later, we were called back to hear whatever David had been working on. He pressed Spacebar/Play and, as the band were listening eagerly, I looked closely at the screen to see the hundreds of micro-edits where drums and bass had been cut into tiny ribbons and moved skillfully into place so that each note was as clock (grid) perfect as could possibly be. Again, I would never want to go down that path, for it reminds me not of rock 'n' roll, but... something else. Oh yes, and I would totally go insane staring at the screen and moving all those tiny chess pieces where they 'theoretically' should have been played in the first place. That was day one and I already had a queasy, uneasy feeling in my stomach.

The next day featured more of the same, me on the couch... asked nothing and saying nothing. After two hours of this stiffness, I had a breakthrough idea that would become more and more a part of my day;

"Hey guys, I'm gonna go out for a walk!"

The first walk was a leisurely hour and I dutifully reported back to my verbally quiet, emotionally turbulent spot on the couch. Two hours later, I felt the strong urge to leave again! I got lunch around Times Square, then went poking around in Sam Ash and Manny's Music.

Occasionally, Julian would ask me to explain something he had in mind to the new engineer, but not very often. We were excited when David Khane would talk with Paul McCartney on his cell phone and we could hear traces of Paul's voice. David told me that very early in his career he'd recorded a Jorma Kaukonen (bassist for *Jefferson Airplane*) solo album. He'd also been head of A&R at Columbia when Jeff Buckley got signed there and, more recently, had scored a massive hit producing an album with Sugar

Ray. This guy had been around and sure seemed to be at the top of the game.

I felt left out, like there was no room for me in this studio anymore, no role left for me to play. When I started to stay away longer and longer, Julian had a chat with me. He saw from the beginning that I had been feeling uncomfortable, but he asked me to please stay to help him. Julian explained that he needed me in case he ran into a problem communicating his thoughts in terms that were technically clear enough to reach David. He even indicated that if I left, they might fire him, and he really wanted a chance to see where the album could possibly go in this new direction. Because I truly cared about the band and Julian's wishes, I agreed to stay. I hoped that perhaps a more involved role for me might emerge in time.

Christmas was coming 'round again and I had plans to celebrate in London. I had made special arrangements with Skin to record a few of her songs at my studio there, just for fun, to see how we got along together for future projects. I was excited to see her and meet the person behind that unique, powerful singing voice.

I went to her house to hear a few more demos, finding Skin to be very chilled out, friendly and bright. The days with Skin and her band in The Silver Transporterraum were dreamy and perfect for me. Four songs were brilliantly finished in five days.

Bing-Bang, Gordon Raphael production method in action. I love finding artists that already sound amazing, just letting them try their ideas and giving them room to shine in the studio. Example: Skin sang a lead vocal. She did it once (like Ian Brown at Chateau Relaxo, years earlier) perfectly. Then she would double that, one time, perfectly. Harmony one, perfect on the first try. Double that, in one take. Harmony two, only one take! Recording Skin singing was effortless. Harmony number three, perfect and its double; the same. The wall of harmonies she created was wide and powerful. On top of her amazing vocal ability, she smiled from the moment she walked into the studio until the day was over. Talk about helping to create an uplifting vibe among her band members! And another wonderful part? Days after the sessions were finished, she was still smiling and hadn't changed her mind! There was no sudden plunge into existential crisis, fearing that what we thought sounded good as a team in the studio was now CRAP in the cold light of one week later. This does happen sometimes, unfortunately.

To celebrate our killer recording sessions and new friendship, Skin invited me, along with her girlfriend, to her beautiful home in Monte Carlo on the French Riviera. We stayed a few nights and ushered in happy new year 2005 together.

The day before I returned to London, I wanted to meet a friend of filmmaker Marc Swadel's called Laurence Vandelli. She said we could meet at a party in the forest surrounding Cannes. I'd never been to Cannes before and I was excited to go there to meet Laurence, as Marc had described her in glowing terms. The party WAS really fun. There was a giant, very beautiful stone house in the middle of the woods and the people at the party were in very high spirits. They were congregating in the various rooms of the house as well as spilling out in the warm night into the majestic woods. Laurence struck me as beautiful and was very warm and friendly to me. I don't strike up conversations at parties, but here everyone was easy to talk with and I felt entirely welcome. I wound up staying overnight there and was offered a ride to Nice Côte d'Azur airport the next morning by some of the partygoers. I had a few days off to enjoy London before going back to my shaky scenario in New York City.

Shortly before midnight of my last day, I was walking in Shoreditch, around Hoxton Square. I tried to remember where Sarah, the girl from Sheffield that I liked, was living. I had only been there once, late at night during the one time we'd ever hung out together. I somehow found her apartment building on Curtain Road and was tempted to ring her bell, but I decided not to. When I got back to my hotel I wrote Sarah an email, even though she'd asked me not to, telling her I'd been thinking about her and that I'd walked past her apartment.

My British Christmas holiday was over, so I took the flight across the Atlantic back to Manhattan. By the time I got home to the Trump apartment building on the Upper West Side and paid the doorman his $5 for opening the taxi door, there was a return email waiting for me from Sarah. It basically said,

"How dare you come around stalking me late at night? I would have been terrified if you had rung my doorbell. And WHY are you even writing to me when I specifically told you not to.... You are very creepy, so get lost!"

Ok, so maybe that wasn't a great idea, for the second time.

39: The End of the Beginning

Everyone said they'd be back in NYC, ready to work by the 13th of January. I landed a week early and visited my Chateau Relaxo studio partner Scott Clark at his new multi-studio, Mercy Sound, on East 14th Street and Avenue C.

There I produced back-to-back sessions with two artists, Gen Blouin, a smashing songwriter/performer from Montreal, and my new friend Skin, over from London to add new vocal parts and do a bit of mixing with me.

It was sweet seeing Scott again and seeing what a phenomenal job he'd done designing the first multi-studio in New York. Mercy Sound offered several different control rooms sharing a single large live room. It was all heavily soundproofed so that three or four producers could be working simultaneously. This was a perfect modern studio philosophy, especially with real estate prices skyrocketing in the East Village. Scott has ALWAYS been ahead of the curve where the future of recording is involved. Recently he quipped that,

"Recording studios are the modern-day VHS rental shop!"

January 13th came and went. Not everyone in our crew had returned from their holidays yet, so I fell back into that dense grey condition called 'waiting around'. I received two interesting emails that week.

The first was from Moses Schneider in Berlin. He sent me a Quicktime video shot by Susie van der Meer, with Moses narrating a walk-through of a gorgeous seven room apartment. It was freshly renovated and painted, yet with its classic 'old world' fixtures left intact. This giant apartment was in the same building that Moses lived in—he was seriously tempting me to move to Kreuzberg, Berlin for fun, culture and music. Wow, that seven-room apartment had twelve-foot ceilings and was available to rent for $800 per month, adjusting for the Dollar to Euro exchange rate which in 2005 was weighted in USA's favor. This was a hilarious bargain when compared to the tiny studio apartment I was currently staying in for $3,000 per month! I told him it looked amazing, but I had no idea when I'd be done in *Strokes*-land, so I had to pass.

The second email was from a singer named Leonardo de Lozanne, who I'd met the year before in London and invited to a party I was throwing. Leonardo is the singer in one of the most loved rock bands in Mexico, called *FOBIA*. They became super famous when they were teenagers and, after years at the top, had taken some time off. Leo was asking me if I would travel to Mexico City and produce their comeback album. *Fobia* also requested that I bring my Arp Odyssey synthesizer and play it on their songs. This was a fabulous opportunity for me as I had never been to Mexico before (I don't count the one night on a *Sky Cries Mary* tour where we crossed the border to Tijuana. There we checked out some awful bars and strip clubs which were more like a subconscious nightmare or frat party in hell). *Fobia*'s offer sounded amazing, but I told Leo that, though I'd love to do it, sadly, the timing wouldn't work.

Then finally came the day in January when I DID meet *The Strokes* at their studio. I was nervous, anxious to see where we were going with this production now that we'd had our holidays and some time apart. Julian, Albert and Fab asked me to go get a bagel with them at a kosher place near the studio, right off Times Square. We sat down and Julian cut straight to the point.

He told me that the band decided they wanted to work with David Khane, without me. Then he asked if I was alright with that. I was a bit shocked but immediately replied,

"Of course, it's your music! I certainly wouldn't like being forced to work with someone on my songs if I didn't want to."

In the clarity of my own mind in that moment I felt a twinge of sadness that our personal, historic and significant bond was going to change now. But that feeling was tempered with the insane relief of not having to sit there in that studio anymore feeling useless or like a leftover! Instantly, on top of that I saw a map of my future like colored stars of light, like magically connecting dots: flying to Mexico City to produce *Fobia*, then moving to Berlin with Moses and finishing the album I had started with Skin in London. Great!

Like the sky opening up over my head, I felt much lighter. Then Julian asked,

"Do you hate us?"

"No, I love you guys," I replied.

Julian then asked, "Would you ever consider working with us in the future if we wanted you to?"

"Yes, of course—any time!" was my reply.

40: What Happened After That?

Once I was let go in New York, everything in my life changed at the speed of a hurricane.

I signed the lease on that seven-room super apartment in Kreuzberg via the internet, which probably would never happen these days. Packed all my recent eBay purchases along with that comfortable California-made bed and shipped them off to Berlin. Flew to Mexico City to produce *Fobia*'s album, *Rosa Venus*, recording in a studio built into the side of a hill with its interior walls covered in volcanic lava—best sound ever! While there, I considered changing my name to 'Pork Taco', for obvious reasons.

From Mexico City, I flew directly to Berlin to set up my new spacious apartment while recording a cool punk band with Moses Schneider, called *Spitting Off Tall Buildings*. Returned to Mexico for *Fobia*'s mixing. Was happy to be invited to Cork County, Ireland to stay with legendary space rock guitarist/singer, Roy Harper, in his beautiful home surrounded by lush green rolling hills. Worked for two more weeks with Skin at my studio in London finishing her album, *Fake Chemical State*. During those UK sessions I was staying in a stylish hotel at 100 Shoreditch High Street. I texted Sarah Maguire and she actually AGREED to meet me at a pub on Bethnal Green Road.

Settling down in Berlin, I totally decked out that huge apartment with two vintage Hi-FI systems, a TV room with a spinning disco mirror ball, recording room, dressing room and my flashy bedroom decorated in 60s Danish furniture and Italian typewriters.

As soon as it was fully finished, Sarah came for a weeklong visit and decided to stay for fifteen years. For a while we were boyfriend and girlfriend, and then not. We remained best friends and when she met and married her husband Graeme, I DJ'd at their wedding—not clearing the floor. In the past six years I have been honored to be called "Bampy" (Welsh for grandfather) by their children Francis Lorca, Phaedra Moon and Koa Bloom. I haven't had kids of my own, thus far, but I am blessed with three lovely grandkids.

My first two productions in Berlin were with *Husky Stash* and *Super 700*. Both bands were perfect for me and I loved their music like crazy. I soon realized that I would NEVER be able to build a studio for myself in that city.

Berlin gave me the feeling that, with techno as KING and laptops as studios, who needs a guy inspired by *Led Zeppelin, The Stones, YES*, Hendrix and Frank Zappa, to set up microphones or work with vocalists?

Just as I really began to despair about no work coming in; Brussells, Paris, Den Haag (The Hague), Los Angeles, Cape Town, San Antonio, San Francisco and Seattle started calling. I became a producer that traveled for most of the year, recording in lovely studios dotted around the world. I've enjoyed this tremendously, especially because I can stay for two weeks or a month in each place soaking up more experience with these new cities, cultures and people.

Musicians in all of these places love *The Strokes* records and Regina Spektor's album that I produced and I fully understand that they call to work with me because they desire to have part of that lineage and magic in the studio with them.

I built several websites before settling on an archaic, never-ending homepage called Gordotronic which is filled with interviews, photos, artwork and links to hundreds of my own songs that languish in psychedelic obscurity. Likewise, I've cobbled together vast quantities of freakish, dazzling videos which hide out on my personal YouTube and Vimeo channels.

In the year 2009, I was invited to Buenos Aires, Argentina to give a talk about guerrilla-style recording (how to make cool sounding recordings without a lot of money). Then I started going back there more and more, recording bands, forming my own bands, playing shows, making friends and having the best times possible. My Argentinian friends, Artistas Sean Unidos, even helped me organize an art show of my paintings and drawings and later, a photo exhibit.

My twelfth visit to Buenos Aires was in 2018 when I produced Rocco Posca for Sony and then also recorded an album for his bassist, Simón Abentin. They are both SO young and talented, representing the highly creative, charged up future of music there.

That same year, my dear friend Andy Chatterley released an album of my music on his London-based Zero Hours label. This album is called, *Sleep On The Radio*, which was recorded with two different bands (one with five guys and one with three total rocker-babes) ...in Argentina! We recorded in three historic and wonderful sounding studios in Buenos Aires—Panda, El Pie and Ion (a renowned Tango studio). After it was released, I embarked on my very first European tour with a band called *The Half Full Flashes*, then continued the celebration touring South America with a band called *The Wild Cards*. The 2018 adventures in Buenos Aires were so energetically high and intense that we filmed and edited a short, sweet documentary. This documentary about my days with Rocco, Simon and *The Wild Cards* is called, *To Argentina with Love* (120 DIAS EN LA CAPITAL FEDERAL) and shall be released as soon as the proper stars align!

In December 2019, I moved back to England where I was granted a Global Talent visa. We're already feeling the next BIG wave of rock music here coming from a brand-new generation, though I'm also a mega-fan of the innovative sound exploration and wild beats that rappers are producing.

I am reminded of *The Strokes* ALL the time, whether it's an artist that I'm working with asking me a question about *Is This It*, a look in someone's eyes when they tell me how much those first two albums mean to them or a row of comments I see on the internet.

I do get a warm fuzzy feeling to this day, when I'm in a shop, bar or café and one of those very special songs starts playing!

41: Reflections on the 20th Anniversary of *Is This It*

All through 2021, the second year of the pandemic, I was busy speaking on blogs, podcasts, radio stations and in the music press, celebrating 20 years of *The Strokes'* debut album. In my personal vinyl collection downstairs many of the albums that I listen to religiously are 20 (or more) years old—I still think about these records and want to converse with people who understand why each one is so UNIQUE. The fact that journalists from around the world wanted to hear stories and get my perspective on *Is This It* for their audiences truly amazes and humbles me. It feels like I was somehow able to give something back to the same powerful, musical energy that inspired me in the first place.

After coming up through three previous decades of music culture, I am mystified as to why the early 2000s sent me *The Strokes* and Regina Spektor. These two collaborations appeared as magical turning points of huge significance in my life. It was already a breakthrough when the sound of those albums was being captured in the studio while recording and mixing. It was yet another revelation when those collections of songs went out into the world and found good homes in the hearts and minds of listeners everywhere.

My own pathway took me from piano lessons to my first band, *Kobyn*. At age 18, Seattle band *The Sorcerer's Apprentice* took me under their wing, kickstarting my glam rock *prima donna* era, and then I landed at the Rosicrucian Lodge where Brian Phraner enlightened and inspired me with his esoteric Medusa 4-track recordings. On I went to endless experiments with synthesizers at my mom's house, followed by seven years of living in Apt. F on Capitol Hill where I started my first two original bands, *Mental Mannequin* and *Colour Twigs*. After being evicted from Apt. F, my punk rock friends and I started living at the church at Ballard that had a great recording studio already built in, but that burnt down

314

after one year. I went to New York with Debe Lazo and we both ended up going in broken circles thanks to drugs. After rehab and trying a year in Hollywood, I took a Greyhound Bus back to Seattle and somehow walked straight into an amazing VICTORY with *Sky Cries Mary*; being signed to a record label and publisher, touring and having a great life, thanks to music. Six years later I met Anne Hadlock and started *Absinthee*, which brought me nervously back to New York. I learned digital music techniques and classic audio equipment near Chinatown thanks to Scott Clark at his Chateau Relaxo. Meeting Moses Schneider and Jimmy Goodman made Transporterraum NYC studio possible. And then came that one day when *The Strokes* walked into that basement.

I'm certain that some human beings can walk a shorter, more direct route to their dreams. For me though, I was lit up by the sounds in my head but seemed to trip through dense forests and muddy rivers before taking the slow bus over bumps and dips in the road. I like to believe that all these twists and curves were necessary for me to get my sound and to write my songs.

Could two people like Jimmy Goodman and I find a derelict, dusty basement in Manhattan and make a glittering artistic recording studio these days? I don't know. We were on the edge of a brand-new technological revolution that allowed us to make certain amazing sounds in a way that had not been widely done before us. There have been thousands of innovations since then that have allowed many more people to create their own music with laptops and phone apps. I hear music continuously, watch videos and see other forms of art throughout my days. I'm happy to report that fresh, challenging ideas, musical virtuosity and the passion for creativity are still blossoming worldwide!

On the first day that I met the fabulous Berlin-based producer Moses Schneider, I asked him, "Why does some music make it out in the world, and some never sees the light of day?" He thought for a minute and then told me:

"It's because of the *Zeitgeist*. That's a German word that means the spirit of the times. Picture it as a giant clock with many, many hands. These hands are spinning at different speeds and if you are in the right place at the right time, one of the hands will pick you up and take you for a ride. In some cases, it's a very long ride, for example—Madonna! In other cases, it's just a little journey for a short time. It's never a good idea to see what's going around and try to copy it, for, by the time you finish, the *Zeitgeist* will have moved on and left you behind."

The Strokes brought the sound of five young musicians playing together in a room like their life depended on it, and the world was startled by that stripped-down, raw sonic impact. Music fans who would never have considered liking a rock 'n' roll sound suddenly changed their minds. In fact, many also changed the way they dressed and went out to form their own bands, because it suddenly seemed fun. The early 2000s gave me a quantum leap in opportunities for my work and applying my creative ideas. Yes, I pushed my own music onto a back burner for a little while because the experience of suddenly being in high demand as a producer and traveling to new places was super exciting.

To be honest, even though I was totally digging my life following the success of *The Strokes*, I did not find the decade of the 2000s to be particularly interesting or energetic. George Bush and Tony Blair led both countries I was most familiar with in highly oppressive, boring and feeble ways (in my opinion). Other than the bands I've already gushed about, I was really not a fan of most of the artists that were getting popular at that time, except for *Bloc Party* and *Yeah Yeah Yeahs*. The club scene was the same as it almost always was, people becoming incoherent and belligerent with alcohol—but now they were wearing the uniform of "indie", whatever that term was supposed to mean, as the main bands were signed to well-funded corporations of course.

Meeting the small music community around Filthy MacNasty's in 2002 was exhilarating but, within two years, the UK music scene was racing towards highly commercial knockoffs of *The Strokes* sound, style and aesthetics. Living in London and finding my way around that vibrant, energetic city was indeed a dream come true. Watching the musical values change from urgent stripped-down aesthetics to slickly (over)produced radio-friendly singles was quite boring and predictable for me.

It was predictable because of this: At age 11, I was listening to KJR radio on New Year's Eve and at midnight, as 1968 morphed into 1969, they played the first new song of the year. I was more than excited to hear a brand-new song, but immediately entered into a shocked state of angry disbelief. I thought, "Wait, this is fake! It's trying to sound like the real music but it's hollow—why would they play this?"

Then it happened in progressive rock in 1976, and again with punk and new wave in 1984. Then, even while wearing the plaid shirt uniform, Seattle grunge became cute and shiny. I felt the same thing happening in the UK in 2004 and suddenly there wasn't much call for me to be working with bands in London. Being willing to help generate slick, palatable blockbuster hits is certainly not my skill set! That is why it was a pretty easy, instant decision to move to Berlin in 2005.

I don't want to give the impression that I don't love bars and nightclubs. Most of the places I've hung around in after dark, for most of my life, plus at least 98% of all the gigs I have ever played or seen, have been at these venues. In Seattle it was The Vogue, The Monastery or Tugs. In New York it was Limelight, The Tunnel, Luna Lounge, Pink Pony and Max Fish. In London it was Camden Barfly, The Dublin Castle, Water Rats and Metro. It certainly wasn't ONLY about witnessing public acts of drunken mayhem; there was a world of connection, romance, friendship, camaraderie and decades of musical inspiration. As my sister Lisa recently reminded me, "one night in a club can change the trajectory of your entire life". So true, so true!

Berlin felt miraculous when I started living there in 2005, a real buzz of excitement at The White Trash Club and with creative people moving there from all over the world. Many of them left that city several years later when they realized that even with very low rent, there was no infrastructure for non-techno sounds, so very few could actually support themselves with their own art/music. Shortly after that, music clubs began shutting down all over the former party areas of Mitte and Prenzlauer Berg as apartments were being renovated and rents skyrocketed. Things CHANGE and sometimes they change rapidly.

Still the beat goes on, and from the tumultuous roller coaster that is the 21st century we clearly see that music and art are essential, vital parts of our lives. Vinyl records are back, Jazz is back and music from the 60s to the 90s is being listened to by millions of people every month. Right now, I'm working with musicians from San Francisco, Manchester, Glasgow, Ecuador, Berlin, Washington D.C., and Florida. I'm excited to discover great new bands and artists, working with them to elevate and expand their sound. Great new songs will be leaving home soon, heading out into the big, wide world. With a little sparkly rainbow magic and plenty of Zeitgeist the world is going to love them.

Always resounding from deep within my heart,

Gordon Raphael

Hebden Bridge, West Yorkshire
January 2022

318

APPENDIX 1

Some of the bands/artists I recorded or worked with:

5 O'Clock Heroes	Chinas Comidas
A Brand	Colleen Green
ADRD	Dame Evelyn Glennie
Absinthee	Damion Anderson
Addie Brik	Damon Albarn
Alin Coen	Darlings UK
Alister Fawnwoda	Dave Allen
Aly Tadros	Deportivo
Amy Hernandez	Detonantes
Animals on TV	Diamond Star Halo
Anna Erickson	Dorit Chrysler
ariel and izzy	Education
Atomic Stop	El Hula
Auditores	Emily Breeze
Audrey Bochsler	entripao
Ben Ireland	Eva Loft
Beatsteaks	Feast of Friends
Big Deal	Fobia
Bingo Palace	Galvanized
Bisons	George Demure
Black Light	Girl Skin
Blonde Redhead	Gods of Blitz
Bundle of Hiss	Green Apple Quickstep
C33X	Green River
Cab Ellis	G.T.F.O.
Calendar	Halcion
Carl Marsh	Hinds
Carol Lund	HQ
Caroline Taucher	Hoodlum UK
Caviare Days	Husky Stash

Hyperlite Driveship
Hysterical Injury
I Ministri
Ian Astbury
Ian Brown
Ill Prospekt
Ithaka Maria
Janus
Jeremiah Bredvad
Jimmy Robinson
Johnny Strahm
Kapetan
Katana
Kennedy
Kid Cola
Kill Kenada
Kitty Solaris
Koyo
La Momo
La Nube Mágica
La Nave de Oniro
Lazy Talk
Lewis Lazar
Lilienthal
Longwave
Lori Carson
Los Outsaiders
Louie "Balo" Guzman
MANKIND
Machina
Maktub
Mama's Weed
Mantik
Marianne Nowottny
Marine
Maris

Millions
Mink
Miss Machine
Modernless
Moped Genius
Mummy's A Tree
Mynde
Ned Dylan
New Silver Girl
Nikita Nippone Noblesse
Olivia Anna Livki
Oscar Mic
Ovejas
Ox.Eagle.Lion.Man
P.M. Tiger
Pablo's Paintings
Pamela Laws
Paris Paris Musique
Petal
Phillip Boa
Plastic Cadillac
Plastic Heroes
Ponte Pilas
Pynch
ray On
Razika
Red Martian
Regina Spektor
Rhonda Star
Rick Szabo
Ricky Berger
Ripe
Rocco Posca
Rockfilia
Rollers of Bedlam
Roxanne de Bastion

Roxanne Fontana
Sara Hawley
Sarah Maguire
Satellites (Cicely Satellites)
Scanners
Scout
Serious Dark Angels
Simón Abentin
Skin
Sky Cries Mary
Sol Flamingo
Sometree
Soundtrak
Spitting Off Tall Buildings
Spring Films
Stefanie Koscher
Stone The Crow
Stormy Lee Rollins
Sue Denim
Super 700
Tangible Green
Tesla Trip
Tetra Splendour
The Alpha Males
The AstroJet
The Bad Apples
The Bellwether Project
The Bisons
The Britanys
The Datsuns
The Dirty Clergy
The Kecks
The Landmarks
The Libertines
The Michelles
The Mondrians

The Moonies
The Nite Howls
The Plastics (S.A.)
The Risin' Sun
The Rollers of Bedlam
The Roman Games
The Scarlet Dukes
The Skuzzies
The Slots
The Sound Explosion
The Strokes
The Tears of Gloom
The Teenagers
The Tellers
The Tempers
The Wildhearts
Three Trapped Tigers
Todd
Toxic Lies
TUSQ
Unisex Salon
Urban Rhythm Unit
VALA
Van Der Meer
Venison
Victoria Celestine
Violet Caste
Warren Suicide
We Leave At Midnight
Wolfy
Yeti
Youloosie
Yung Heazy
Zen
Zeno and The Stoics

Appendix 2

Bands I was in or played with (* indicates my own songs)
In order of appearance!

Kobyn
Fly
Journey
Apple Corps
The Steve Kirk Band
Musk Floral Ensemble
The Dave Head Band
The Sorcerer's Apprentice
Medusa
Masala
The Force
Mental Mannequin*
Refuzors
Colour Twigs*
Pronoia
500 Prisoners
Red Masque
Room 9
Perfect Circles
The Tears of Gloom*
Hollywood Bums*

The Divine Comedy
    with David Hillis
Sky Cries Mary*
Nigel Green Mystic Mood Orchestra
Justine and the Pussycats from
    Outer Space
COCA – Velvet Underground band
Absinthee*
The Psychedelic Furs
Black Light*
Analog Poodle*
Sarah Maguire
The Angelheaded Hipsters*
Paris Paris Musique
    featuring Gordon Raphael*
Atari Teenage Riot
His Argentinian Brothers*
Ovejas*
The Half Full Flashes*
The Wild Cards*

Acknowledgements

Valentines For All That You Do

I want to thankfully acknowledge every human being that I speak of with glowing fondness and respect within the pages of this book. Double shout outs to: my Aunt BB who gave me $500 so I could record my band, *Mental Mannequin*, in 1980. Eternal love to my two sisters, Lisa and Cherron; to Sarah, Graeme, Francis, Phaedra and baby Koa Maguire; to Manny, Joe, Ann and Ryan of the Hadlock/Bear Creek family! Sincere thanks to Lucy Tertia George and Tedd George at Wordville for all the help and encouragement with this book. Oh, and rock star Ned Dylan who hooked me up with the publishers.

I am grateful for *The Strokes*—thanks for walking into my life at that moment and taking me on such an amazing journey. Major merci to Regina Spektor. Thanks-a-million for the inspiration to: Steve Kirk, Brian Phraner, Barbie and Ben Ireland, Tor Midtskog, and Michael Davidson, Pony Maurice (*Meng*), Upchuck, Alley Lovell, Ms. Lazo in San Francisco, Barb, Ava, Lacinda & Karen from the Rosicrucian Lodge.

Thanks, Scott Clark, for showing me the way, and Jimmy Goodman for taking the next step. Clapping of the hands and smiles to Moses Schneider for your musical imagination and some well-timed wise words. Tom O'Horgan and Wendy Carlos: I am touched that you shared some of your energy and experience with me.

Blessings to my teachers: David Arntzen (improvisation) and Donald Denegar (classical piano and theory).

Writers Kurt Vonnegut, Ceanne DeRohan, Allen Ginsberg and Richard Brautigan opened my mind to new colors of light.

Physics student Mike Holder at Sammamish High School: Thanks for having the patience and psychic reception to program the synthesizer sounds for *Lissajous Fingers*, my first ever electronic composition and gateway to the Arp Odyssey synthesizer that has remained forever by my side.

Toby L and Chad Swahnberg—thanks for being rare, incredible friends!

Kenny Weller, Forest Kinney, Will Adams, Kevin Helppie, Scott Levitin, Tom Vigal, Lori Johnson and Kenda Schafer: Thanks for being in my musical circle growing up in Robinswood. What a difference it makes at that age to find friends on your same wavelength!

Griff Stevens, Tom Morrison, Larry Tuttle, Robert Puff, Mimi Sturman, Robbie Stoneman, Josie Dombrowski, Jack Chatham, Lauri Miller: I can't leave you out here for the unimaginable contributions you gave to me by pushing my musical mind over the edge.

Index

Lightning Source UK Ltd.
Milton Keynes UK
UKHW021820250922
409421UK00004B/113